IMAGES
of America

SILOAM SPRINGS

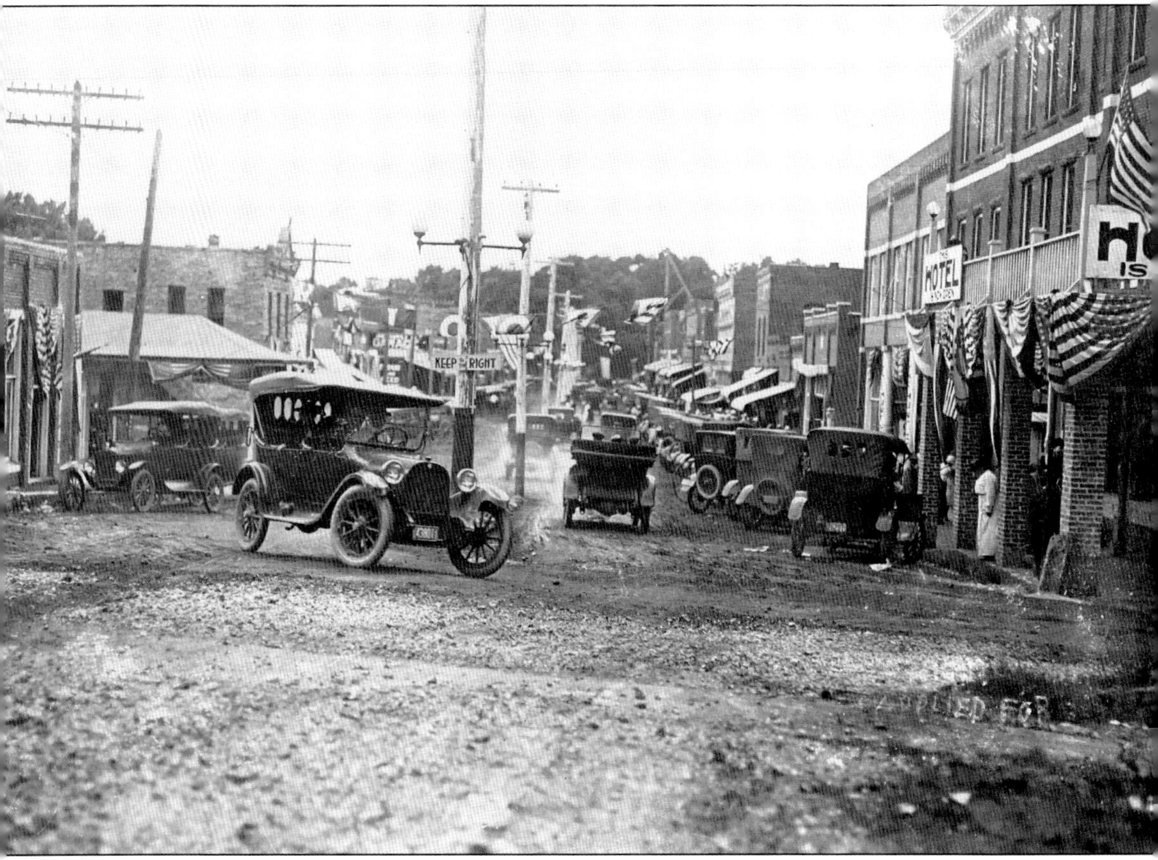

This is the north end of St. Nicholas Avenue (now Broadway) looking south in about 1925. The car in the foreground is a 1921 Dodge touring car, owned by Tony Brooks and driven by Olney Storey. The poles in the middle of the street not only divided the northbound and southbound lanes but also provided space for additional parking. (Courtesy of Siloam Springs Museum.)

On the Cover: Jennie Heath Sparks and her son William Clark Sparks are seen in a buggy in the Sager Creek bottom below the dam in about 1906. The rockwork along the tree-lined bluff is at the Siloam Springs. The champion surrey horse was named Frances. Jennie's husband, Marion, bought, sold, and traded mules and horses, and their beautiful home still stands at 604 South Maple Street. (Courtesy of Siloam Springs Museum.)

IMAGES
of America

SILOAM SPRINGS

Don Warden

ARCADIA
PUBLISHING

ISBN 978-0-7385-9429-3

Published by Arcadia Publishing
Charleston, South Carolina

Printed in the United States of America

Library of Congress Control Number: 2012942639

For all general information, please contact Arcadia Publishing:
Telephone 843-853-2070
Fax 843-853-0044
E-mail sales@arcadiapublishing.com
For customer service and orders:
Toll-Free 1-888-313-2665

Visit us on the Internet at www.arcadiapublishing.com

Dedicated to the people of Siloam Springs who have donated their photographs, objects, and stories to be preserved in the Siloam Springs Museum.

Contents

Acknowledgments 6

Introduction 7

1. Pioneering Sagers and Town-Building Gunters: 1839–1860 9
2. Civil War and Reconstruction: 1861–1878 13
3. Siloam City from Boom to Bust: 1879–1893 17
4. Saved by the Railroad: 1894–1929 23
5. The New Deal: 1930–1941 57
6. From World War II to the Bypass: 1942–1962 71
7. Downtown versus the Bypass: 1963–Present 91

Acknowledgments

This book would not have been possible without the generous donations citizens have made over the years to the Siloam Springs Museum. I am grateful to Helen "Johnnie" Johnson for her 20 years of volunteer work to catalogue and index the museum's collection. The museum has been collecting the history of Siloam Springs since 1969, including most of the photographs in this book and many more that could not be included here. Unless otherwise noted, all images appear courtesy of the Siloam Springs Museum. I am also grateful to Sammye Lou Gunter and the late Bub Gunter for generously sharing their family photographs and stories. I am grateful to Don Cundiff for sharing some important photographs from his collection. I am grateful to Bob Wasson for allowing use of an image of Sager Cabin that he made years ago. Finally, I am grateful to Simone Monet-Williams of Arcadia Publishing for her guidance and encouragement, especially at critical points in this process.

INTRODUCTION

Siloam Springs is literally a city on the edge. The town's western boundary is on the Arkansas-Oklahoma state line, which is also the western edge of Benton County. Western Arkansas and eastern Oklahoma are in the transition zone between the woodlands to the east and the Great Plains to the west, and patches of prairie were important in the early white settlement of the area. A few of these patches still have the distinctive "prairie bumps" that are often confused for prehistoric Indian mounds. In 2000, the Arkansas Natural Heritage Commission recognized an 80-acre prairie remnant near Siloam Springs as the Chesney Prairie Natural Area.

It is thought that the first white settlers in Benton County were on Beaties Prairie, near present-day Maysville, in the northwest corner of the county just before 1830. Other families soon joined them, and a post office was established in 1840. During the Cherokee Trail of Tears, one detachment traveled through Maysville on their way to the Cherokee Nation in Indian Territory (now Oklahoma).

Rivers were another focus of early white settlement. By 1839, Simon Sager and family were living along Sager Creek in what is now Siloam Springs. There is more about them in the first chapter. Other early settlement in western Benton County was along Flint Creek, which is at the north edge of Lindsey's Prairie north of Siloam Springs. Lindsey's Prairie Post Office was open from 1842 to 1845. Key Lodge No. 7, Ancient Free and Accepted Masons, which still meets in Siloam Springs, was chartered on Lindsey's Prairie in 1854.

Until Oklahoma became a state in 1907, the border area with Indian Territory was a legally complicated area. Cherokee laws and law enforcement regulated the Cherokee people, but federal laws and law enforcement were required if a white person was involved. Arkansas law enforcement stopped at the state line, so town marshals in Siloam Springs often also served as US deputy marshals who could follow white lawbreakers into the Indian Territory.

In the 1870s and 1880s, resorts were developed around springs at several places in the Ozarks of Arkansas and Missouri. These resorts relied on testimonials from those who claimed cures. One such place was Eureka Springs in Carroll County, and the success of that resort probably inspired John Valentine Hargrove in March 1880 to have his land along Sager Creek surveyed into a new town that he called Siloam City. There is more about this in the third chapter.

In 1880, a railroad was built through central Benton County, and part of Hargrove's promotion of Siloam City was that a railroad would surely soon be built through western Benton County. As a Hico merchant, Hargrove knew first hand about the large volume of trade that stores could expect to get from residents of the Cherokee Nation. It was on this three-pronged promotion of springs, train, and trade that Siloam City boomed in its first few years of existence.

In 1881, the town was incorporated as Siloam Springs. But by the mid-1880s, some people were beginning to wonder if the railroad was ever going to be built through western Benton County after all, and if maybe Siloam Springs was overbuilt, so they moved away. The devastating flood of 1892 was the first recorded flood in the town and probably increased the anxiety of those who were still living here. After these events, it is easy to imagine the joy of learning that the railroad was beginning to build south, despite the national economic problems of 1892 and 1893. The railroad arrived in Siloam Springs in December 1893 and ushered in a period of prosperity. Most of the buildings now standing downtown were built between 1894 and the beginning of the Great Depression.

From this town's founding through the 1960s, it was known as a "Sundown Town," meaning that there were signs on the outskirts of town warning African Americans not to remain in town after sunset. There are no known photographs of these signs, but there are numerous reports of their existence. There are also tourism brochures promoting the town as a place where African Americans were not seen. In more recent years, large signs were placed at the outskirts of town reading, "Welcome to Siloam Springs Where Jesus is Lord. Welcome to God's Country."

Agriculture is the base of the area economy. Through the 1870s and 1880s, Benton County produced commercial quantities of tobacco, and in some years, this county produced more tobacco than any other county in the state. From the 1880s into the 1920s, apples were the main cash crop, and 1919 was the peak year of production, when Benton County produced more apples than any other county in the nation. Since the 1920s, chicken broiler production has topped the list of agricultural output, and for several years, Benton and Washington Counties took turns at top place nationally in broiler and egg production and were near the top in turkey production. These products are still important in Benton County, as are beef cattle. Milk cattle were once important here, and Siloam Springs had a Pet Milk plant.

The end of World War I brought a flu epidemic that closed local schools. Then, in 1919, John Elward Brown opened his college with a three-fold concept of higher education. The Great Depression brought bank failures and New Deal construction projects. World War II brought ration books and stars in the front windows of local homes. The postwar years brought new street names, a new hospital, and more. The bypass devastated the downtown and led to development of a Main Street program to revitalize the downtown while preserving the look and feel of this National Register Historic District.

In May 2012, *Smithsonian* magazine named Siloam Springs one of the 20 best small towns in America. In the same month, *US News & World Report* ranked Siloam Springs High School as no. 22 in Arkansas. Once again in 2012, *US News & World Report: America's Best Colleges* named John Brown University as one of the best regional colleges in the South. JBU has been ranked in the top three in each of the past five years and in the top 10 in each of the past nine years. In recent years, *Forbes* magazine has ranked JBU as a best value in higher education.

One

Pioneering Sagers and Town-Building Gunters 1839–1860

Simon Sager (1802–1864); his wife, Willminea (1805–1871); and their first five children were born in Germany. The youngest of these children was born in 1836, so their trip to the new world was after that. The family arrived in Baltimore on January 1, 1837, and the next child was born in Missouri on April 7, 1837, which shows that the family made this trip in three months or less. On November 12, 1839, Simon Sager filed a Declaration of Intention to become a citizen in Benton County, placing him here by that date, and he is thought to be the first white settler in what is now Siloam Springs. The family's first child born in Arkansas, Mary Ann, was born in 1840.

Their cabin, now standing on the John Brown University campus, was the family's second cabin, built in 1844–1845. The family conducted subsistence agriculture, and for the small amount of cash needed, Simon Sager bought oxen from local farmers and sold them in Kansas City.

As a child, Nancy Ward traveled west with her family on the Trail of Tears. In 1845, she married Caldeen Gunter, who had moved to the area a few years earlier. They established the town of Hico, using a Cherokee word meaning "clear" or "sparkling water," a reference to the springs that emerge in the vicinity of the town. The primary trade for Hico businesses was with people from the nearby Cherokee Nation in Indian Territory, and the 1889 Goodspeed *History of Benton County* describes Hico as "the leading place" in southwest Benton County until Siloam Springs was established. A post office was established at Hico in 1855.

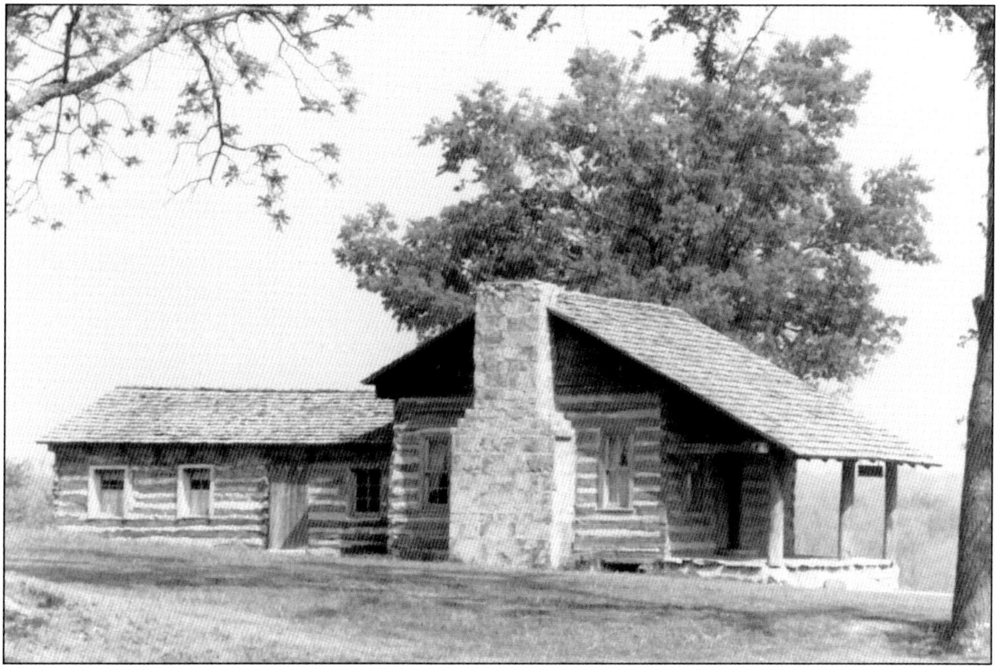

Sager Cabin sits today in the middle of the John Brown University campus. Bob Wasson shot the image above so that nothing modern would appear in the background. The wood sample seen below is from a log in the front section of the cabin. University of Arkansas tree-ring specialist Dr. David Stahle found that this tree was a sapling in 1730 and was cut down in 1844. This is also the date on the land patent for the first piece of property Simon Sager owned, so this cabin probably originally stood on that property, which is north of Sager Creek. The third piece of evidence that points at this same year is Mary Ann Sager Britt's memory of moving into this cabin with her family in 1845. (Above, courtesy of Bob Wasson; below, courtesy of Siloam Springs Museum.)

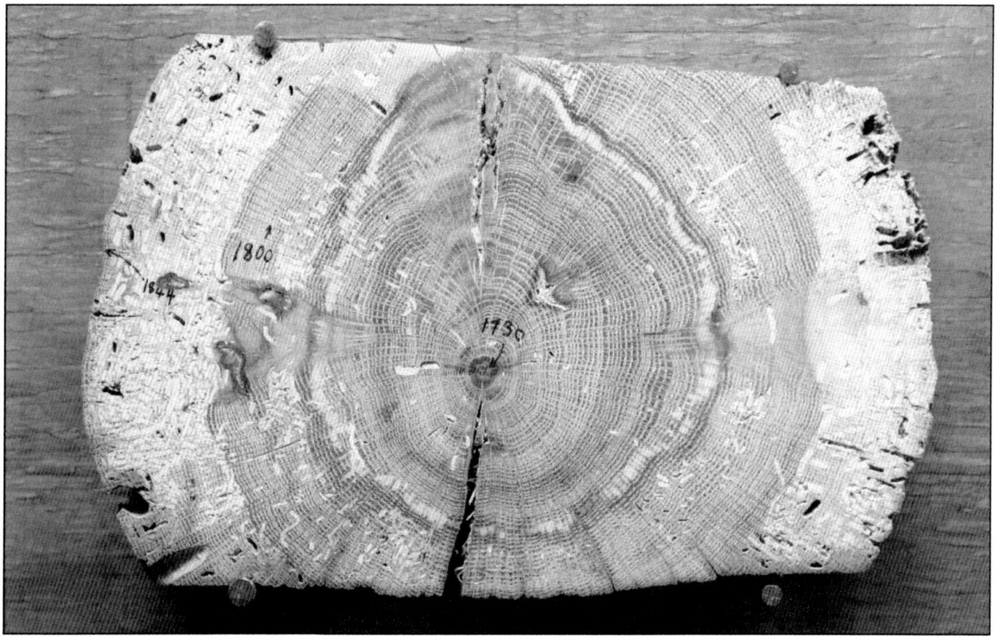

Caldeen Gunter (1818–1898) was born in Tennessee and raised primarily in Alabama where he learned to farm. He settled in Benton County in the early 1840s and married Nancy Ward (below) in 1845. During the Civil War, he fought for the Confederacy. He was a Mason and in 1889 he still owned between 900 and 1,000 acres of land near Siloam Springs. (Courtesy of C.L. "Bub" and Sammye Lou Gunter.)

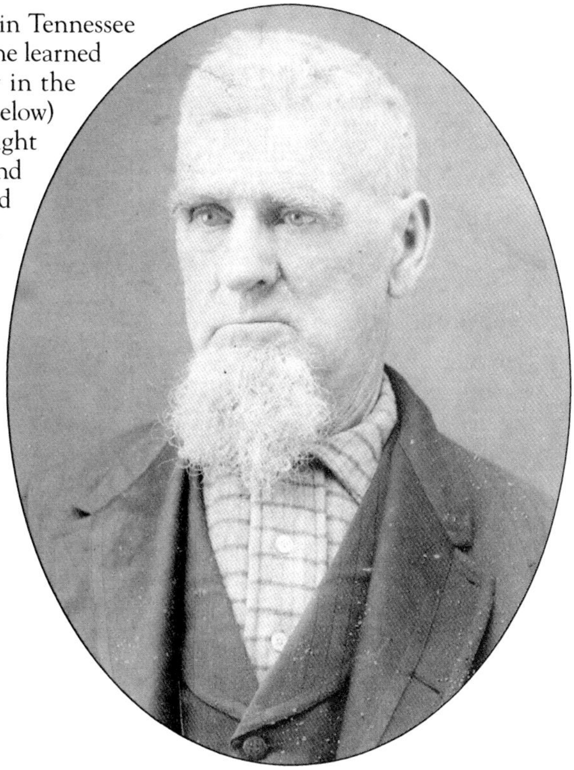

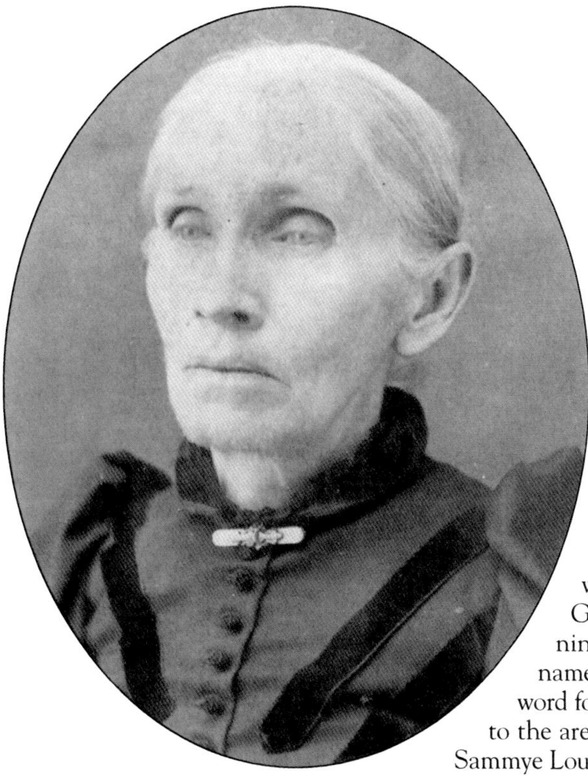

Nancy Ward Gunter (1830–1907) was born in Georgia. Her father was Cherokee, and the family was removed to Indian Territory while she was still a child. She married Caldeen Gunter (above) in 1845, and they had nine children who lived to adulthood. She named the town of Hico, using a Cherokee word for "clear" or "sparkling water," referring to the area springs. (Courtesy of C.L. "Bub" and Sammye Lou Gunter.)

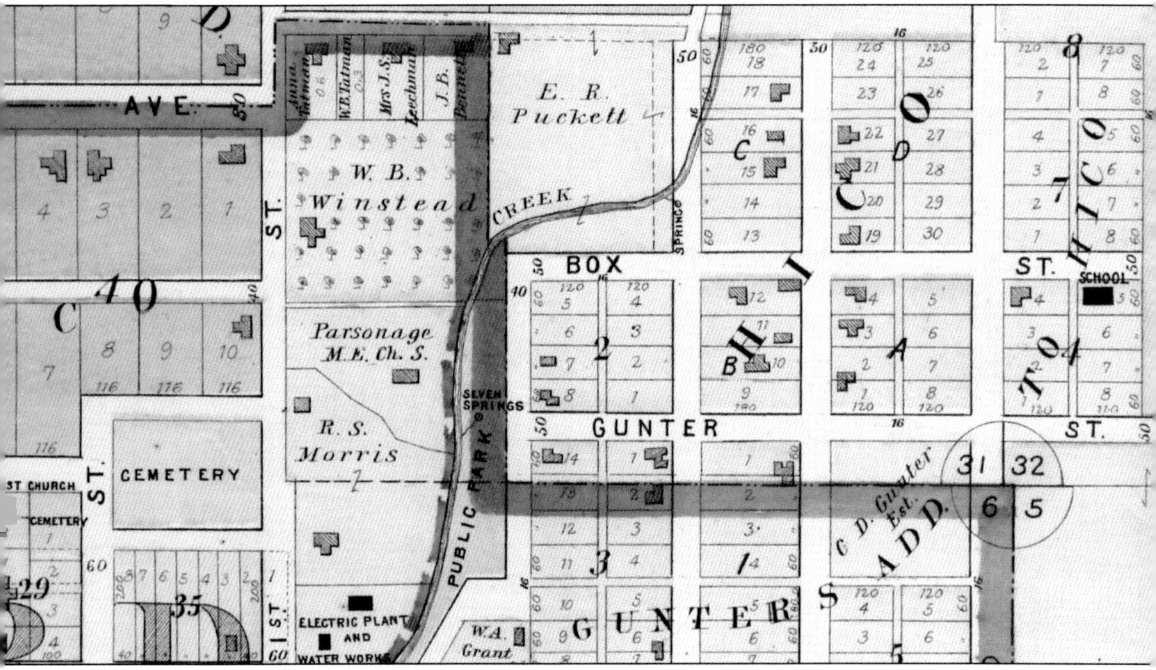

This detail from the 1903 map of Siloam Springs shows the location of the original four-block Hico townsite, labeled here as blocks A, B, C, and D. On this map, Hico is still outside the city limits of Siloam Springs, but some of the additions to Hico had already been annexed into Siloam Springs. Siloam Springs and Hico stood as two separate communities for 24 years, and at times, each town had its own post office. The Hico Post Office was closed in 1882, when the Siloam Springs Post Office opened, but then was reopened from 1885 to 1894. By 1889, nearly all of the businesses that had been in Hico had moved to Siloam Springs. In 1904, Siloam Springs annexed the Hico townsite. Today, the south edge of this four-block area is Tahlequah Street, and the east edge is Hico Street. Hico cemetery is on the other side of Sager Creek from the townsite.

Two

Civil War and Reconstruction 1861–1878

During the Civil War, regular troops moved through western Benton County, especially along the Military Road that ran between Fort Smith, Arkansas, and Fort Scott, Kansas, and beyond. But the larger story in this area was the impact of irregular troops that supported one side or the other and took what they needed from area citizens or destroyed food and other valuable resources so that they would not fall into the hands of the other side. There were also outlaws who took advantage of this turbulent time. Citizens were forced to become creative in their methods for hiding things, especially food. After the end of the war, it took several years for the local economy to recover.

The Civil War divided the Cherokee Nation as sharply as it divided the United States. Stand Watie was a Cherokee who rose to the rank of general in the Confederate Army and was the last Confederate general to surrender. In contrast, the Cherokee Pin Indians fought for the Union by scouring northwest Arkansas looking for those who supported the Confederacy and taking or destroying their food and, in some cases, even killing them.

Mary Ann Sager (1840–1925) married James J. Britt (1837–1902) in 1856, and during the war, he joined the Confederates. Two sons of Simon and Willminea Sager also fought for the Confederacy.

Caldeen Gunter served in the Confederacy. He gave two trusted slaves a supply of gold to use while taking his family to Texas for the duration of the war. When they returned, he rewarded them with enough money to buy land in Adair County, Oklahoma. During the Civil War, Nancy Ward Gunter carried the charter for Key Lodge No. 7 for safekeeping. This lodge still meets. The original Gunter house was destroyed during the war, and it took the family until 1870 to be able to begin construction on a new house.

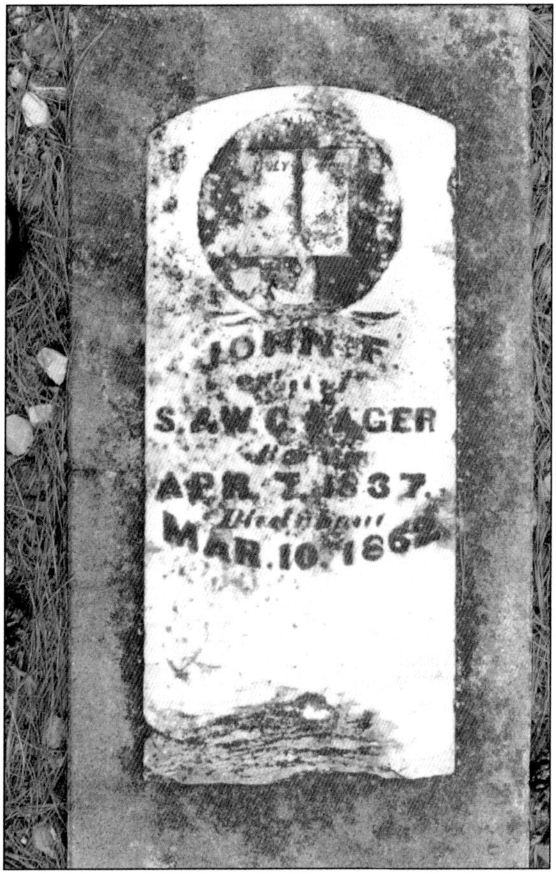

On about March 10, 1862, John Sager (1837–1862), his brother Samuel (1842–after 1880), and two other men were returning to their homes near Hico following the Battle of Pea Ridge, which was in northeastern Benton County. They were members of a Confederate volunteer unit, 2nd Company A, 2nd Regiment, Arkansas, and they were traveling at night and hiding during the day. They were hiding in the woods above the spring pictured below, which is in Sleepy Hollow along what was then known as the Springtown to Hico Road, now Dawn Hill Road just west of Highway 59, when they were attacked by a group of Pin Indians, members of the 2nd and 3rd Cherokee Home Guards. John Sager and two other men were killed in the attack. Only Samuel Sager escaped.

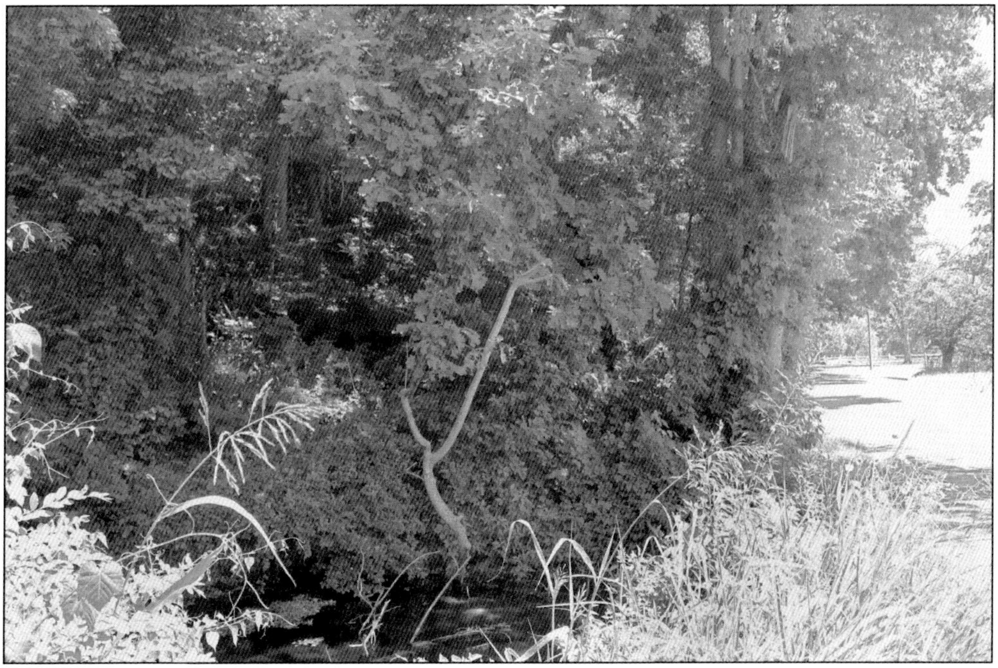

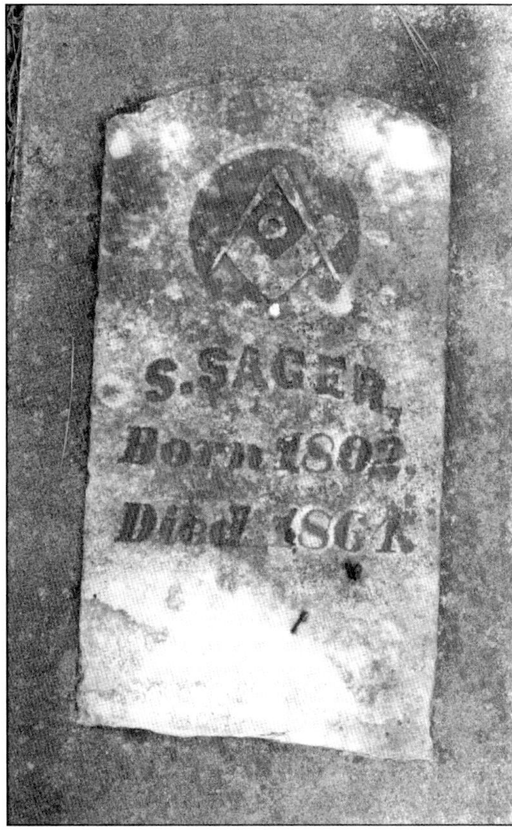

Pin Indians also killed Simon Sager (1802–1864). In 1851, he sold his 1844 cabin to John DeArmond and moved his family to a cabin near Box Spring on what is now the Siloam Springs Country Club. This spring is the headwaters of Sager Creek, so it was a reliable water source for the family. The photograph below was taken during a severe drought, and even then, there was always water in the creek downstream from this spring. In the summer of 1864, a group of Pins called Sager from his cabin, led him a short distance from the cabin, and fatally shot him.

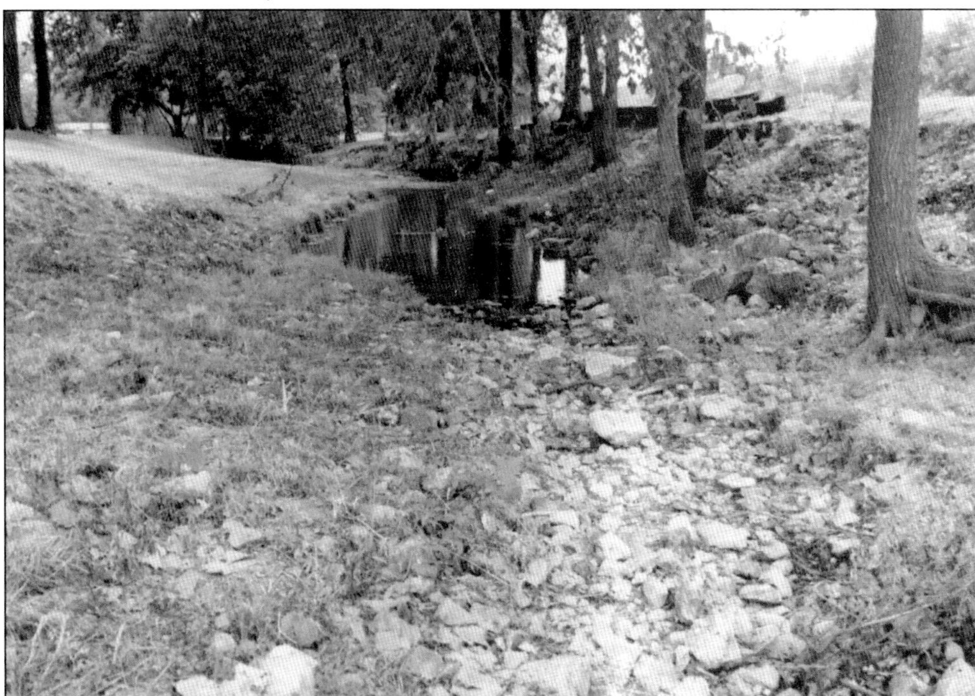

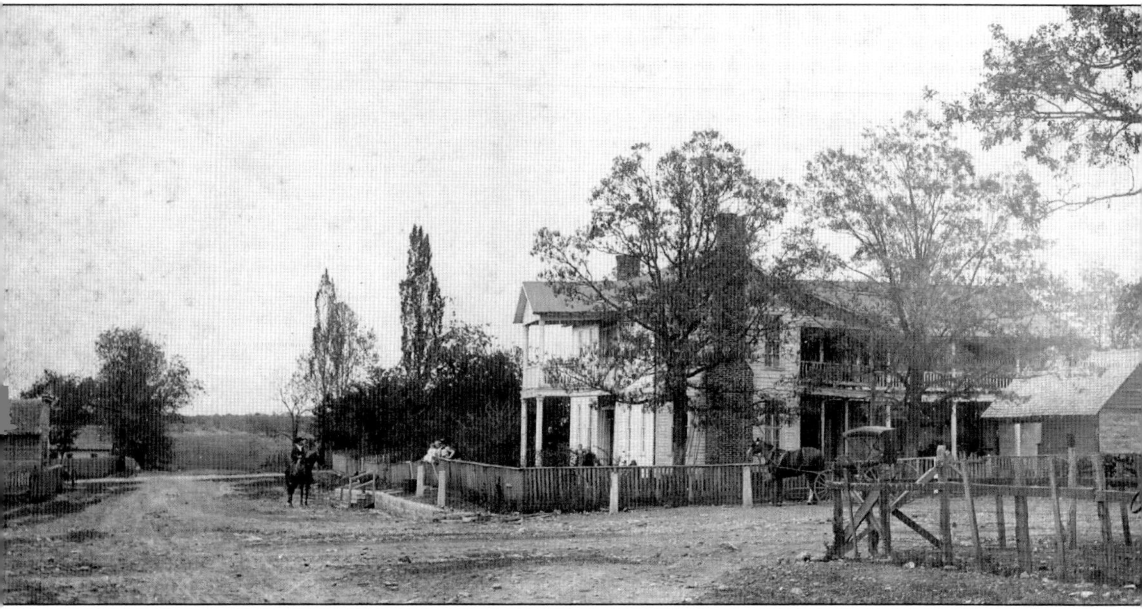

This is the house the Gunter family built in about 1870 in Hico. It stood on Block A, lots Nos. 1 and 2, and this is the view looking north. The pre–Civil War Gunter house was destroyed during the war, and the stone outbuilding near the house was all that survived. The four hitching posts around the house reflect the amount of entertaining the family did. The low stone wall beside the street at the front of the house would have made it easier to get into or out of a wagon or buggy. This is described as the largest home in the area and was the site of many weddings and parties. The house stood until about 1970, and tearing it down revealed construction details like the six oak corner posts extending vertically 30 feet from foundation to roof. The frame was held together with wooden pegs and wedges. (Courtesy of C.L. "Bub" and Sammye Lou Gunter.)

Three

Siloam City from Boom to Bust 1879–1893

In 1879, the city of Eureka Springs was gaining a reputation as a health resort, and it seems likely that the success of that Ozarks town helped to inspire Hico merchant and Union veteran John Valentine Hargrove to plan a similar resort. Resorts are built on testimonials, and the first testimonial about the springs here featured a man who drank from the Siloam Springs and did not suffer the pain he usually felt after eating or drinking anything. His physician, Dr. H. Perry of Hico, named this the Siloam Springs, drawing the name from a healing described in the gospel of John (9:7).

Hargrove owned land in the Sager Creek valley that included this spring and had it surveyed into lots and a town he called Siloam City in March 1880. Main Street ran north near the spring.

The population of the new town boomed in its first few years of existence, reaching a peak of 2,264 in the summer of 1881 when it was incorporated as Siloam Springs. Owners of property surrounding the new town had plats surveyed and made additions to Siloam Springs in 1880, 1881, and early 1882. But by the mid-1880s, an increasing number of people who had come to Siloam Springs to establish businesses were beginning to seriously wonder if the railroad was ever going to be built to this town, and they began to move away.

By the 1890 census, the population had dropped to 821. This was probably the bottom of the slump in population, because the number would start to increase once it was certain that a rail line would soon be built to the town after all.

Even before the arrival of the railroad, there were apple-related businesses in and near Siloam Springs, including an evaporator to dry apples, an apple brandy distillery, and a cold storage plant.

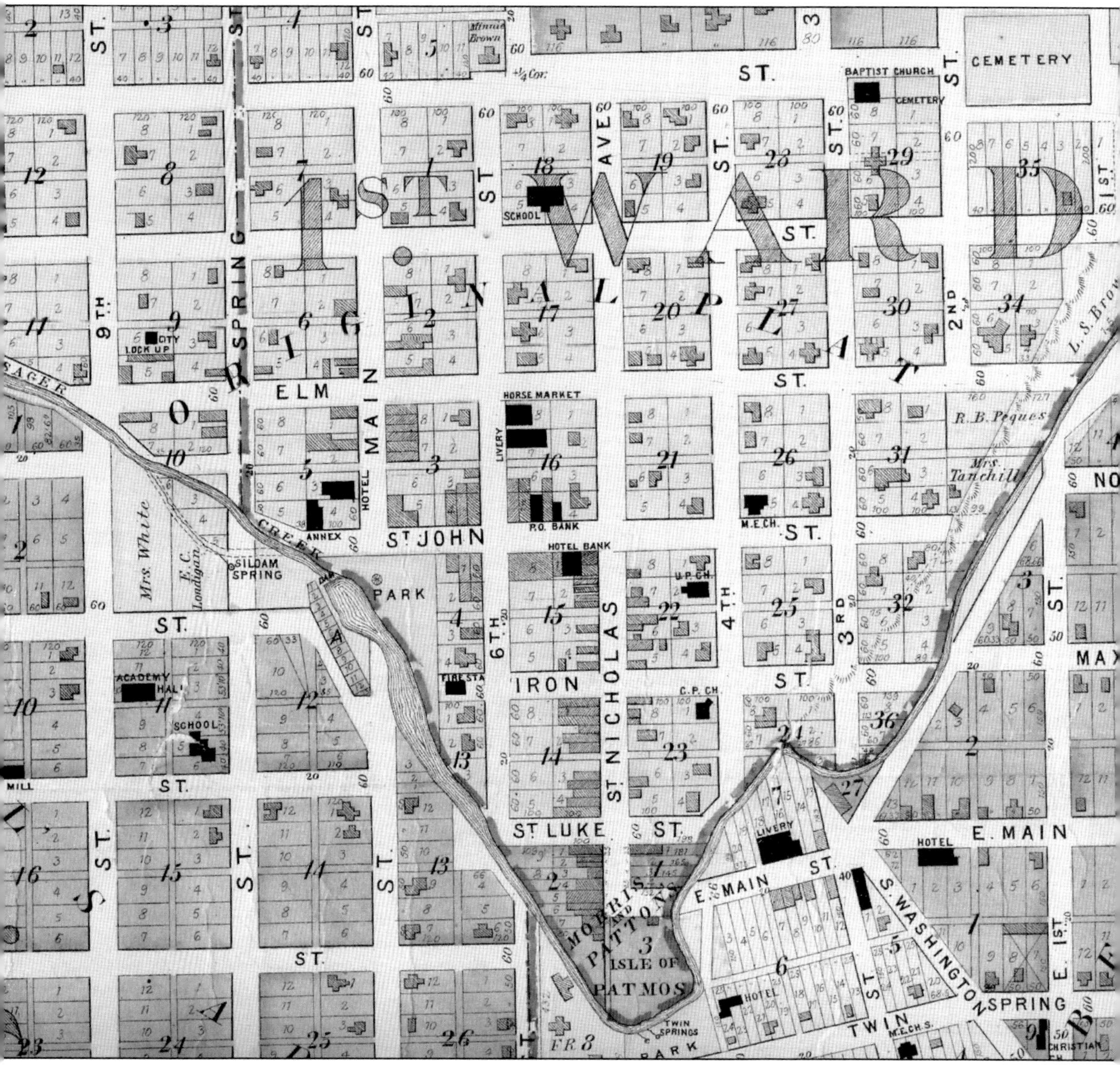

This detail from the 1903 map of Siloam Springs shows the original plat of the town, surveyed for John Valentine Hargrove in March 1880. The original plat runs from St. Luke Street on the south (now Alpine Street) to Tahlequah Street on the north (near the top edge of this image) and First Street on the east (now North Hill Street) to the block on the west side of Ninth Street (now North Maple Street). The dashed line near the Siloam Springs is probably the course of the creek before the 1892 flood. Hargrove moved his general store from Hico to Main Street. But when the Morris-Patton Addition between St. Luke Street and Sager Creek at the Twin Springs was added to the town, the business district was pulled east to include St. John Street and St. Nicholas Avenue. Between 1880 and 1882, owners of the land surrounding the new town surveyed and platted additions to Siloam Springs.

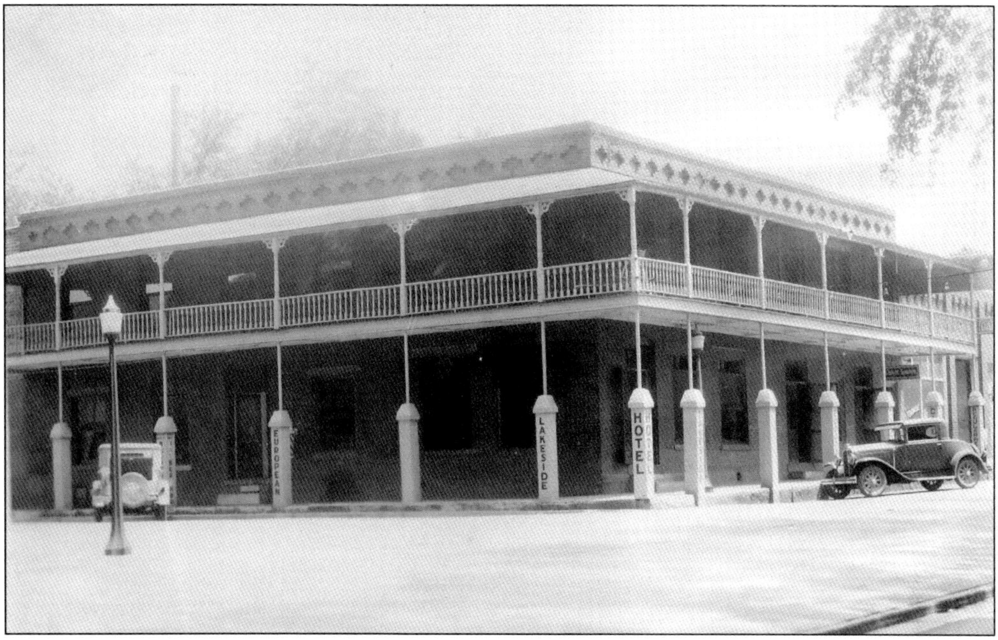

The Lakeside Hotel (now Crown Hotel) was built in 1881 and is the oldest building downtown. Its original name is probably a reference to the lake formed by the dam on Sager Creek. It represents the need for housing during the initial population boom and, later, the need to house summer visitors who came here to drink at the springs.

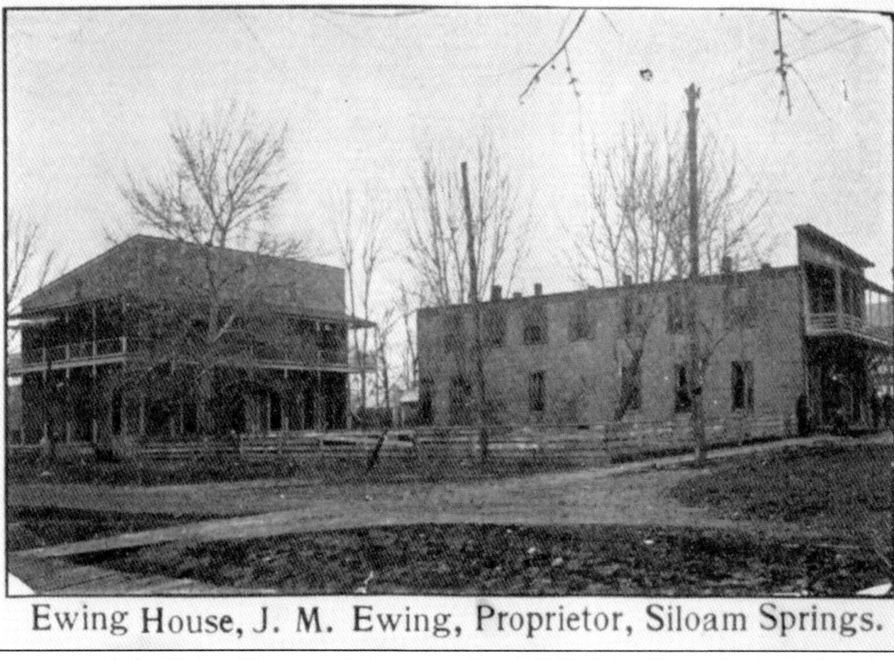

Ewing House, J. M. Ewing, Proprietor, Siloam Springs.

This picture of the Ewing House and Annex is dated 1903. John Ewing built the hotel on the right (the Ewing House) in 1882 and added the hotel on the left (the Annex) before 1897. The building on the left is still standing today and has served for several years as a restaurant.

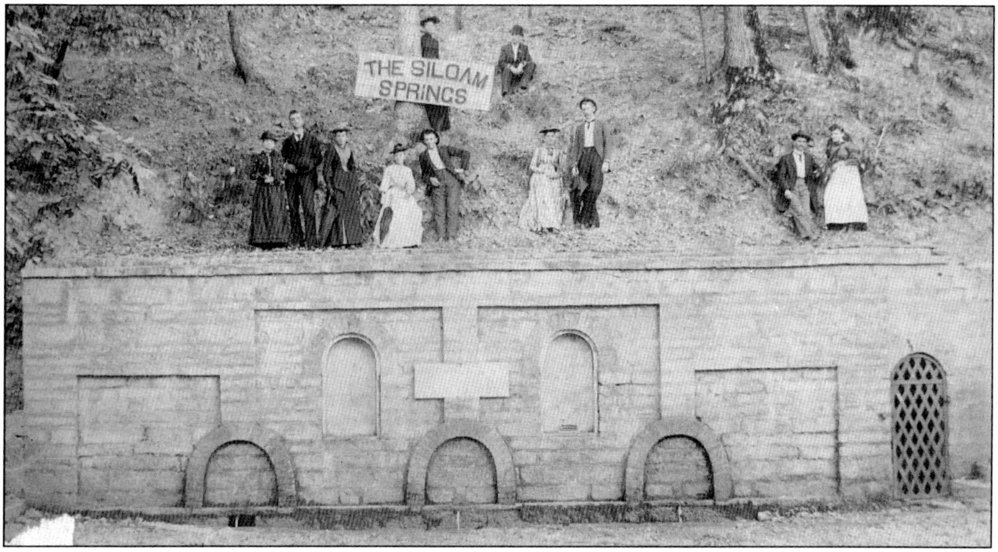

This wall stood at the Siloam Springs from 1882 to about 1895. Three pipes along this wall allowed spring water to flow out, and the grate doorway allowed workers to rearrange the pipes and dams behind the wall to keep the water flowing where they wanted it to go. The spring itself is under a rock shelf behind this wall.

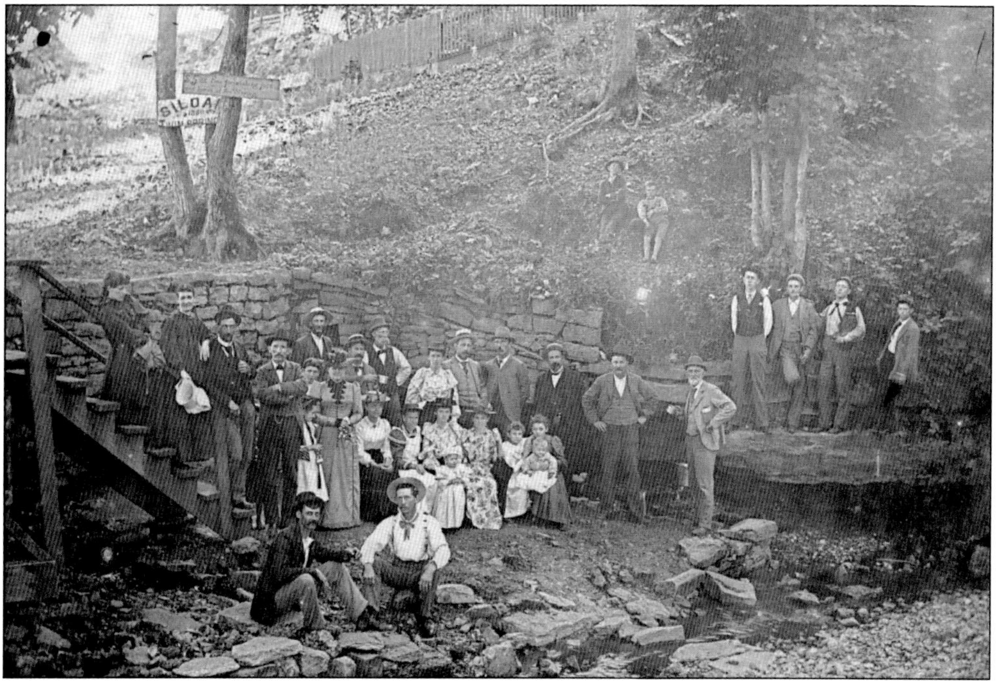

This is the wall at the Twin Springs in about 1885, when wooden steps provided access to the spring. Note that a hand-painted sign in the background threatens a $5 fine for those who wash their face and hands at this spring. There was a similar sign at the Siloam Springs. They may have been trying to keep the water clear for drinking.

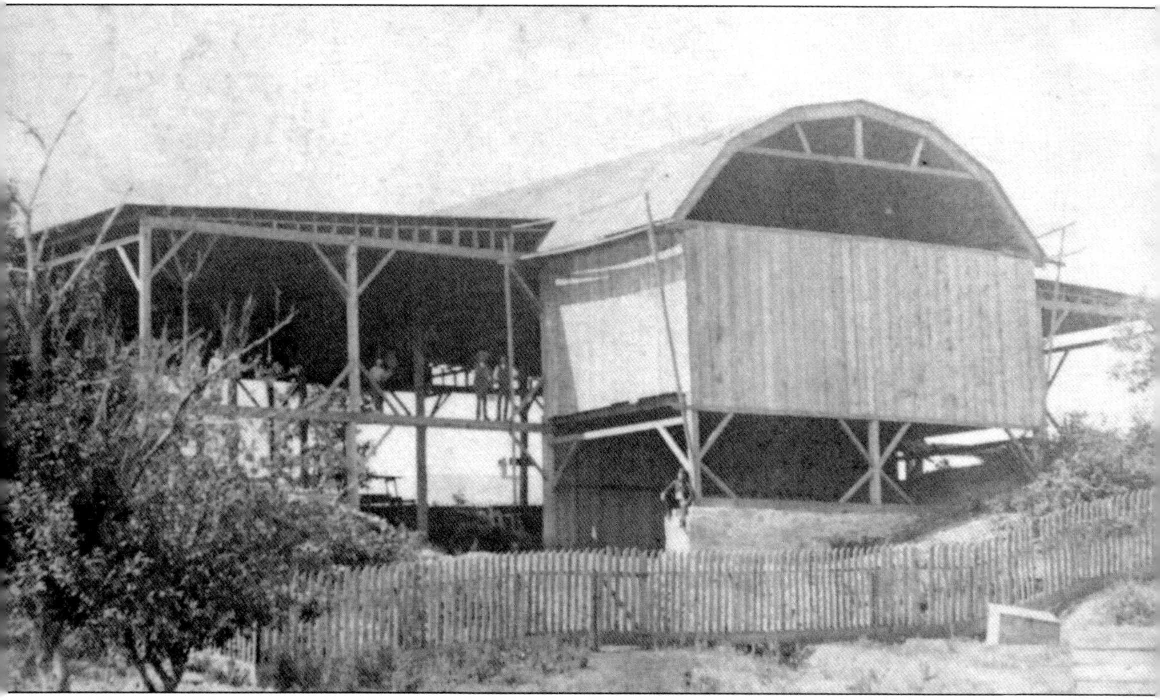

The first Chautauqua Building was 160 feet long, 120 feet wide, and could seat 2,500 people. It was completed in time for the 1885 summer program, and the Rev. John Heyl Vincent traveled from Lake Chautauqua, New York, to dedicate it. Lake Chautauqua is where the Chautauqua movement began in 1874 as a series of educational and inspirational programs for Methodist Sunday school teachers. Organizers soon opened these programs to a more general audience, and they became so popular that communities across the country were inspired to develop their own Chautauqua programs. There was also a year-round mail-order self-education program called Chautauqua Literary and Scientific Circle and a four-year course of study with continuing self-education through Seal Courses. Programs for children included the Loyal Temperance Legion, and there was an organization for teenagers. The initial phase of the Siloam Springs Chautauqua included all of these elements and lasted until 1890.

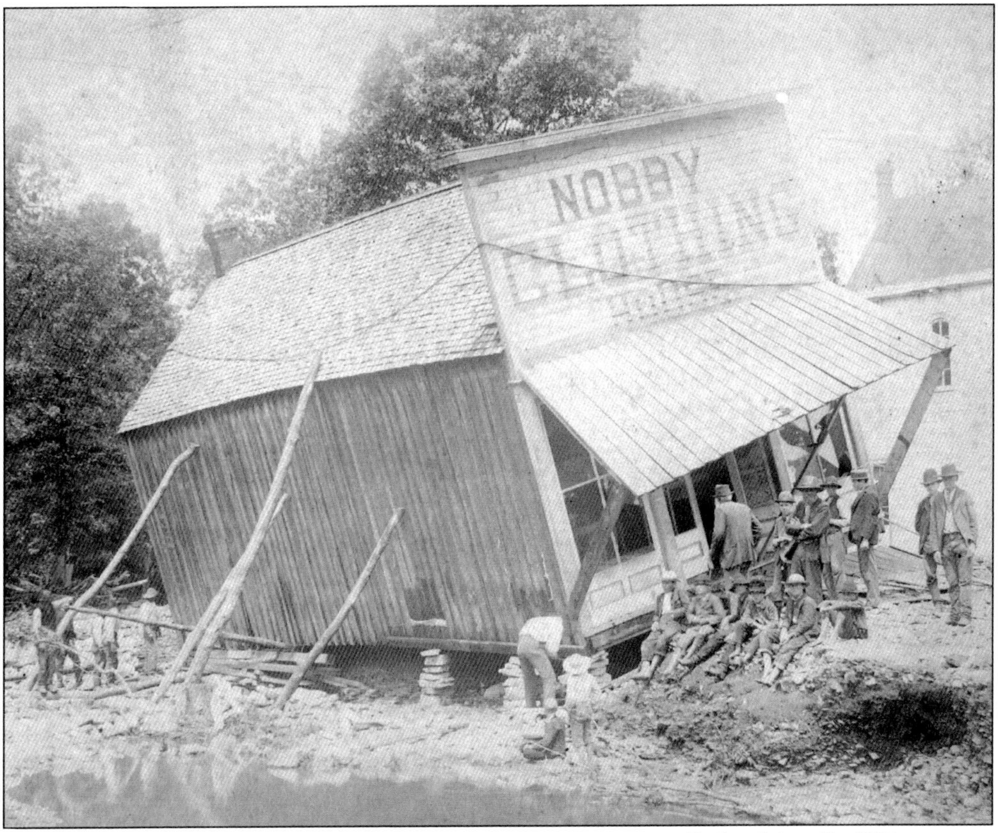

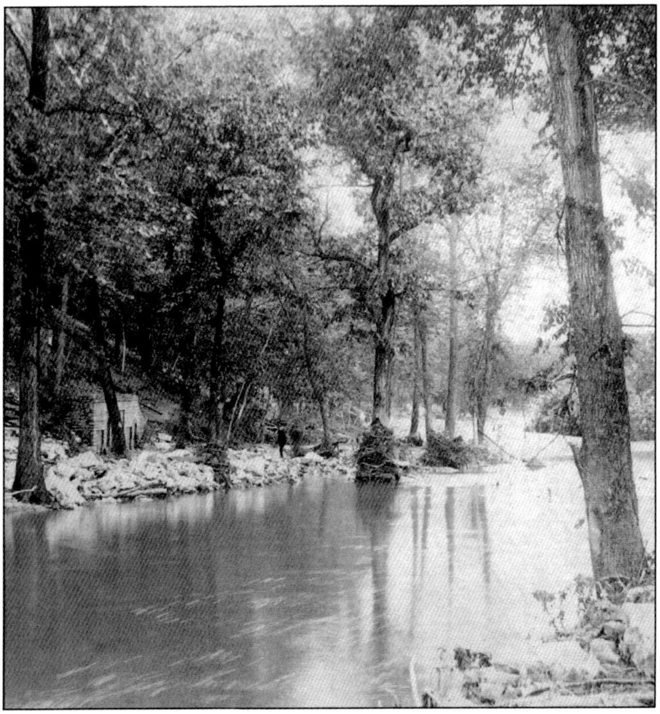

Friday, May 13, 1892, was the first recorded major flood in the Siloam Springs downtown. Three people were killed, and there was an estimated $28,500 in damages. Debris from buildings upstream caught at the curve of the creek at the Twin Springs, forcing the water to cut a new channel across the south end of St. Nicholas Avenue (now Broadway), which destroyed the businesses there and undermined Nobby Clothing, as seen above. The photograph below shows the area around the Siloam Springs after the water began to recede, but the debris caught on the trees shows how high the water was at the height of the flood.

Four

Saved by the Railroad 1894–1929

The Kansas City, Pittsburgh & Gulf rail line reached Siloam Springs on December 15, 1893. The town's business leaders pledged $20,000 to secure the railroad, plus land for the depot and for the rails through town. In 1900, this rail line was reorganized as the Kansas City Southern, which is the name it still has today. The railroad led to a sustained period of growth for the town that lasted until the beginning of the Great Depression. Most of the buildings now standing downtown were built during this time.

In 1898, citizens petitioned the city to install a system of electric lights. It took several years to fully install the system downtown, but within a few years, streetlights and some lights in businesses began to be seen. At about this same time, wires from the Siloam Springs Telephone Company also began to be seen downtown.

Apples were still the most important agricultural product of the area, and in 1919, Benton County produced more apples than any other county in the United States. But into the 1920s, orchards were so close together that diseases and pests spread easily from orchard to orchard, and attempts to control them led farmers to spend more and more on spray, until it reached a point that they were no longer making a profit. Most farmers left the apple-growing industry and destroyed their trees.

The apple industry was already in decline when the city of Rogers started an Apple Blossom Festival, and Siloam Springs participated each year. This town sent floats for the parade, complete with contestants for the Apple Blossom queen contest, and in 1925, Helen Duckworth of Siloam Springs was crowned queen.

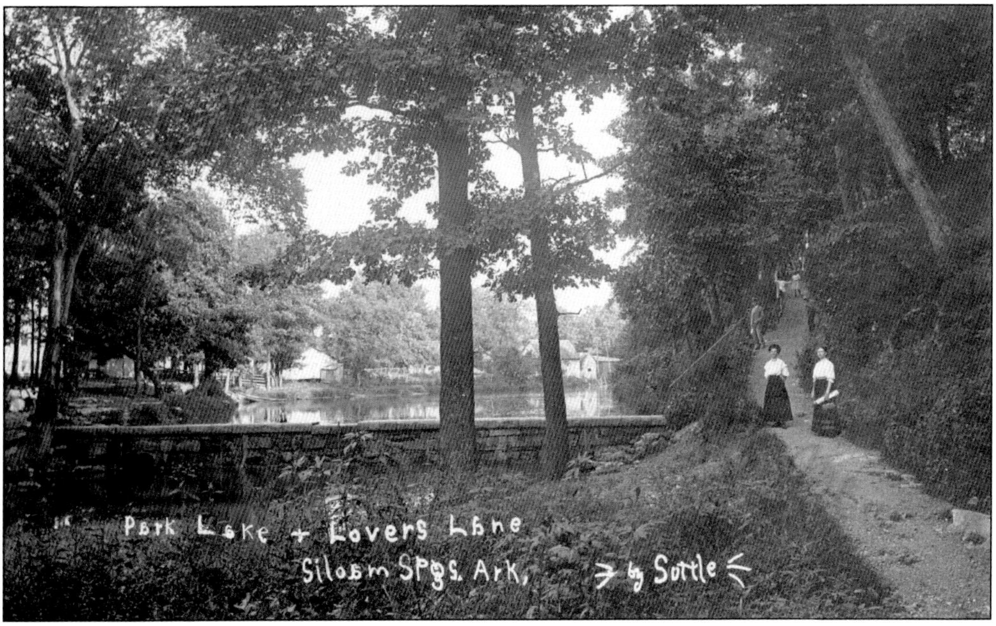

Lover's Lane was once a wide, well-maintained path along the bluff above Sager Creek. In the photograph above, it appears to have a fresh coat of gravel. The land it used belonged to the homeowners at the top of the bluff. Over the years, some of them began to restrict access to this path, and Lover's Lane has now largely returned to forest. The first dam on Sager Creek was built in the first few years after Siloam Springs was established and was lower than the dam that was built later. There are probably several members of the photographer's family featured in these photographs.

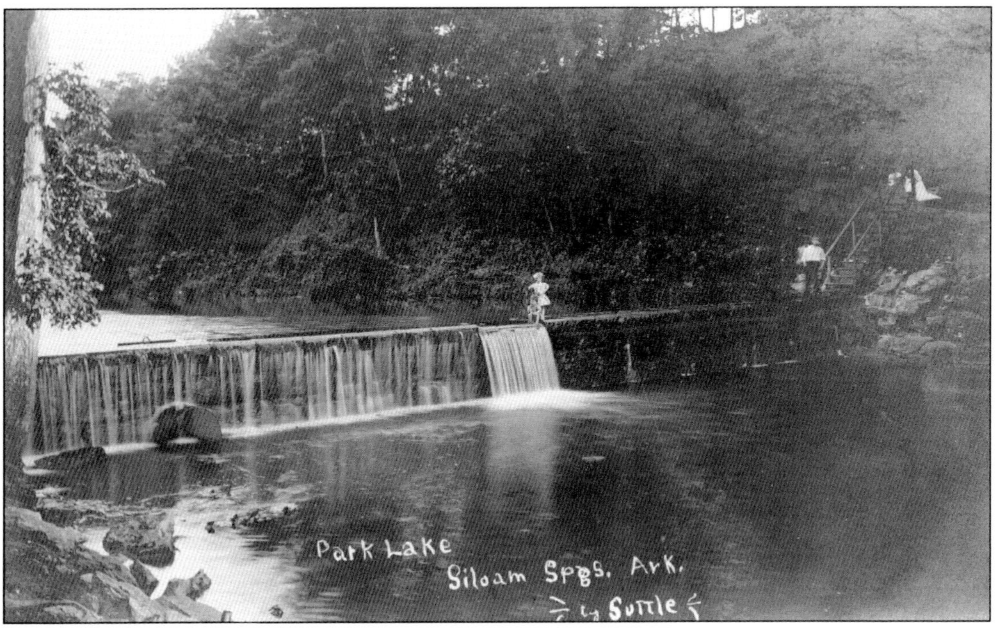

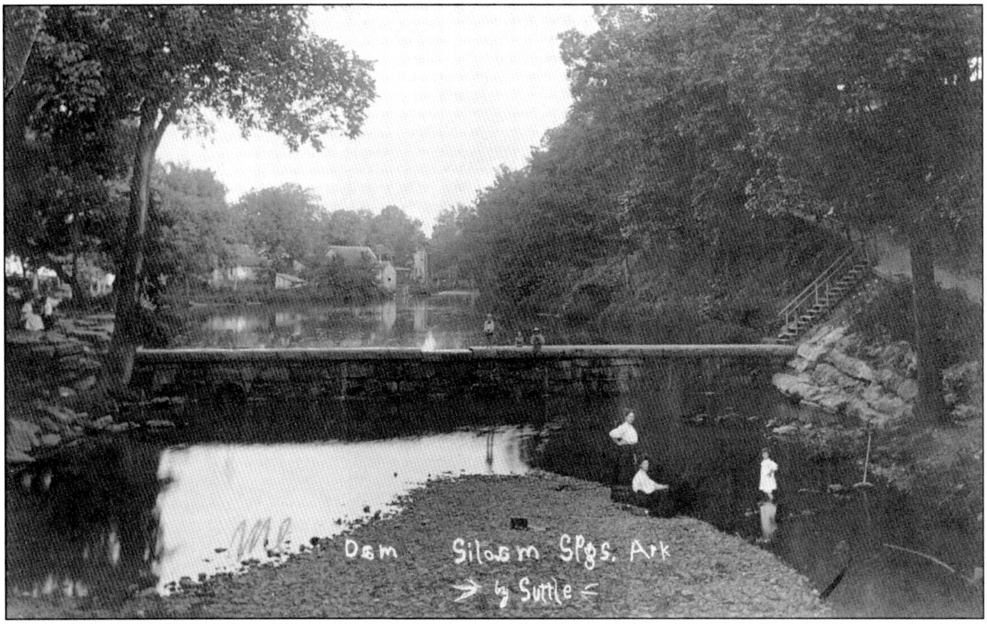

Sager Creek and the lake formed by the dam provide a cool retreat from the heat of summer, as seen in several of the photographs appearing in these pages. But photographs of people skating on the creek are rare. There probably have not been many winters that stayed cold enough for long enough periods of time to form ice thick enough to support a large group of skaters, like the group in the photograph below. But note that the water below the dam is not frozen, and there is still open water near the spillway. These photographs were taken from about the same spot on the footbridge spanning from the park to the Siloam Springs.

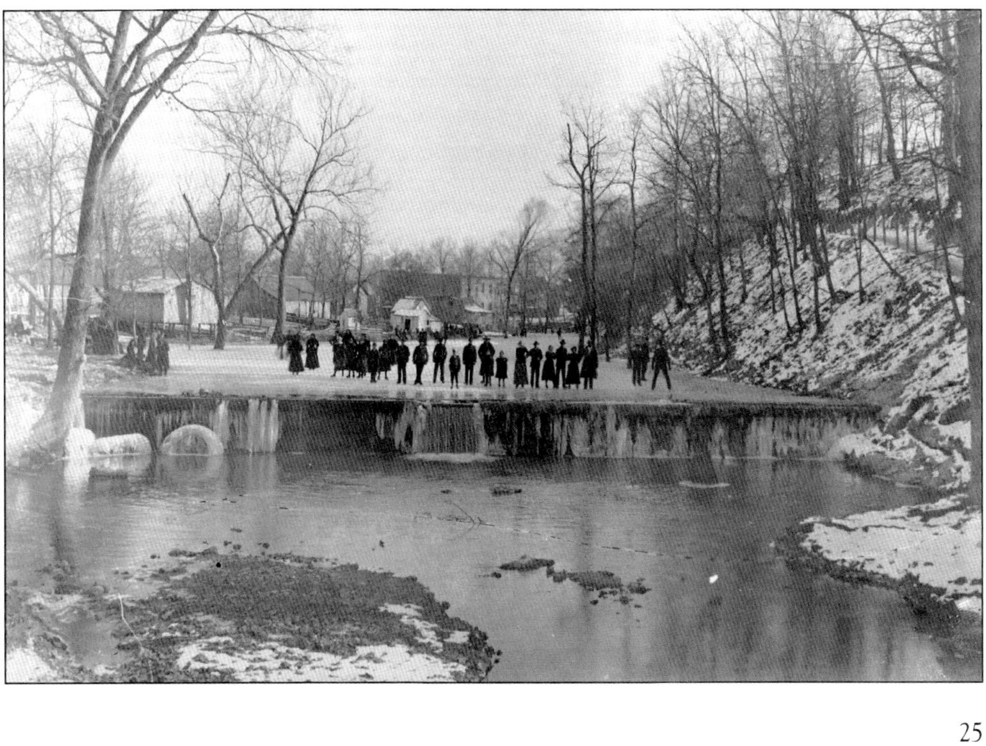

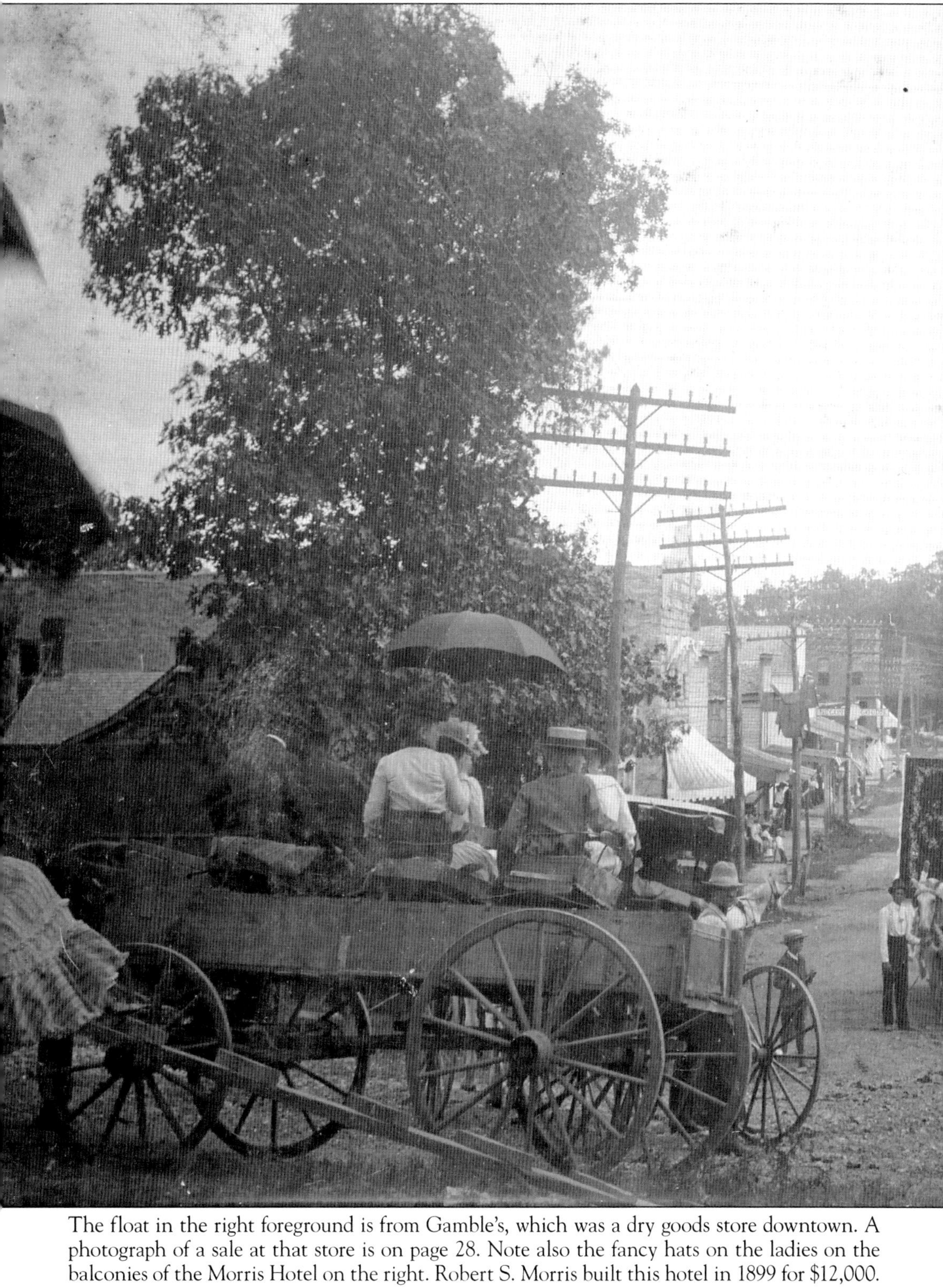

The float in the right foreground is from Gamble's, which was a dry goods store downtown. A photograph of a sale at that store is on page 28. Note also the fancy hats on the ladies on the balconies of the Morris Hotel on the right. Robert S. Morris built this hotel in 1899 for $12,000.

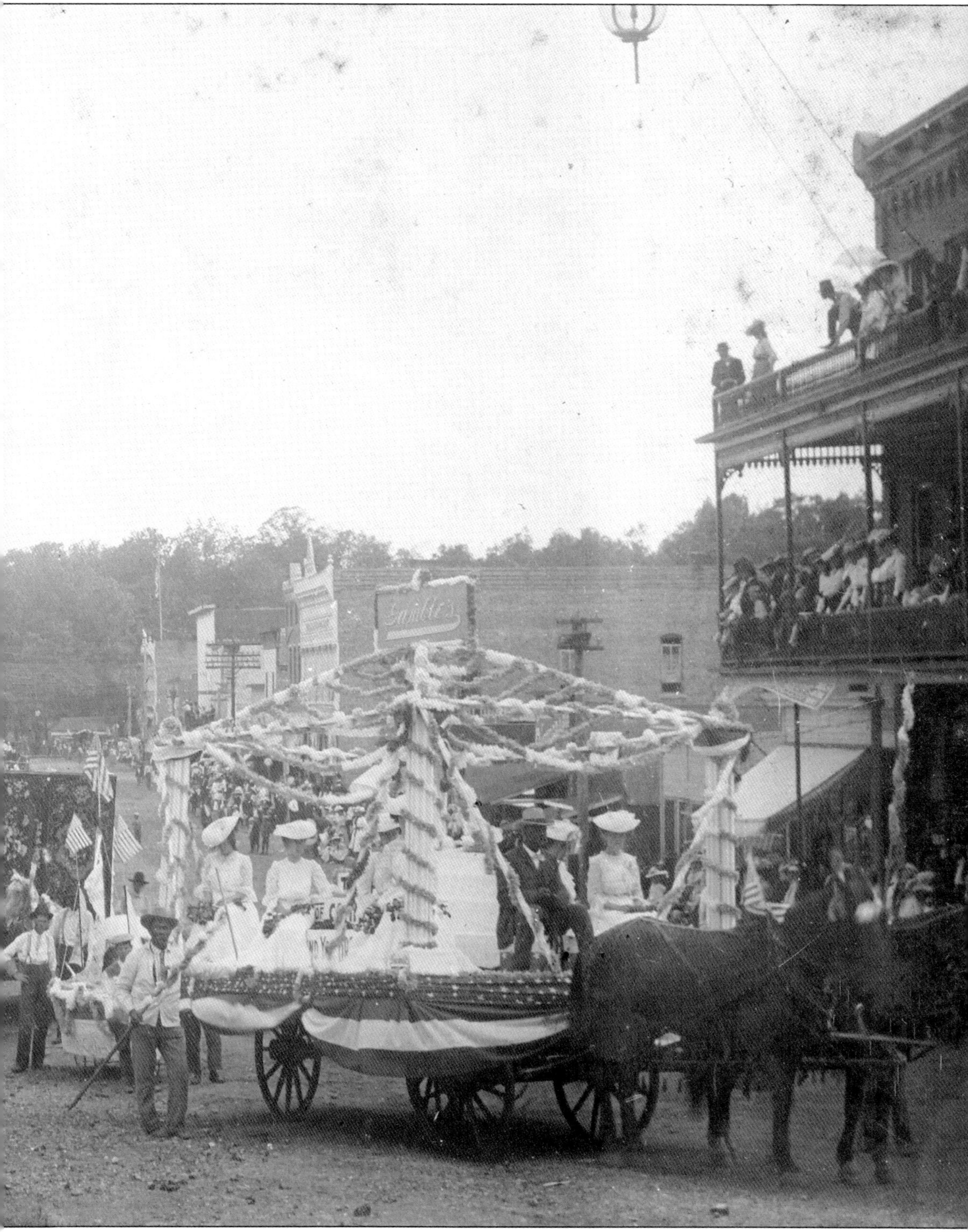

This building also contained the Bank of Siloam. Morris was a major backer of the town and improvements to it since he established his bank in 1881. Note also the streetlight over this intersection and the poles with wires for electricity and telephone service.

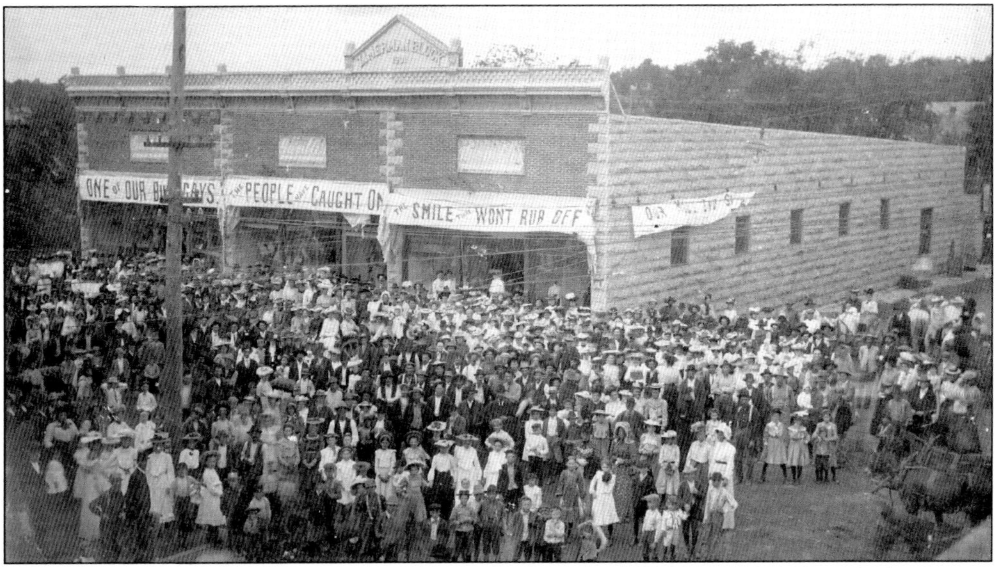

Gamble's was a dry goods store. This building was completed as the Zimerman Block in 1901. This photograph was taken on a Saturday afternoon, which was the last day of the big sale in the spring of 1904. This building still stands at the northwest corner of Mount Olive and University Streets. Only the building on the left (west) end of the row retains the facade seen here.

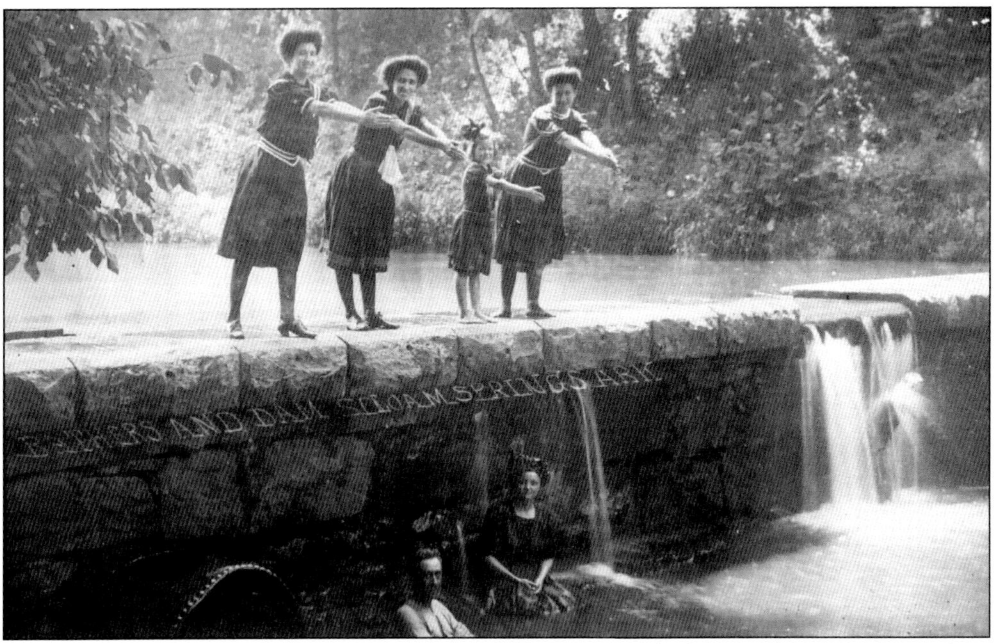
These divers are wearing the latest in swimming dresses, though they may not want to get their shoes wet. Several photographs from the early 1900s show women posing as if about to dive off this dam. Today, Sager Creek, the spring walls, and the gazebos are still popular backdrops for photographs.

The date 1894 is prominently displayed on the front of the building in the photograph at right. This is 113 North Broadway, which in recent years has been a dentist office. On the 1897 Sanborn map, the business shown in this building was a saddle, harness, and trunk shop. The building seen in the photograph below has some similar architectural features, so it may have also been built about 1894. This was the beginning of the post-railroad building boom when most of the brick and stone buildings downtown were constructed.

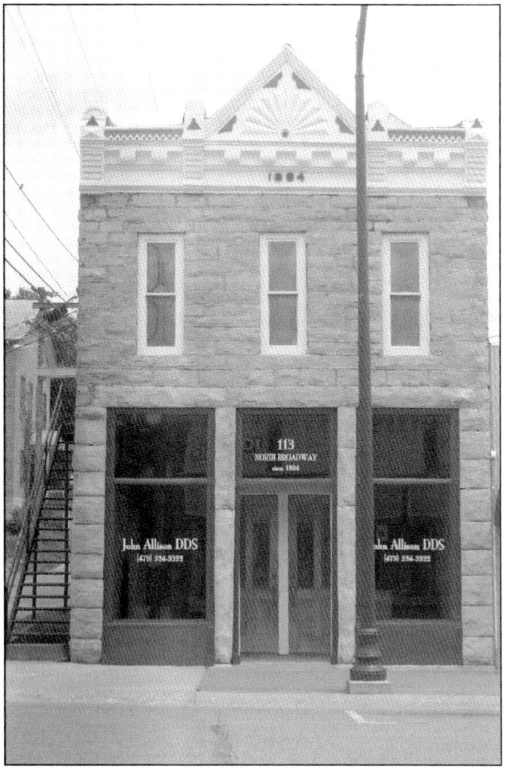

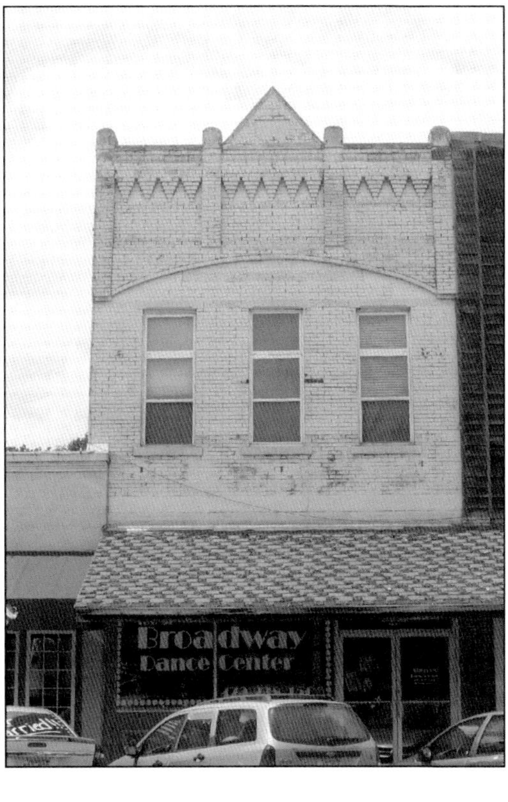

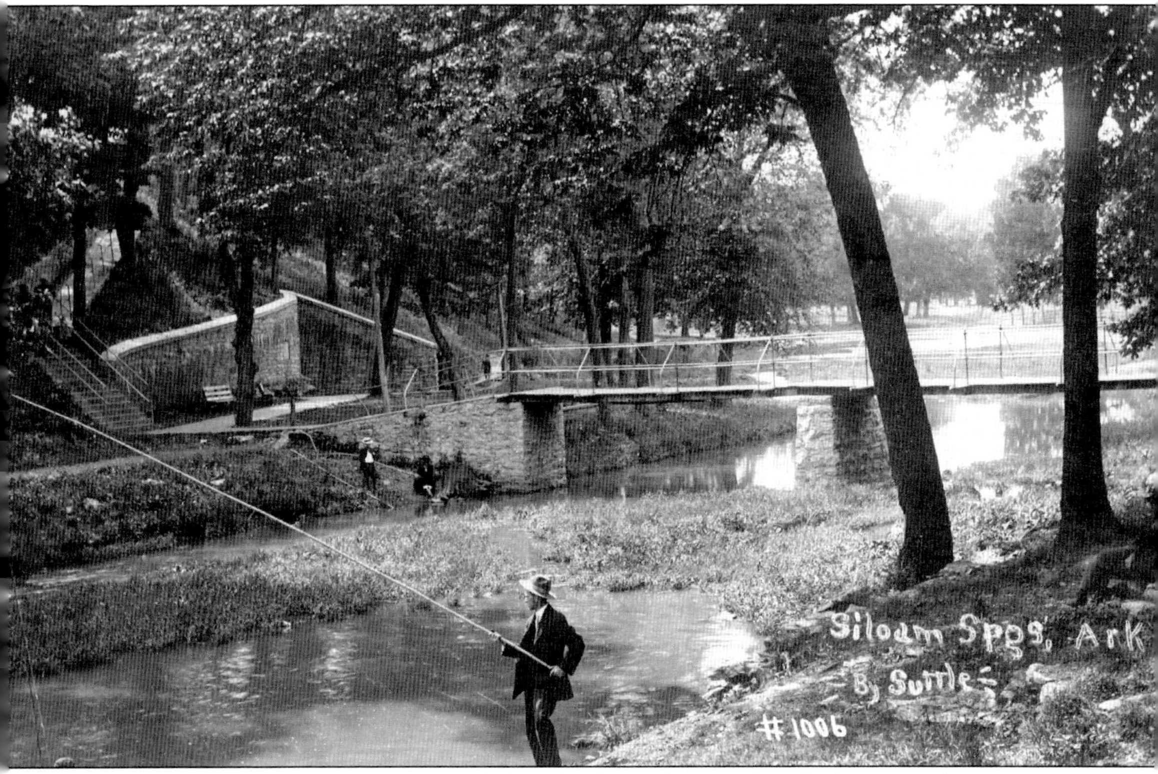

This remarkable image was taken just below the dam. The steps beside the 1897 Siloam Springs wall appear to be the ones there now, which are dated 1911, and the 1926 University Street Bridge is not yet in place, meaning this photograph was taken sometime between those years. A footpath along the bank beyond the Siloam Springs wall probably leads to the next spring. The graceful curves of the Siloam Springs wall stand out in this photograph and are still visible today. This photograph is labeled as taken by Suttle. Members of the Suttle family, including J. Henry and J.E. Suttle, were some of the leading photographers of Siloam Springs from about 1890 to about 1915. They partnered at various times with other local businessmen and had a studio for a while in Prairie Grove. (Courtesy of Don Cundiff.)

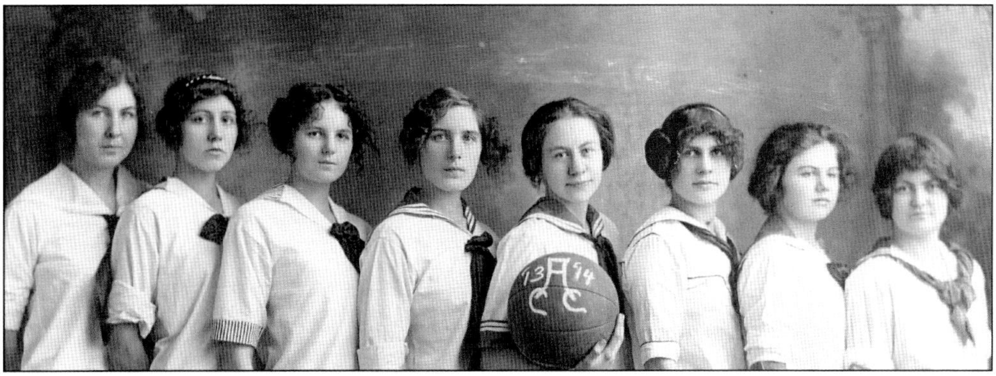

Arkansas Conference College (ACC) was the college of the Methodist Episcopal Church of Arkansas. The school opened in 1899 and offered academy (high school–level) classes and baccalaureate programs, primarily in teaching. Most students were in the academy, but there were almost always some students in the college program. The members of the ACC women's basketball team in 1913–1914 are, from left to right, Vera Cruse, Ethel Mead, Vera Smith, Ann Holland, Eula Keiser, Pauline Andrews, Ethel Whitehead, and Kate Williams. ACC did not have an indoor gymnasium, so practices were weather dependent. The 1915 yearbook optimistically states, "We expect a good indoor court and a champion team next year."

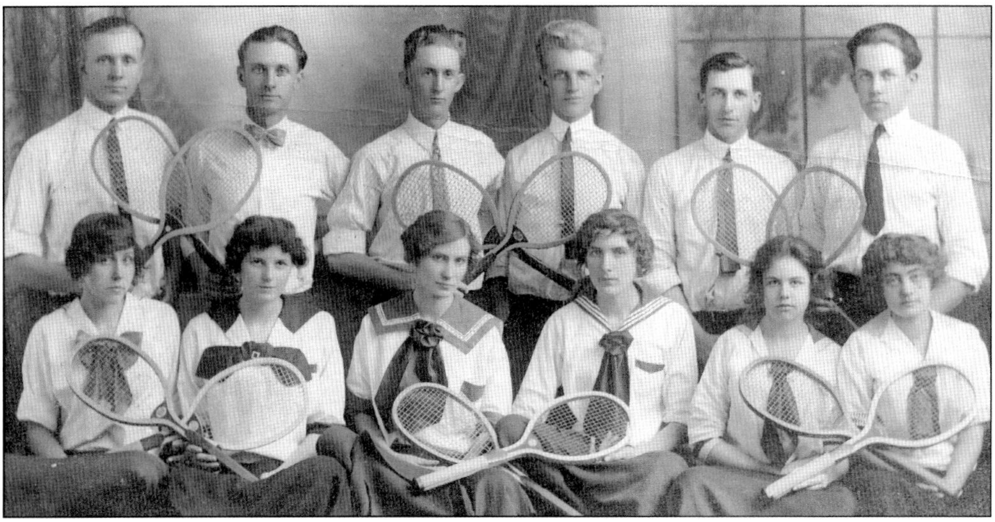

The ACC tennis club included (first row) Ethel Mead, Vera Smith, Ola Miller, Ann Holland, Ethel Whitehead, and Hazel Steinbrenner; (second row) Paul Brice, Emmett Brice, Floyd McMaster, Byram Kinsey, Otis Chamberlain, and Mark Green. To encourage the spiritual growth of students, ACC also offered YWCA and YMCA groups, which conducted devotionals and Bible studies for each gender.

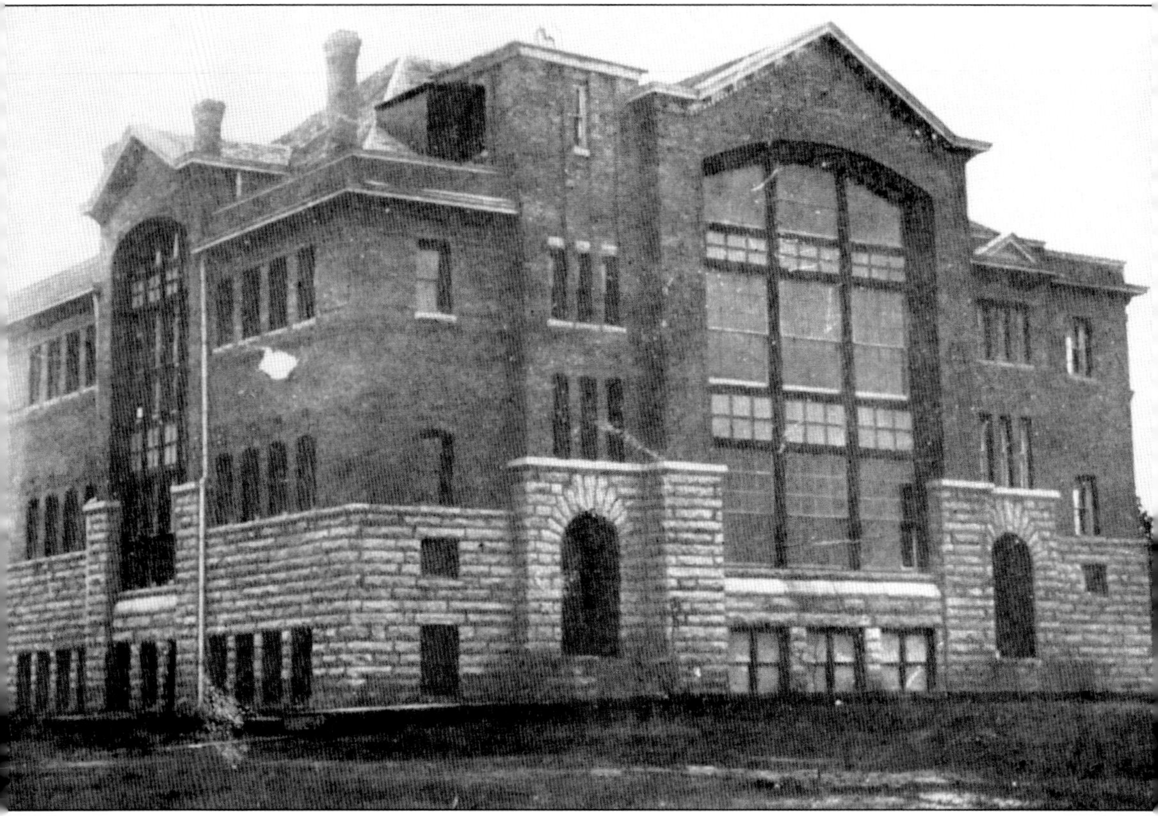

The Arkansas Conference College Building stood about where Southside Elementary School stands today along Tulsa Street at the end of College Street. ACC was always in a difficult financial condition but was able to remain open until 1917. The Siloam Springs School District bought the building to use as the public high school, which opened in the fall of 1918 and was in use until the 1940 high school opened immediately north of this building (about where the Southside Elementary School parking lot is today). Sports at ACC included football, basketball, baseball, tennis, and track and field.

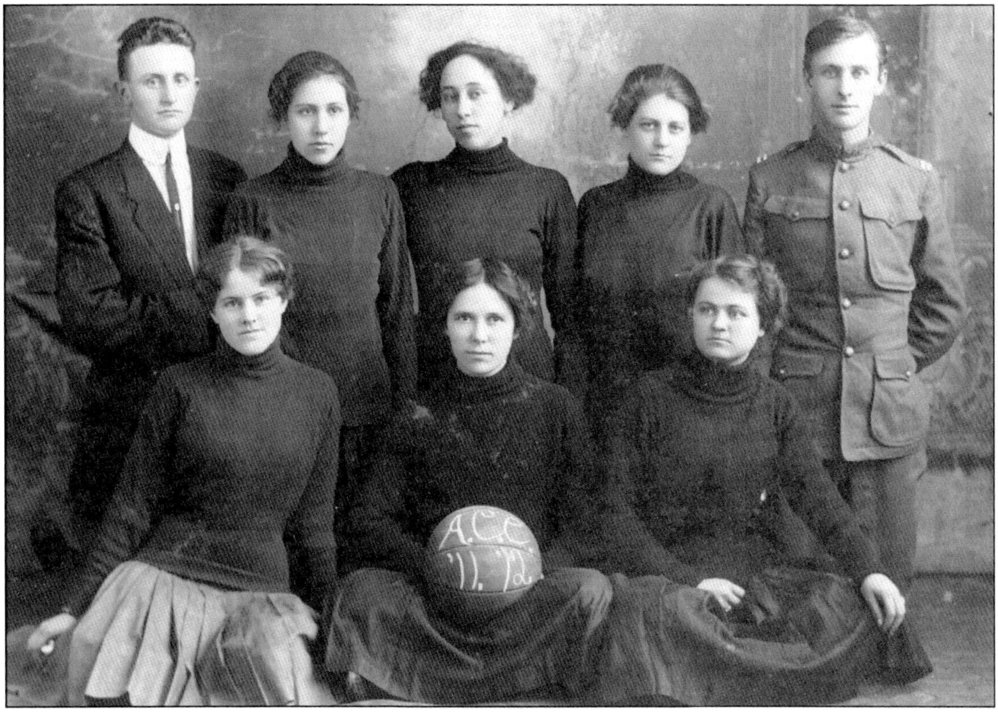

The Arkansas Conference College women's basketball team in 1911–1912, pictured above, included, from left to right, (first row) Leila Keith, Stella Martin, and unidentified (second row) Charlie Tucker, Ethel Mead, Margaret Mead, unidentified, and Emmett Brice. ACC also had several literary societies over the years, and the Zeomathian Literary Society of April 1910 is pictured below. From left to right are (first row) Bernice Miles, unidentified, Madge Chamberlain, Beula DeWitt, Clarence Elrod, and ? Ragan; (second row) Alice Duskin, Jessie Darling, Elmo Mead, Bess Walker (president), Faye Chamberlain, Mabel Hansard, and Zetsy Harmon; (third row) Beryl Huffmon, Fred Moulton, Gertrude Chamberlain, Nell Casey, Anna Mason, Huler McCulley, and unidentified; (fourth row) Stella Martin, Icy McCulley, Herbert Davis, Roy Chesney, Charley Davis, Ethel Mead, and unidentified.

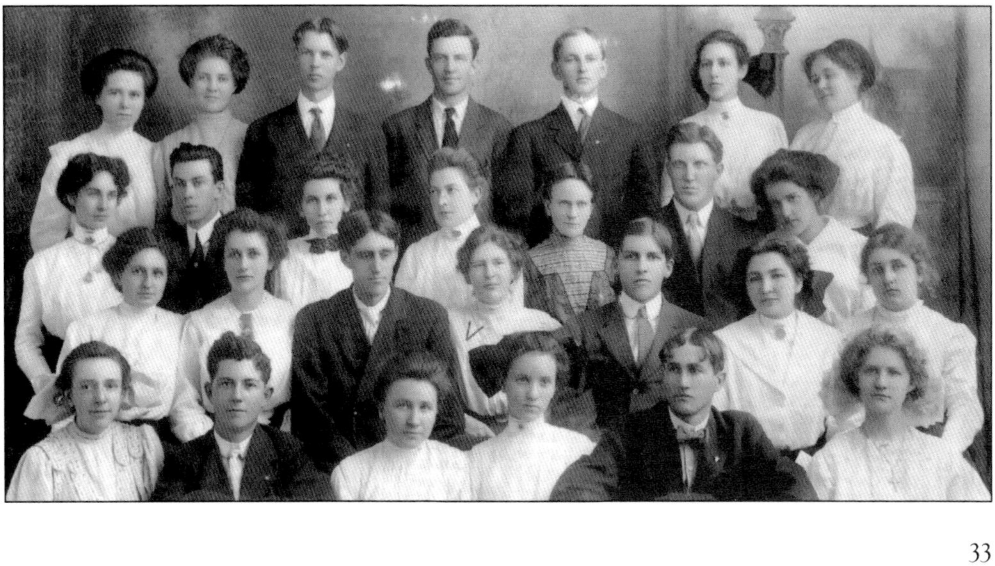

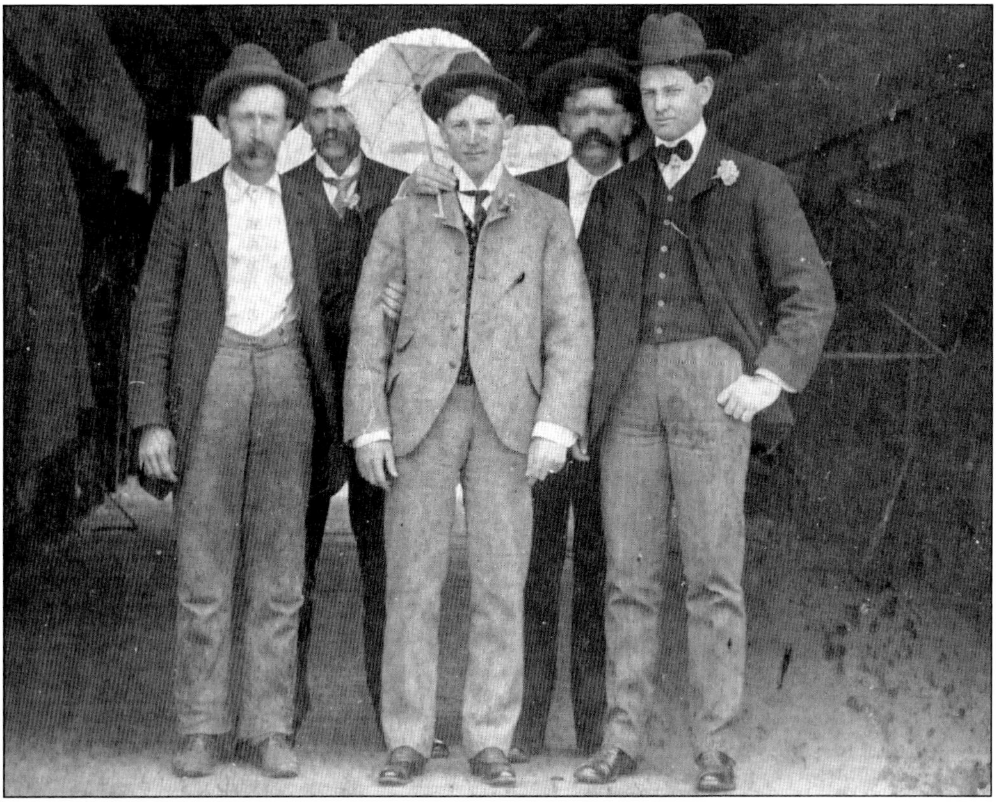

In the middle of the front row is Charles Marion Sparks (1878–1935) on the day he married Jennie Oates Heath (1880–1965), who appears with one of their sons on the cover of this book. Also in this photograph are Brooks Sparks, ? Alley, and Caldeen Gunter II (1873–1937), who is in the back row at right, holding the parasol on Marion's shoulder. (Courtesy of C.L. "Bub" and Sammye Lou Gunter.)

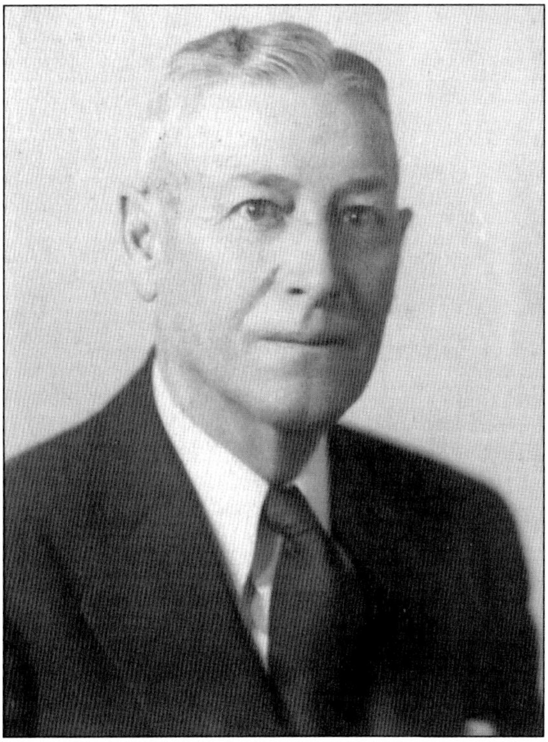

This photograph shows Charles Marion Sparks later in life. He made his living through horse and mule trading. He and Jennie Oates Heath had two sons, William Clark Sparks (1902–1976) and Charles Marion Sparks Jr. (1910–1993). (Courtesy of C.L. "Bub" and Sammye Lou Gunter).

Jennie Oates Heath Sparks's father was John G. Heath (1829–1888), a farmer who, in 1866, became one of the first half-dozen white settlers on Lindsay's Prairie, where he eventually owned 420 acres. In 1854, he married Sarah Kilgore (1839–1901). They had six children, and Jennie was the youngest. (Courtesy of C.L. "Bub" and Sammye Lou Gunter.)

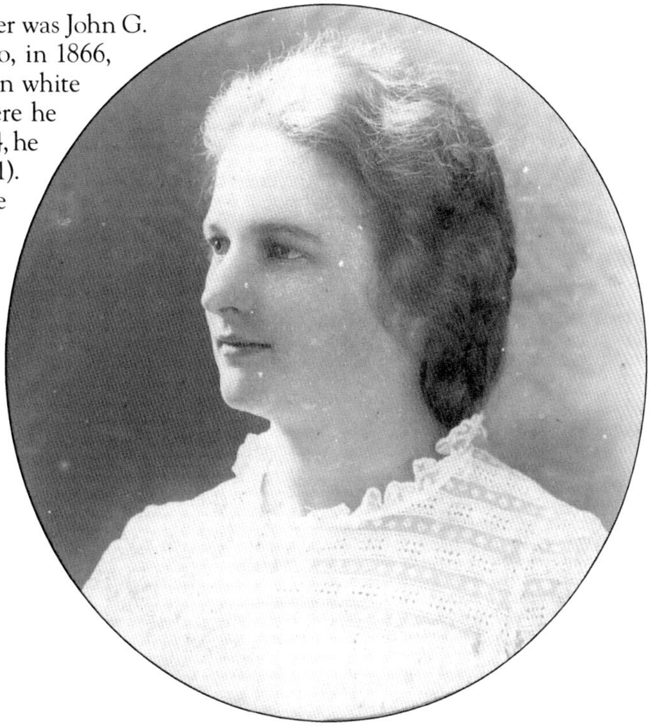

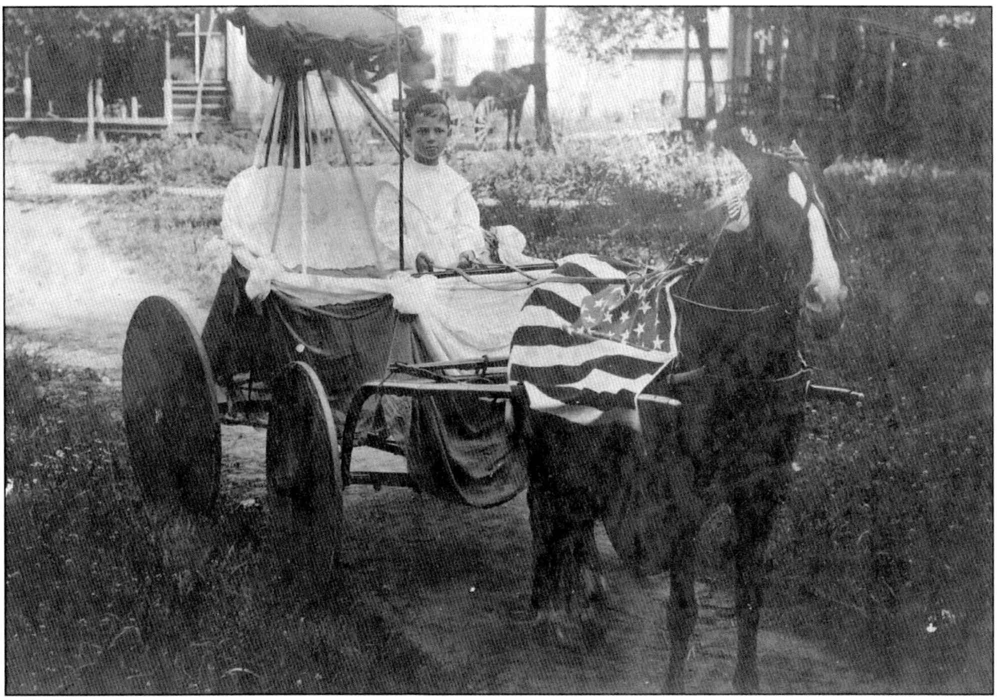

William Clark Sparks (1902–1976) drives a buggy and small mule, perhaps ready for a Fourth of July parade. He was the son of Marion and Jennie Sparks and grew up in the house at 604 South Maple Street. He was named after his paternal grandfather. In 1927, he made a successful application to the Sons of the American Revolution. (Courtesy of C.L. "Bub" and Sammye Lou Gunter.)

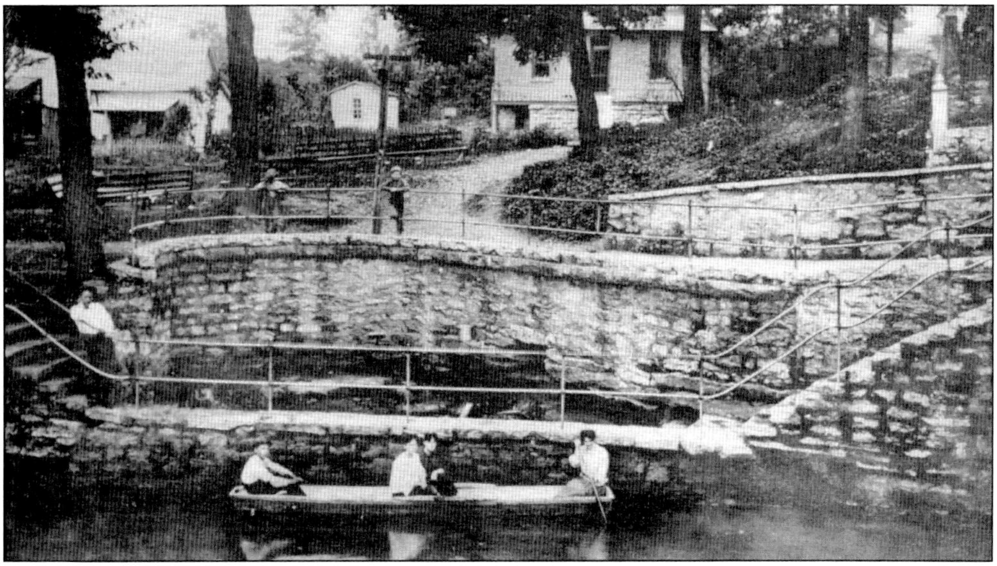

This postcard of the Twin Springs and vicinity is postmarked 1906. This shows that by around 1900, the rockwork at this spring was about how it is today. The wall next to the canoe was built to keep the creek water out of the spring and not to form a pool at the spring. In the background are some of the businesses that were once open in this area.

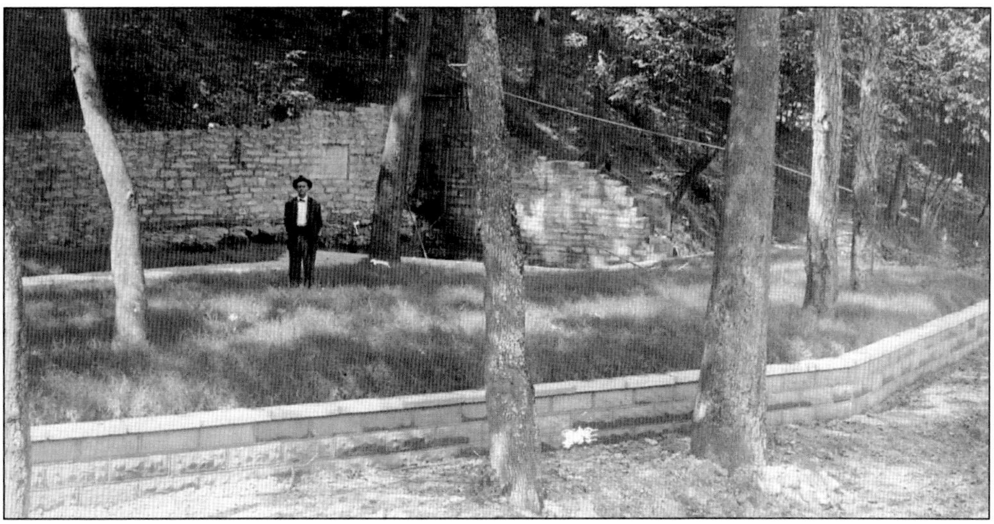

This postcard of the Siloam Springs is postmarked 1907. The plaque in this wall is dated 1897 and reminds viewers that the first celebration of the new town took place on June 24, 1880. By tradition, this is held to be the date on which the city of Siloam Springs was born. For many years, June 24 (St. John's Day) was celebrated every year with an annual picnic and homecoming.

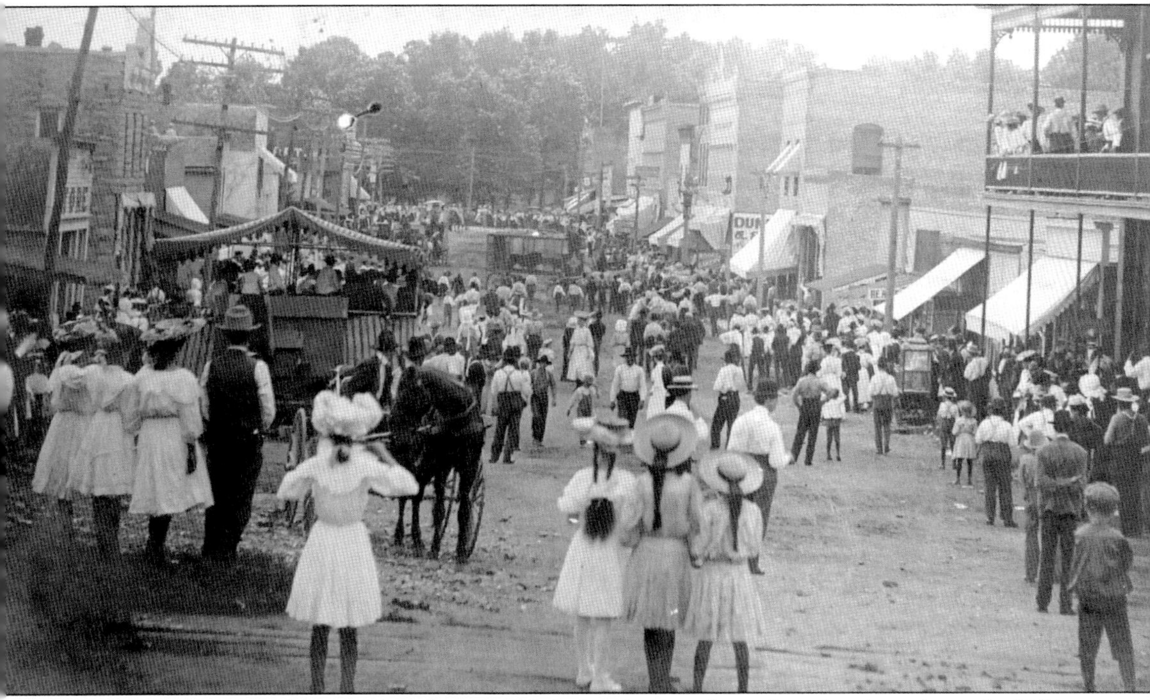

Here, a large crowd has gathered on St. Nicholas Avenue (now Broadway) in the early 1900s. Everyone seems to be looking at the wagon in the middle of the street, but humans and horses are keeping a safe distance. Magnification shows that this wagon contains a male lion. Imagine a roar echoing off the buildings downtown. Over the years, many different circuses have come to town. Another photograph in the museum collection shows a large crowd gathered along St. Nicholas Avenue in about 1915 to watch a Yankee Robinson Show coming to town with wagons and two elephants. In this photograph, there is still a dense growth of trees in Twin Springs Park, which helped to make this and other parks a cool getaway for summer visitors who came here to drink at the springs and enjoy the other entertainments available in town, like the circus.

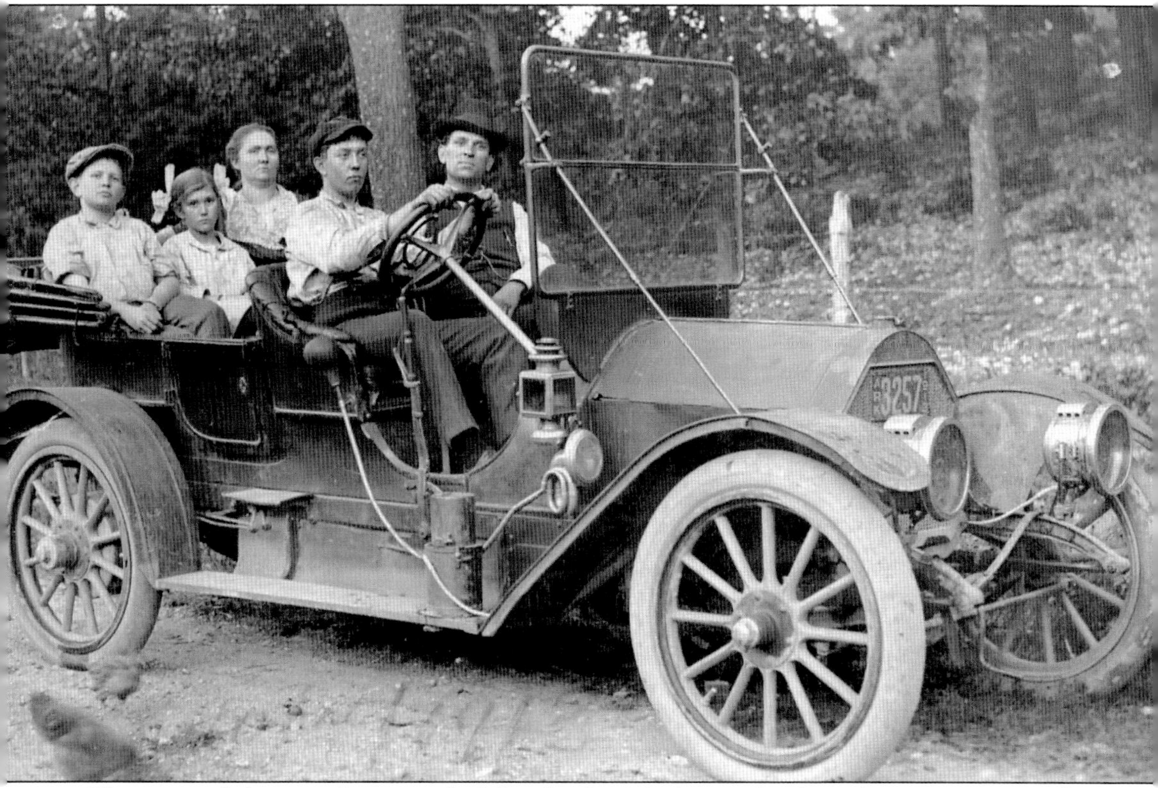

This postcard photograph, postmarked October 7, 1913, shows a family in their touring car with the top down for a day trip. The car has a 1913 Arkansas license plate. In the note on the back, Ida (last name unknown) tells the recipients that this photograph was taken after a trip from Siloam Springs to the nearby towns of Bloomfield and Cherokee City. "The wind had blown us to pieces but it's us any way." Bloomfield and Cherokee City are each several miles north of Siloam Springs and were once much larger than they are today. The Bloomfield Post Office was open from 1875 to 1904. The town had a large public square, several stores, and an academy. The Cherokee City Post Office was open from 1871 to 1953. Due to its springs, this town had a boom in the early 1880s as a summer resort.

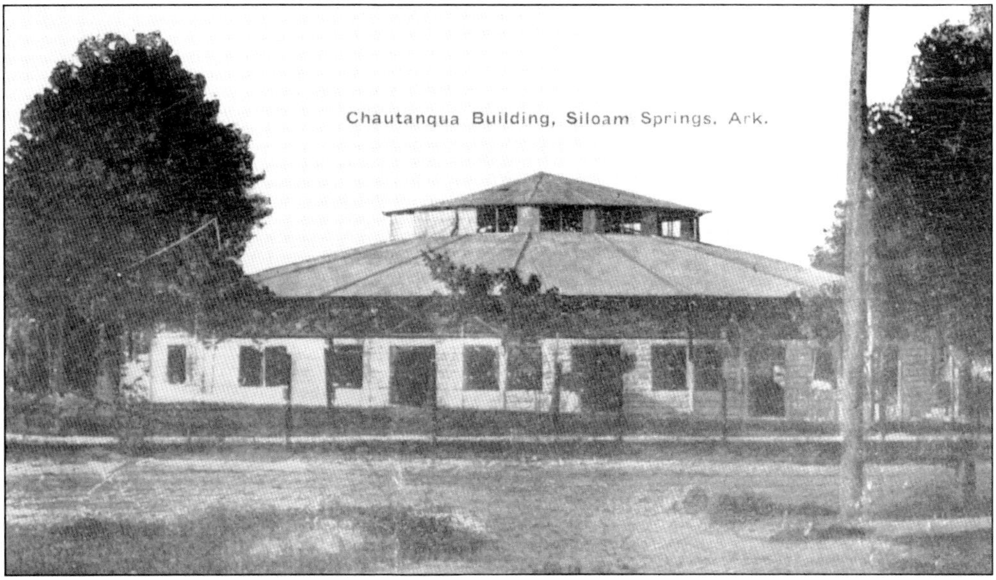

The new round Chautauqua Building (above) opened in 1907 with a blockbuster program, headlined by William Jennings Bryan (No. 1 in photograph below). Posed next to Bryan are local Chautauqua organizer Frederick W. Bartell (No. 3) and his wife, Daisy (No. 2), and behind them is Connelly Harrington (No. 4), a local merchant, banker, and town promoter. There are probably other prominent local citizens in this photograph that have not yet been identified. Bartell developed a circuit of 17 Chautauqua assemblies in Arkansas, Oklahoma, Missouri, and Kansas. The Bartell circuit lasted until 1910, when the failure of the Bank of Siloam forced Bartell into bankruptcy.

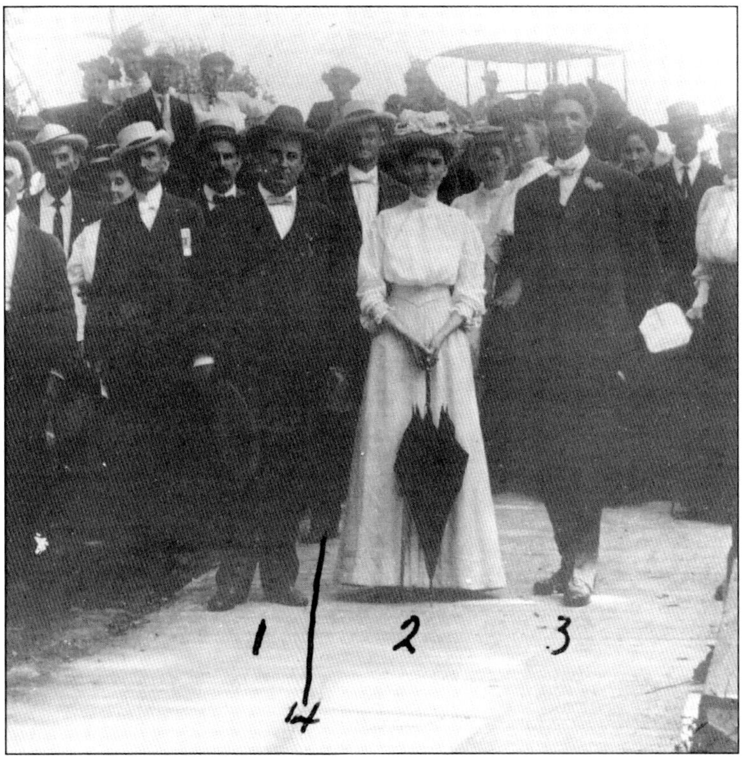

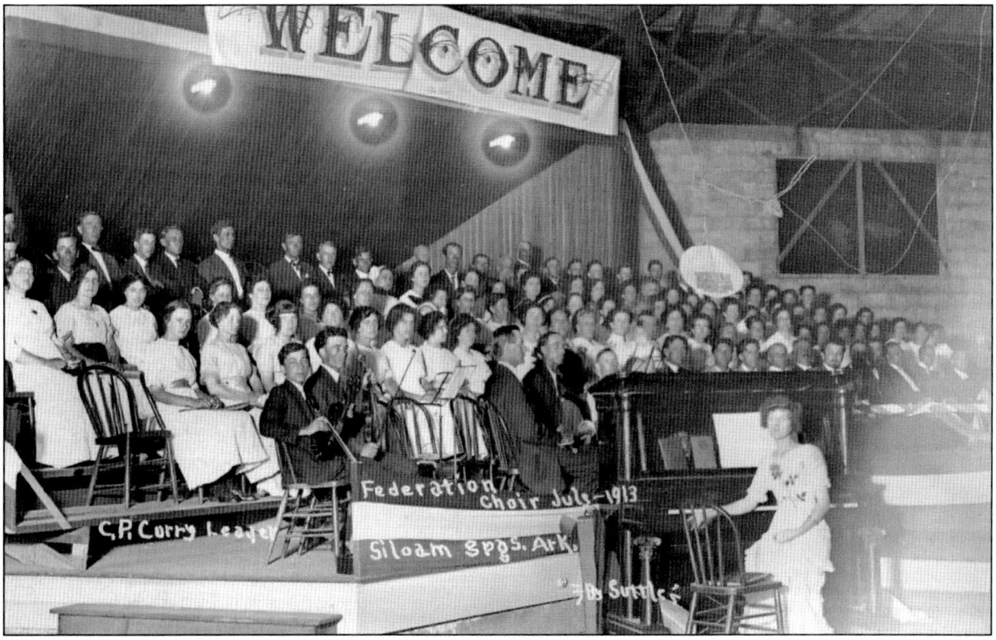

This photograph by Suttle shows the inside of the Chautauqua Building in July 1913 during the first annual convention of the International Federation of Christian Workers, which was organized by John Elward Brown (1879–1957). Summer visitors to Siloam Springs were invited to attended this free convention and urged to "combine inspiration with your vacation; education with your outing."

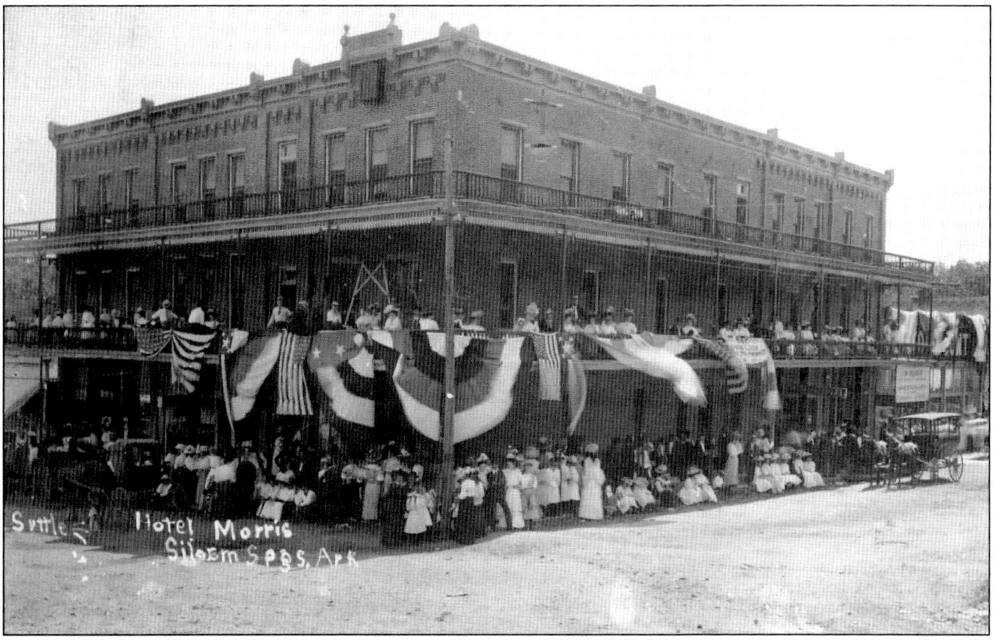

This photograph by Suttle shows the Hotel Morris during a patriotic event. Flags and a variety of bunting decorate what was then by far the largest hotel in town. This building also housed the Bank of Siloam, which was the first bank in Siloam Springs. Robert S. Morris (1837–1915) opened the Bank of Siloam in about 1881 and then built the Morris Hotel in 1899 for $12,000.

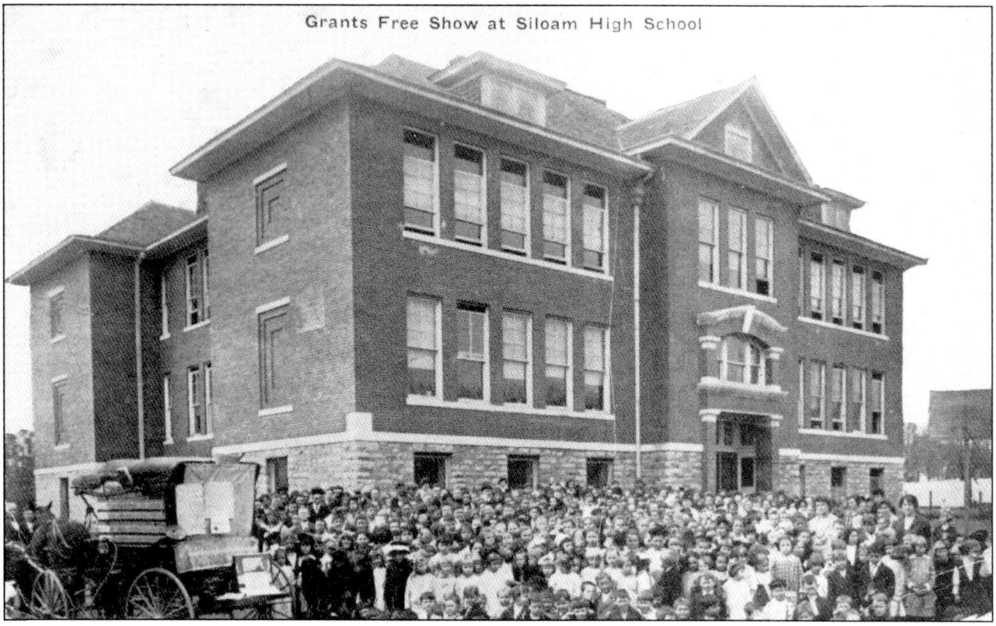

The 1907 public school building originally contained one room for each grade from the first grade through high school. It stood south of Tahlequah Street between Mount Olive and Broadway. By the fall of 1918, it was overcrowded, and the high school classes moved into the former Arkansas Conference College Building. The 1907 building later became known as Central Elementary.

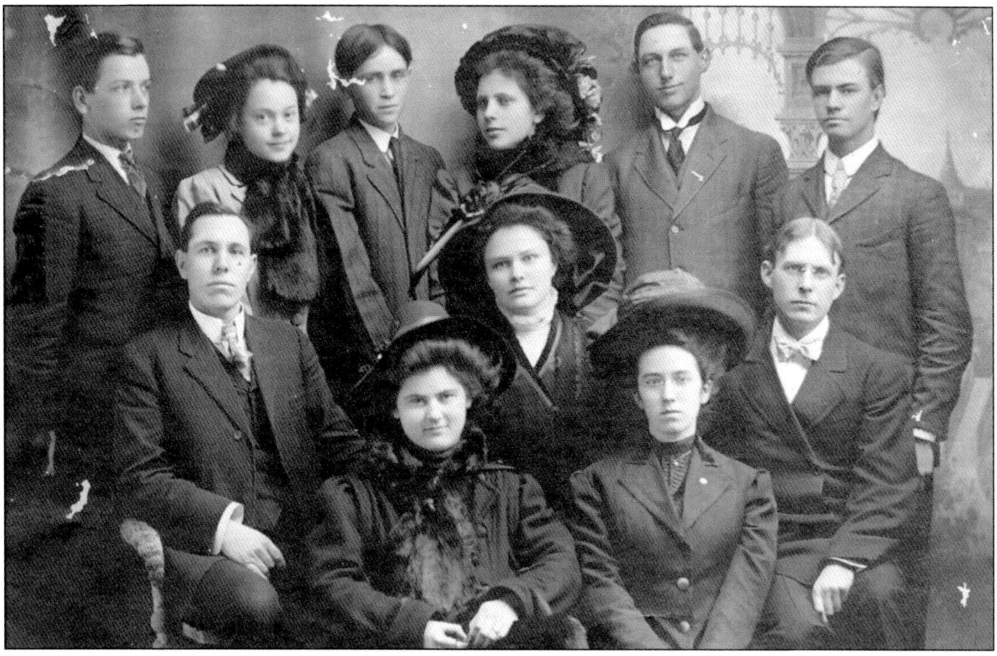

In 1909, Rex Williams and Grace Wisner became the first two graduates of Siloam Springs Public High School. In this photograph they are joined by the high school faculty and students. From left to right are (first row) Faye Williams and Grace Wisner; (second row) Prof. Denton R. Woods, Mayme Brockman, and Prof. Earl McClaren; (third row) Wilbur Orton, Frances Martin, Rex Williams, Ruby Andrews, Roy Shannon, and Leslie Hurlock.

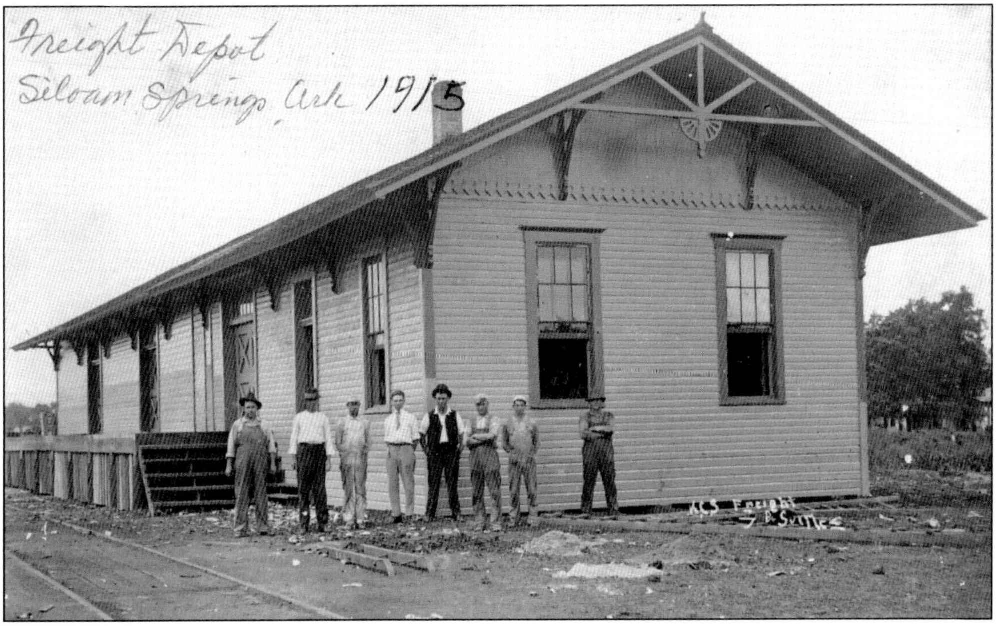

The Kansas City Southern Railroad freight depot is seen here in 1915. It seems to have been the first railroad depot in Siloam Springs. It originally stood along the tracks just south of Jefferson Street. When a new passenger depot was planned, this depot was moved farther south, where it could serve as the freight depot.

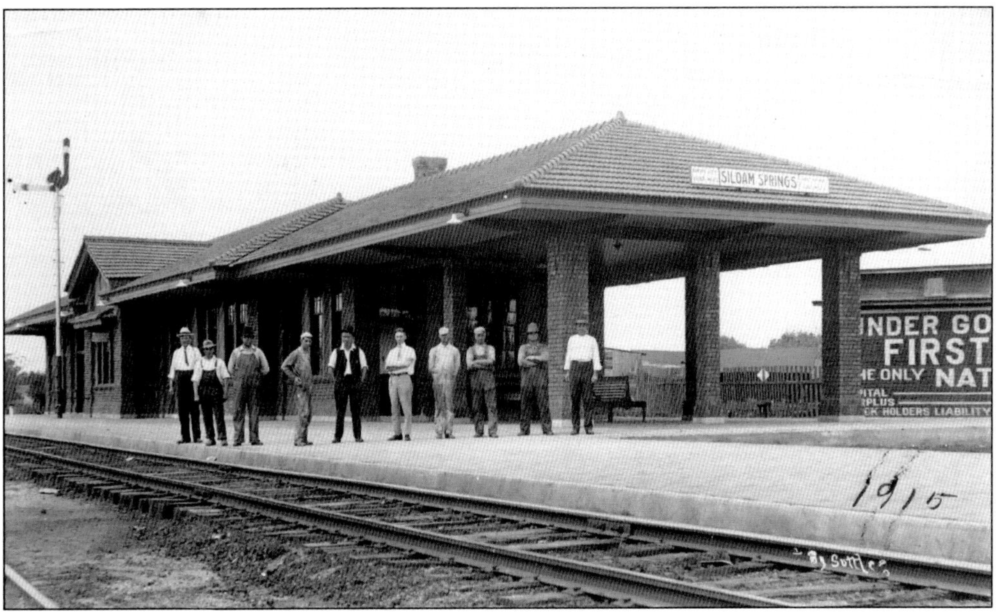

Built in 1915, this is the Kansas City Southern passenger depot, located just south of Jefferson Street. Some of the paving brick and roofing tiles from this building have been reused at the Arkansas State Welcome Center on Highway 412. The ticket window and counter, telegraphy counter, semaphore levers, and other materials from the old depot have been reused at the Welcome Center as part of a small museum display.

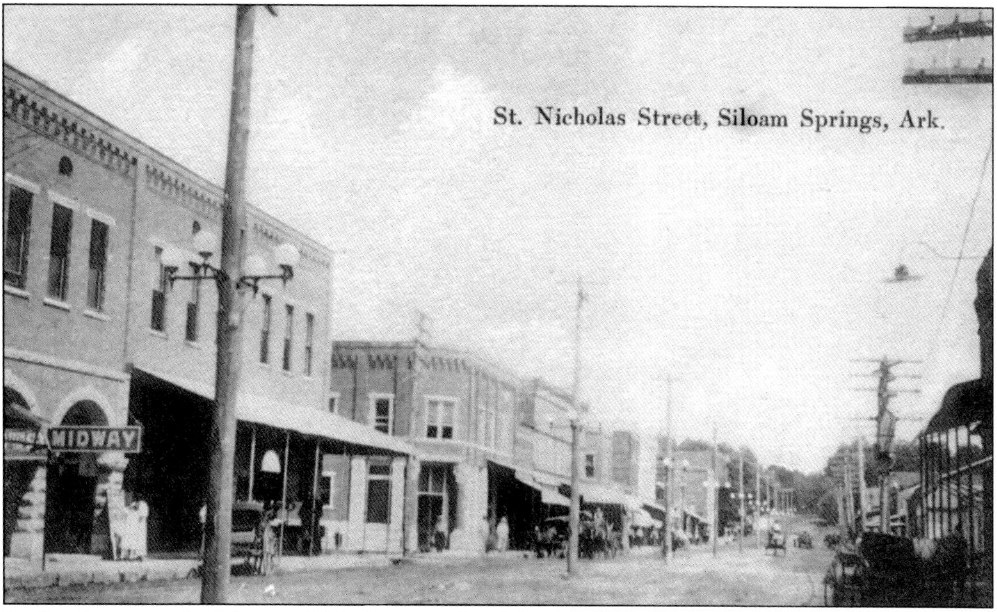

In the foreground of this c. 1915 photograph of the south end of St. Nicholas Avenue looking northwest is a sign for the Midway, the first movie theater in town. It was later called the Rialto, which burned on March 3, 1948. Next to it was McCulloch's Grocery; a ghost sign for this business survives on the north wall of the building (see page 64). (Courtesy of Donald Cundiff.)

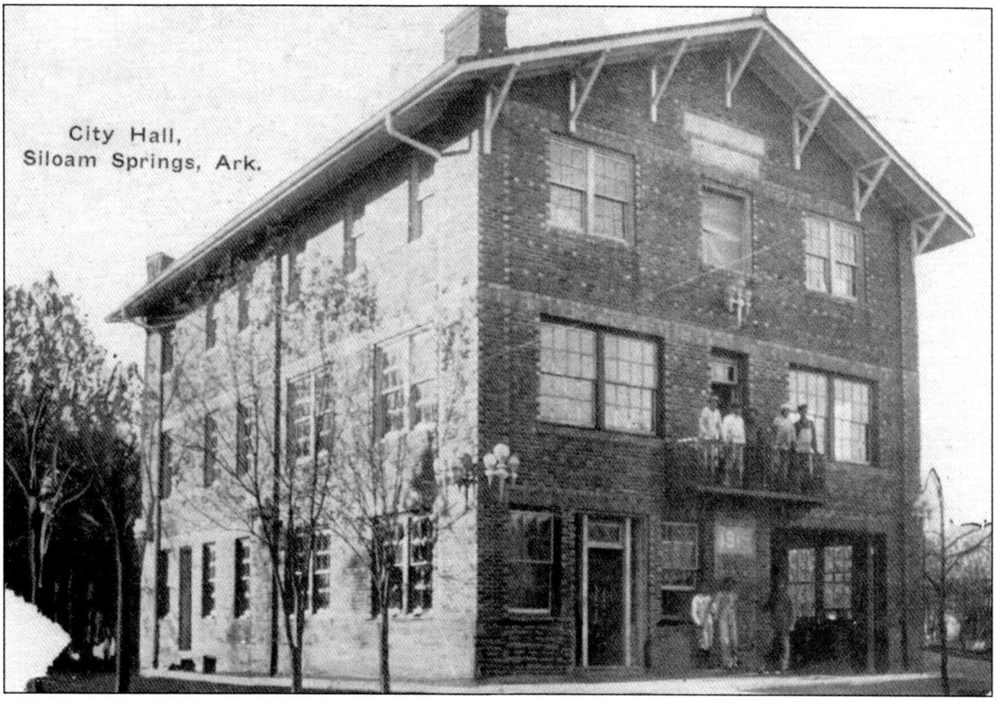

The first Siloam Springs City Hall was built in 1915 and stood where fire station No. 2 is today at Mount Olive Street at Central Street. The first floor housed the fire and police departments, on the second floor were the city offices and public library, and the third floor was the city hospital. This building stood until about 1965. Fire station No. 1 (now No. 2) was dedicated in 1967.

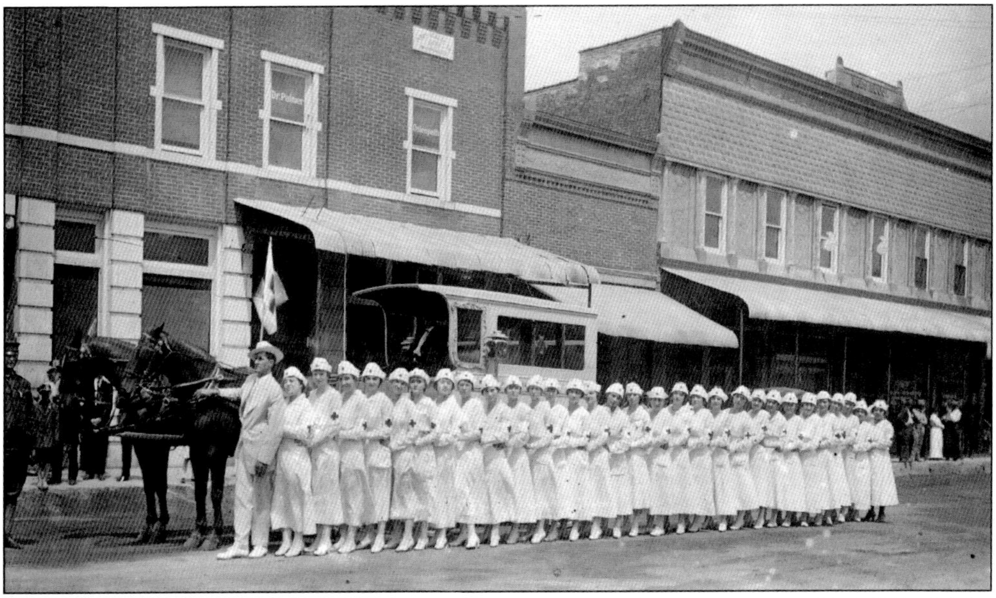

Dressed in white from head to toe, these young women were volunteer nurses in World War I. The red crosses on the ambulance window, the nurses' hats, and their armbands all look homemade. There is also a red cross on the flag between the horses. World War I started in 1914, and the United States joined the war in April 1917. Armistice Day was November 11, 1918.

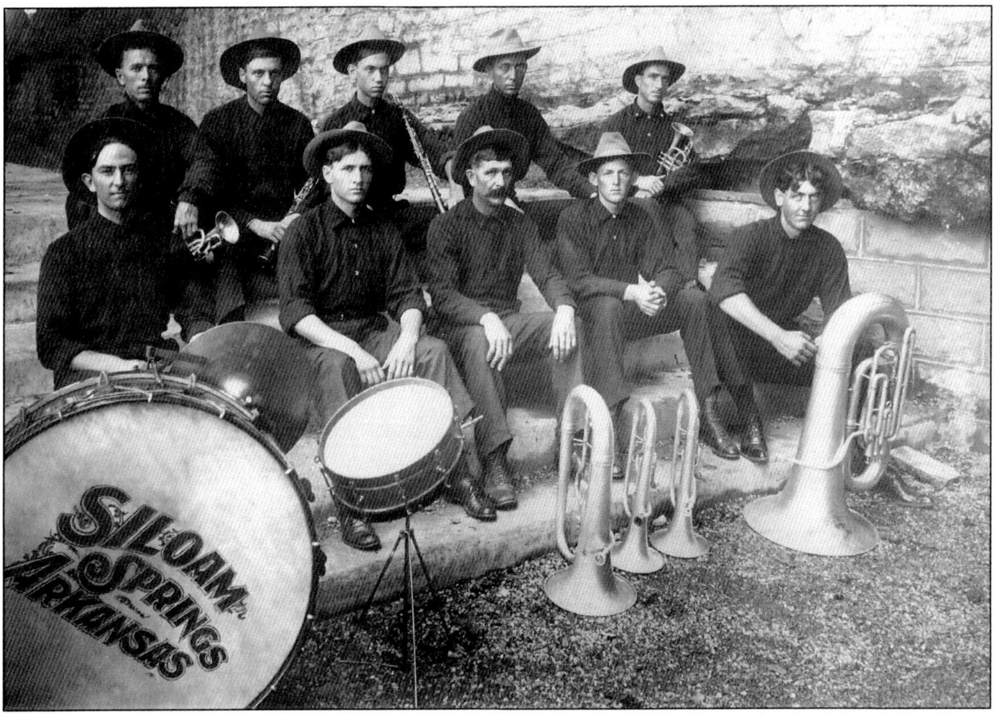

From the beginning of this town to the present, summer nights in the parks are often filled with music. In this photograph, Kemper's Coronet Band poses next to the wall at the Siloam Springs. In 1899, Alex G. Black, bookkeeper for Farmers Bank and former deputy Benton County clerk, was leader of Kemper's Military Band, which was probably a related band.

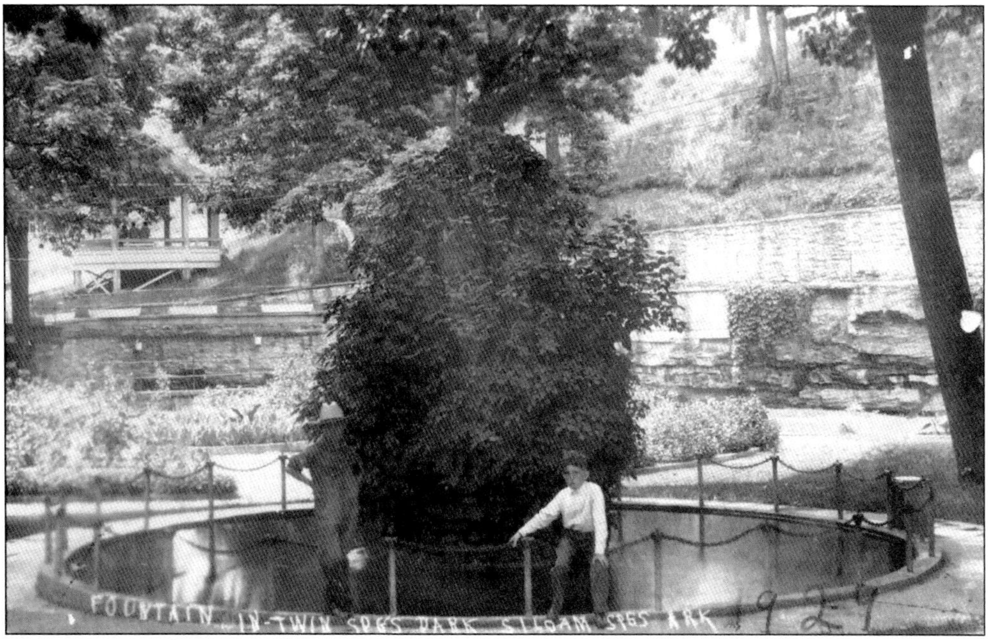

The postcard of Twin Springs Park shown above is postmarked 1929. Here, the vines on the 1913 fountain have grown out. Note also the flower circle in the background, which also dates to about 1913. This area is temporarily flooded in the photograph below. Under magnification, the 1913 date on the fountain is visible in this photograph. The gazebo in both photographs was later moved to a more level part of the park. The plants in the flower circle were later changed to canna lilies but have since been changed back to a mixture of plants of different sizes, shapes, and blooms.

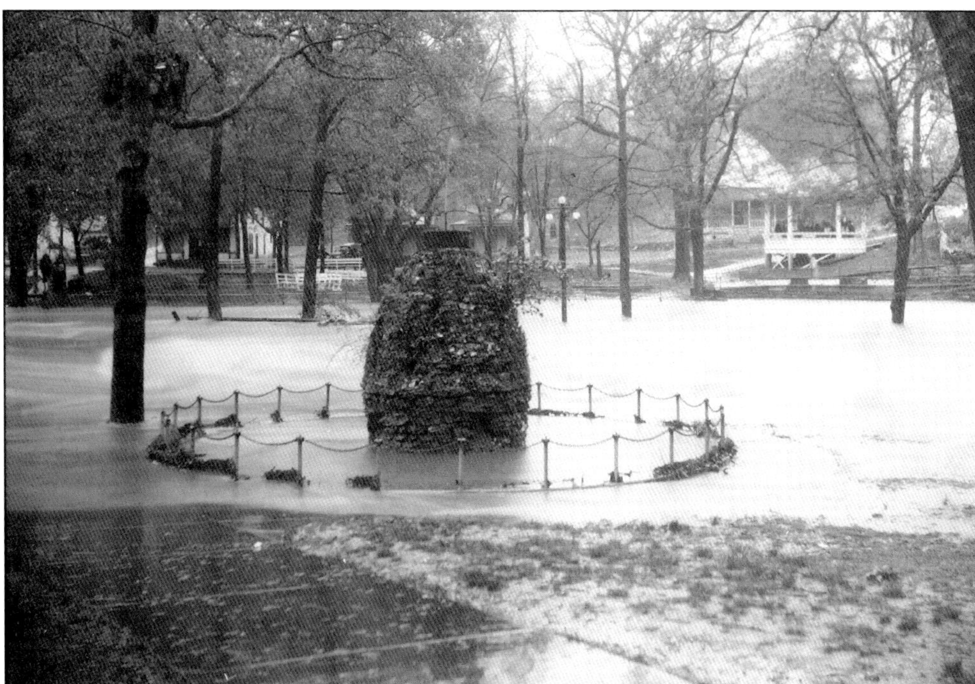

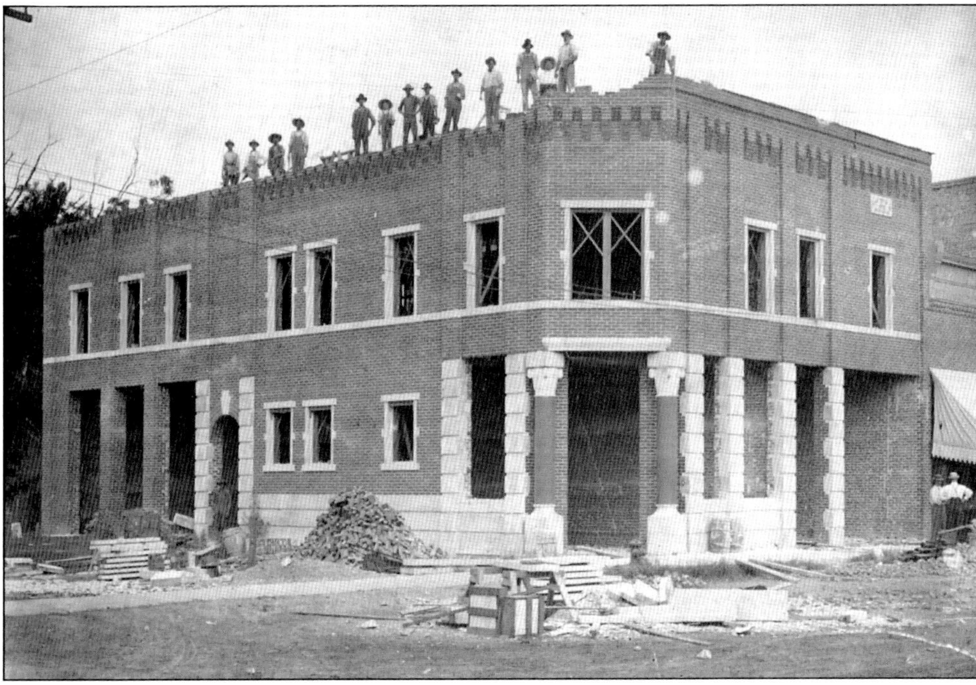

The Allen brothers, Harry, Everett, and Bert, built many of the stone-and-brick buildings still standing in Siloam Springs. In the photograph above, the brothers and their crew are nearing completion of the exterior of the State Bank Building in about 1910. The beautiful columns of this building were covered for several years but are once again visible. The building still stands along Broadway at Alpine Street. The photograph below shows the sturdy scaffolding needed to build the columns on the Methodist Episcopal Church South in 1920. When the North and South parts of the local Methodist Episcopal church reunited, they used this building at the corner of Twin Springs and Maxwell Streets.

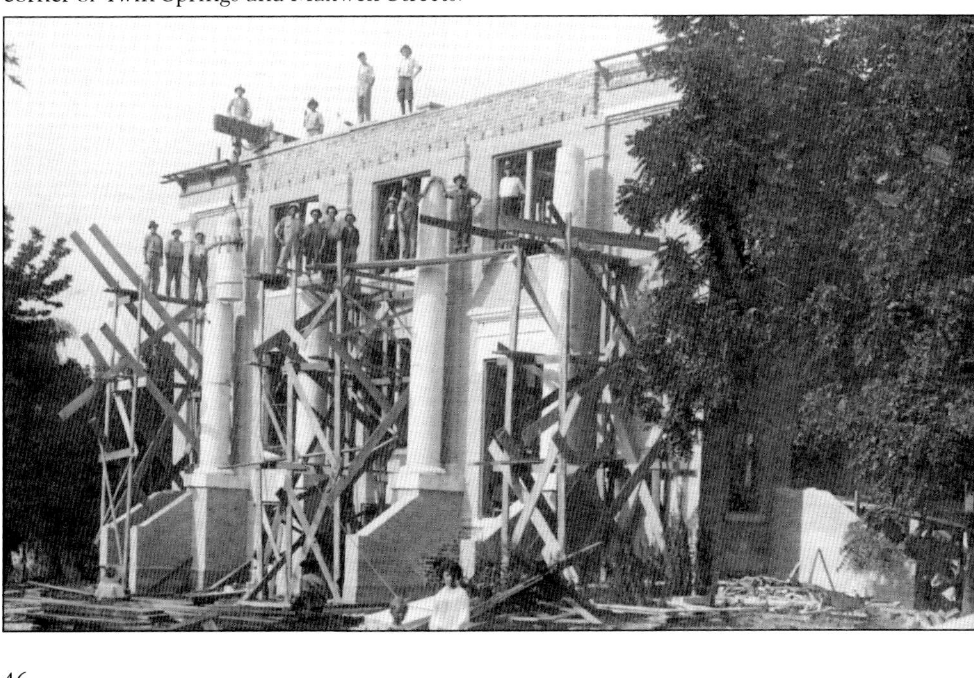

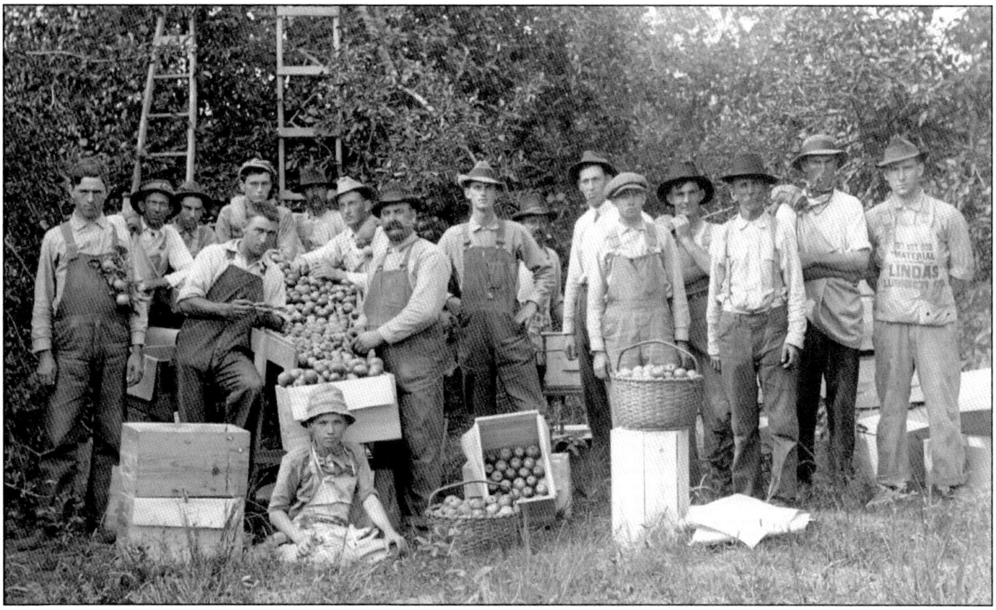

Apples were an important crop in northwest Arkansas into the 1920s. There were large orchards near Siloam Springs, and apple processing facilities in town. The photograph above shows an apple-picking crew as well as its crates and ladders. The photograph below shows some of the ways in which apples were processed. The vent stack on the left is from the box where sulfur was used to bleach apples that were to be dried. The women in the middle are at machines used to peel and core whole apples, and the men on the right are at a cider press. In town were evaporators where apples were dried, cider and vinegar plants, a distillery, and ice plants to cool the apples that were shipped whole.

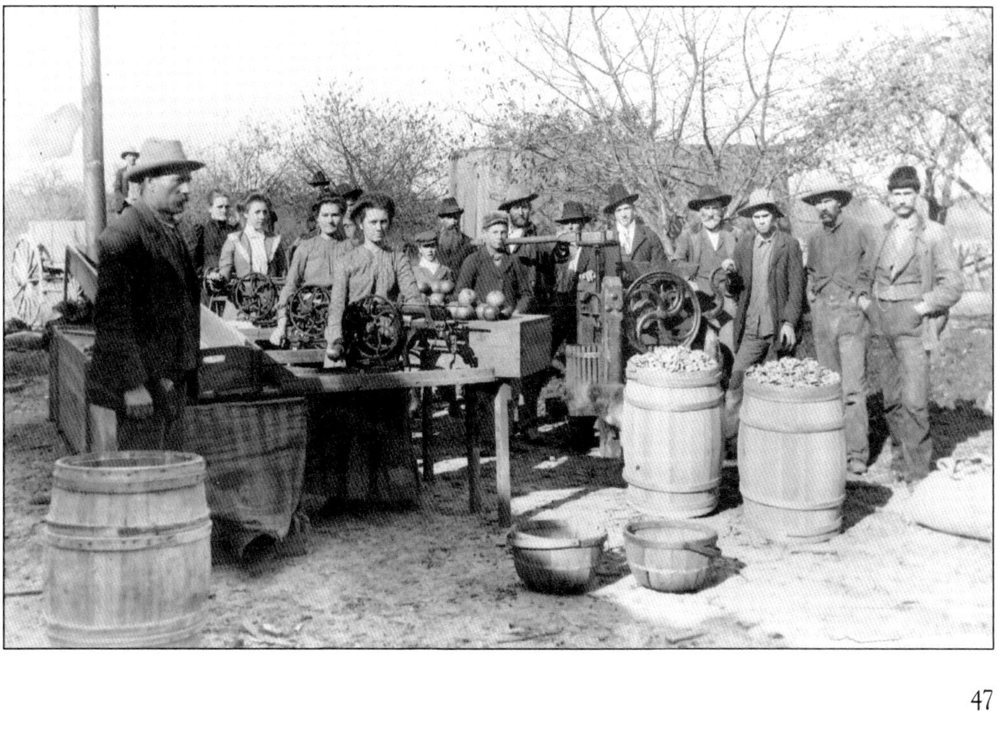

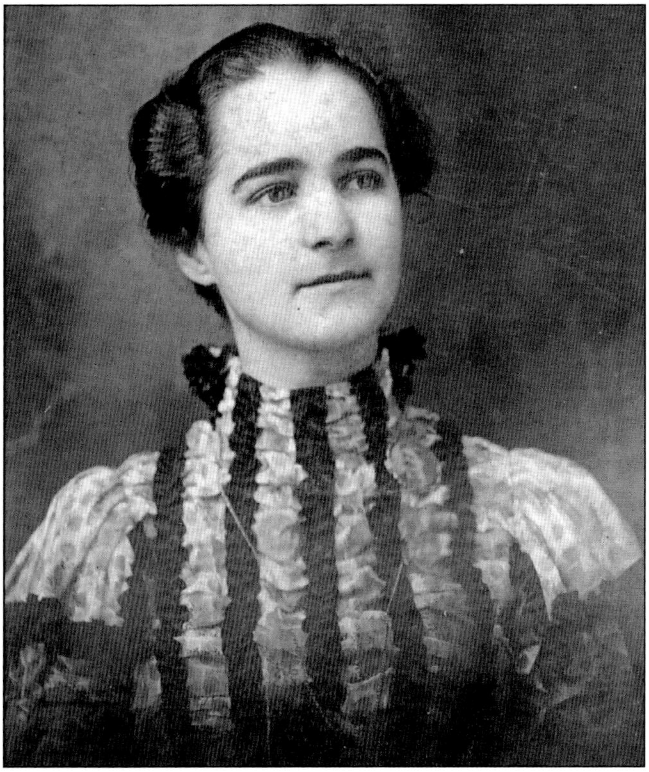

Effie Porter Gunter (1879–1953), shown at left, married Caldeen Gunter II (1873–1937), shown below. While they were courting, they worked at competing dry goods stores. They had four children who lived into adulthood. One son, Caldeen Gunter III (1911–1977), became a physician who collected family photographs and histories and produced voluminous files on the history of this area. Another son, Porter (1913–1937), fathered Bub, who preserves these files. Caldeen II was a builder. One of his Depression-era projects was to build the Lake Frances dam higher; a photograph of that project in progress is on page 66. (Both, courtesy of C.L. "Bub" and Sammye Lou Gunter.)

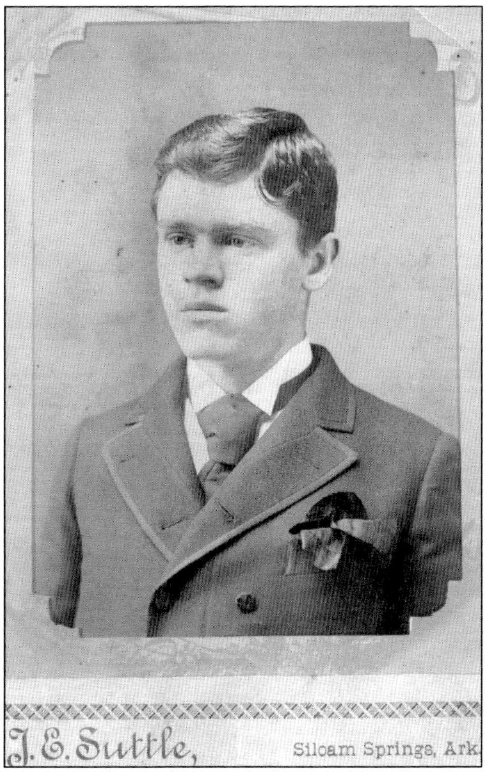

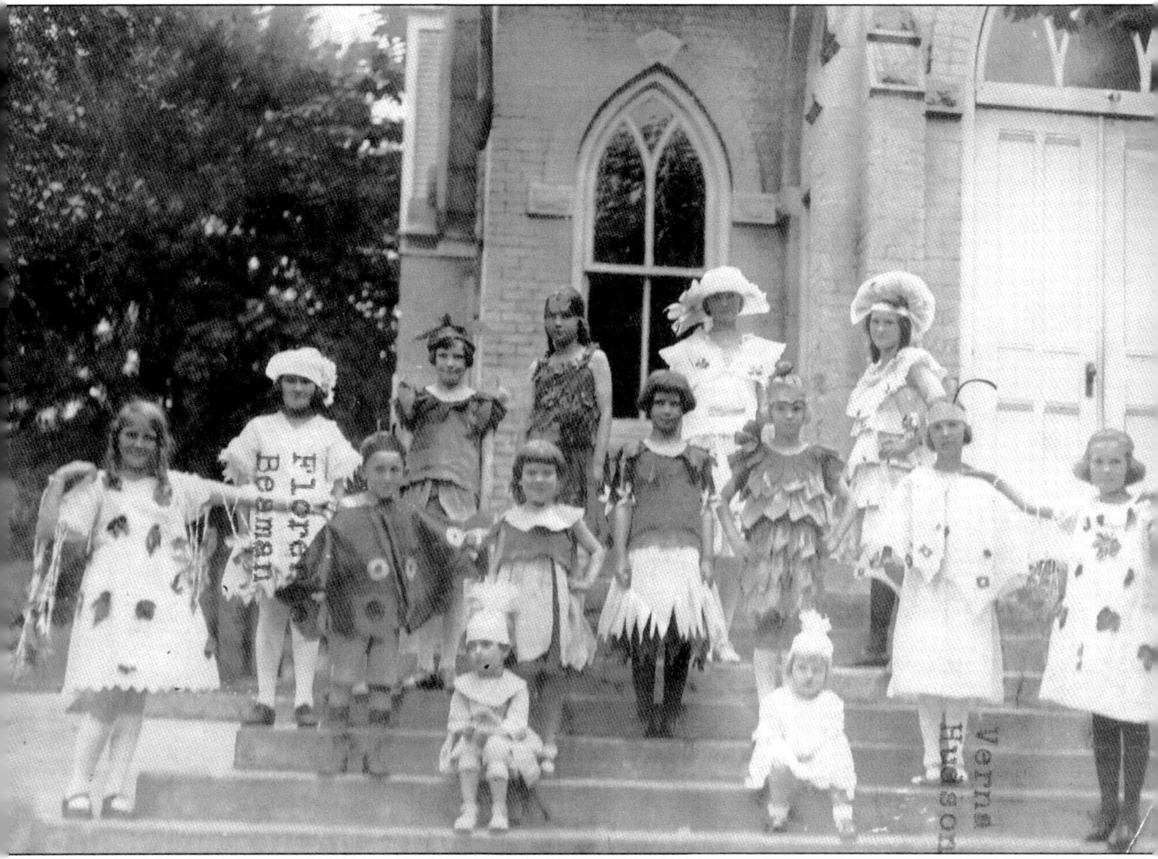

In the early 1920s, these children performed in the Methodist Episcopal Church North, seen behind them. The building still stands at the corner of University and Maxwell Streets. It was built in 1895 for $3,000. Florence Beaman is second from the left, and Verna Beaman Hudson is second from the right. Florence Beaman remembers that their play divided the church because many of the older people thought it was "dancing in church." In 1948, she was still attending the Methodist church and was in the choir. She was also in the Nesika Study Club, which was one of the women's federated clubs in this town for many years. Verna Beaman went on to marry Loyce Hudson and became a registered nurse. She supervised the move from city hospital in December 1950 and was superintendent of Siloam Springs Memorial Hospital for the first several years it was open.

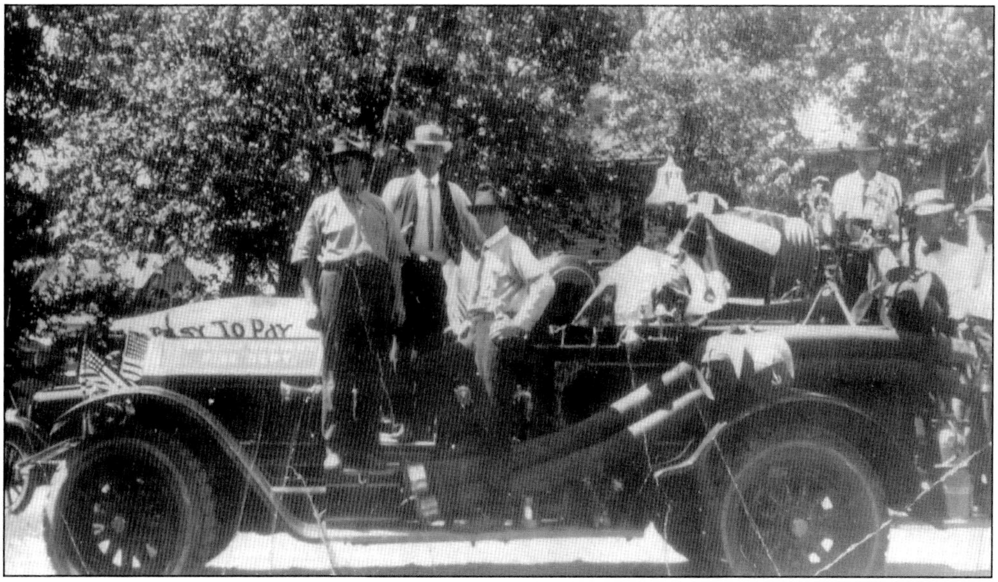

Siloam Springs's first fire truck was this 1919 American LaFrance model. This was a major development for the local fire department. According to the Sanborn maps, the fire department's equipment consisted of two hose jumpers and one hook and ladder truck, with "horses hired when needed," in 1914. The 1922 map notes the hose on the truck, plus the hose trailer and a hose cart at the railroad depot.

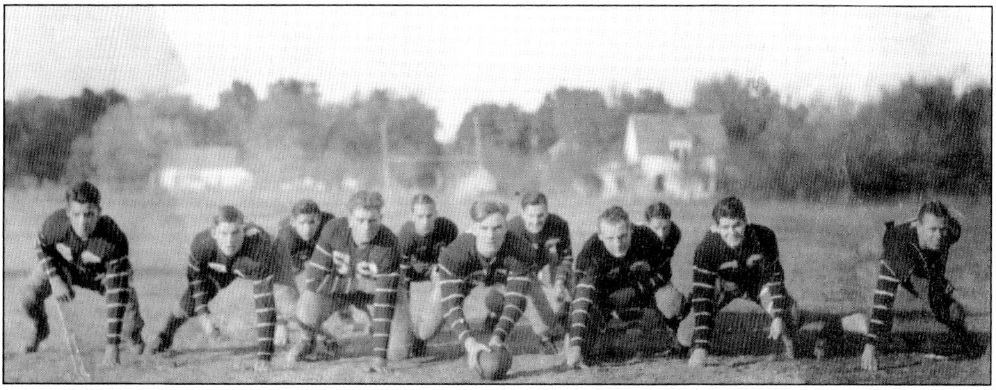

The undefeated 1928 Siloam Springs High School football team included, from left to right, Chester Gilliland, Roy Wolfe, Dago Guthrie, Tiny Ward, Ralph "Slick" Henry, Lee "Athletic" Elrod, Cecil "Beardie" Elrod, Zeke Cecil Camp, Caldeen Gunter III, Vol Smith, and "Peter Taz" Paul LaFollette. Part of the team yell went as follows: "Hippety hus, hippety hus! What in the hell is the matter with us? Nothing at all, nothing at all! We're the gang that plays football!"

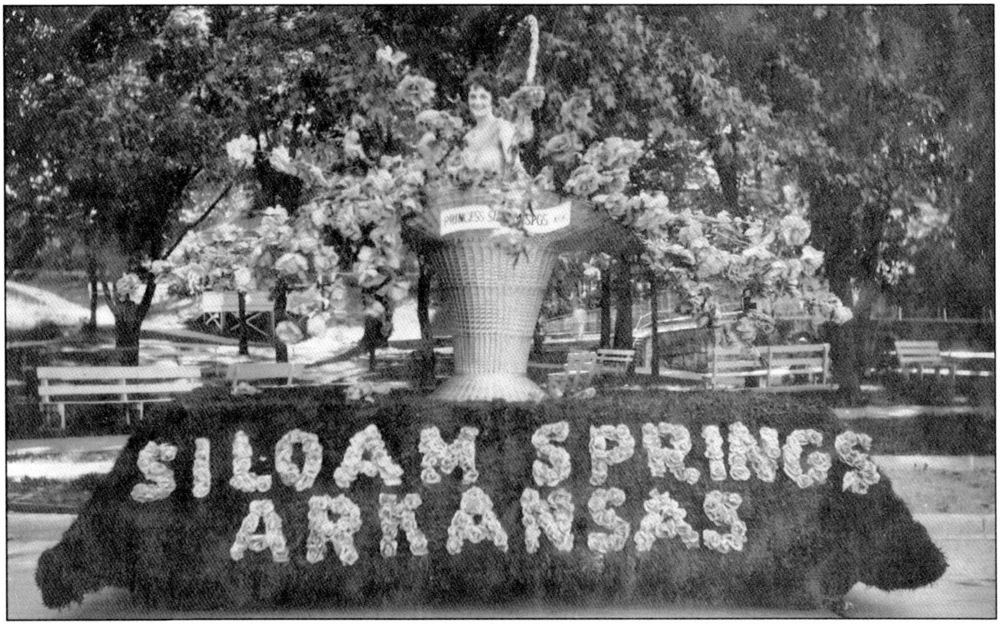

The city of Rogers held an Apple Blossom Festival from 1924 to 1927. The photograph above shows Willa Mae Maxwell on the 1924 Siloam Springs float at Twin Springs Park. Helen Duckworth of Siloam Springs was queen of the 1925 festival. The picture below shows the Siloam Springs float from an unknown year in front of First National Bank (now Arvest Downtown) in Siloam Springs. The women on the float are, from left to right, Bonnie Fretwell Blake, Louise Brown Jones, Ruth Dunlap, and Dorothy Masters Leach. J. Dickson Black reports that the joke during these festivals was that they were great rain-getting events.

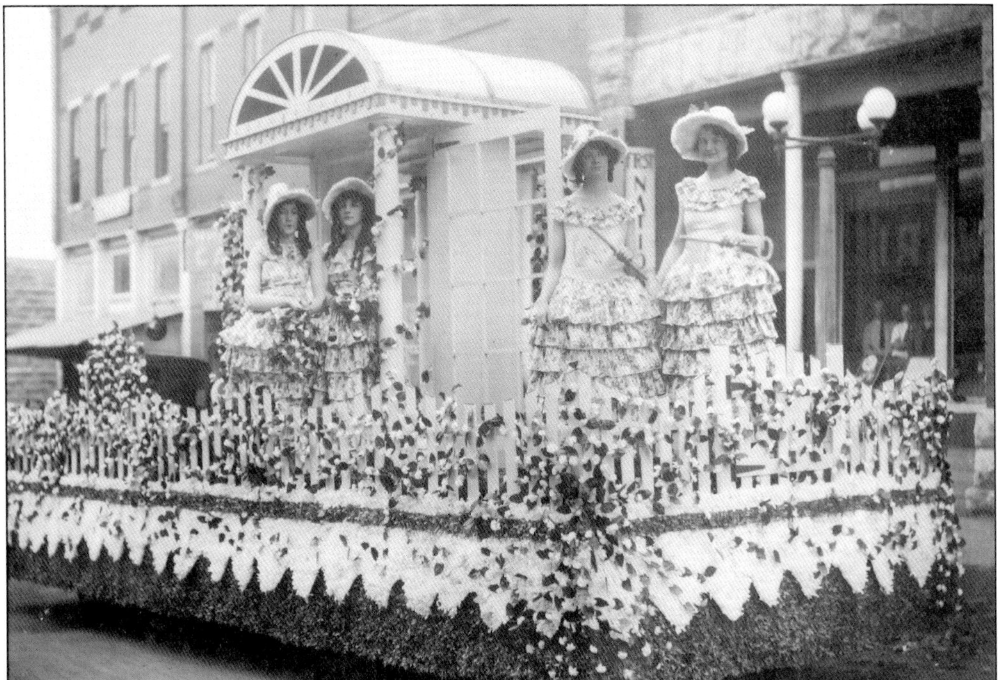

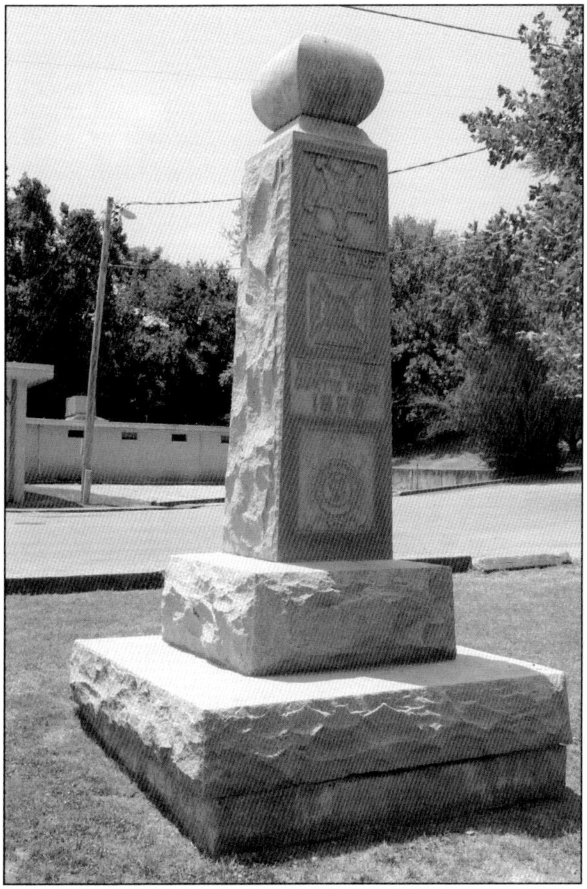

The 1928 Grand Army of the Republic monument stands near the south edge of Twin Springs Park. The GAR was established in 1866 for Union veterans of the Civil War, and the local group was Curtis Post No. 9, chartered in 1884. It was a large and active group. The women's auxiliary of the GAR was the Women's Relief Corps, established in 1883.

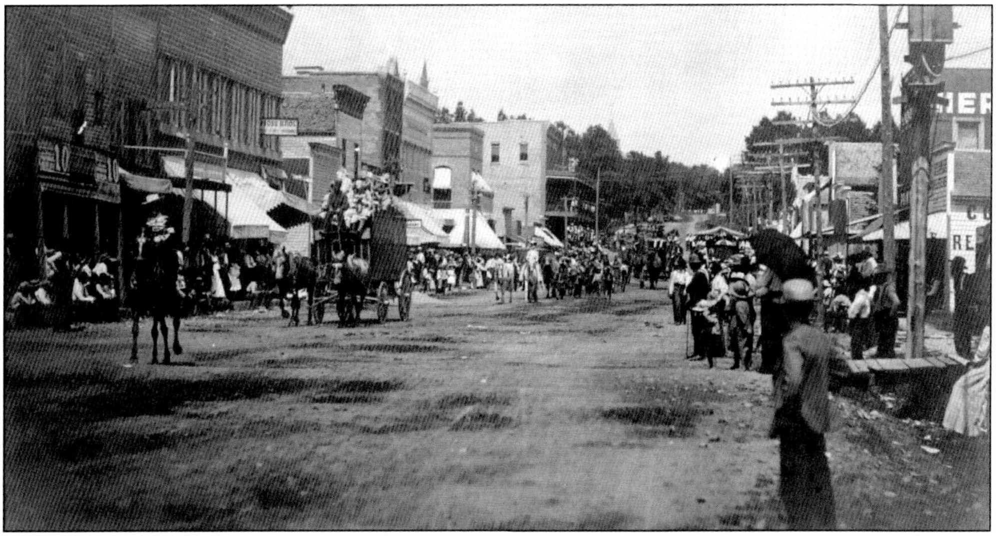

This postcard is postmarked 1907 and shows another show coming into town along St. Nicholas Avenue (now Broadway). Notice the clowns on the first wagon, who have put on their full makeup for the trip into town. Large crowds of children and adults were gathered along the street to watch the spectacle.

The photograph at right shows John Elward Brown Sr. (1879–1957) in 1924. Brown became convinced that higher education ought to follow a three-fold course that trained the head, hand, and heart; that is, academic and vocational instruction grounded in a strong base of Christian belief and practice. He put this philosophy into practice in the Southwestern Collegiate Institute, which opened in the fall of 1919. The photograph below shows Southwestern Hall, which housed classrooms, offices, dormitories, and everything else for that first academic year. For the next academic year, the name of the school was changed to John E. Brown College. After accreditation, it became John Brown University.

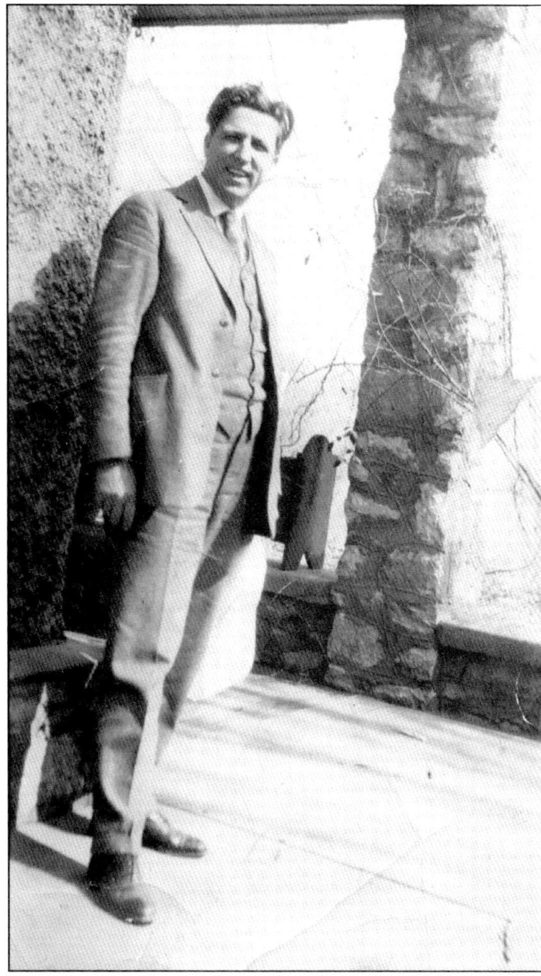

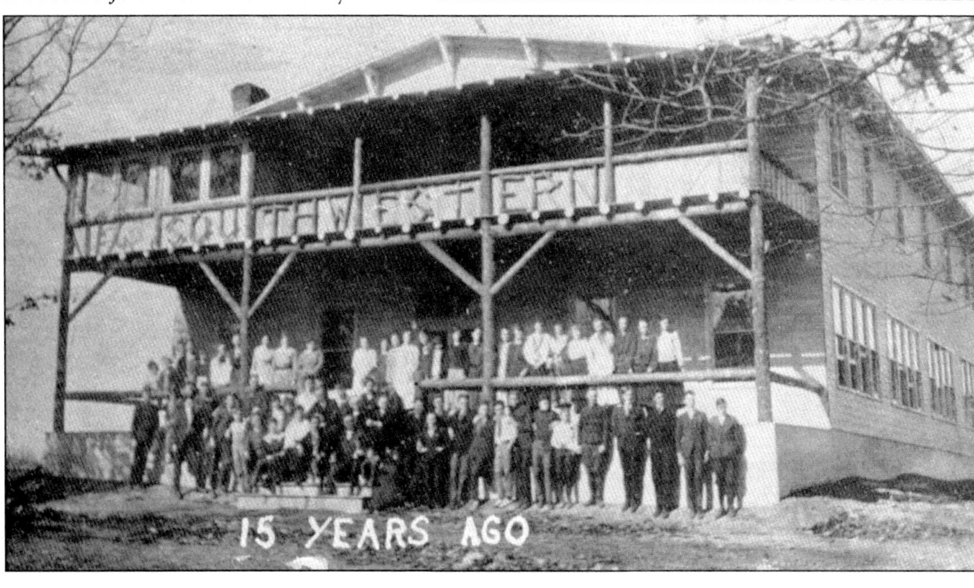

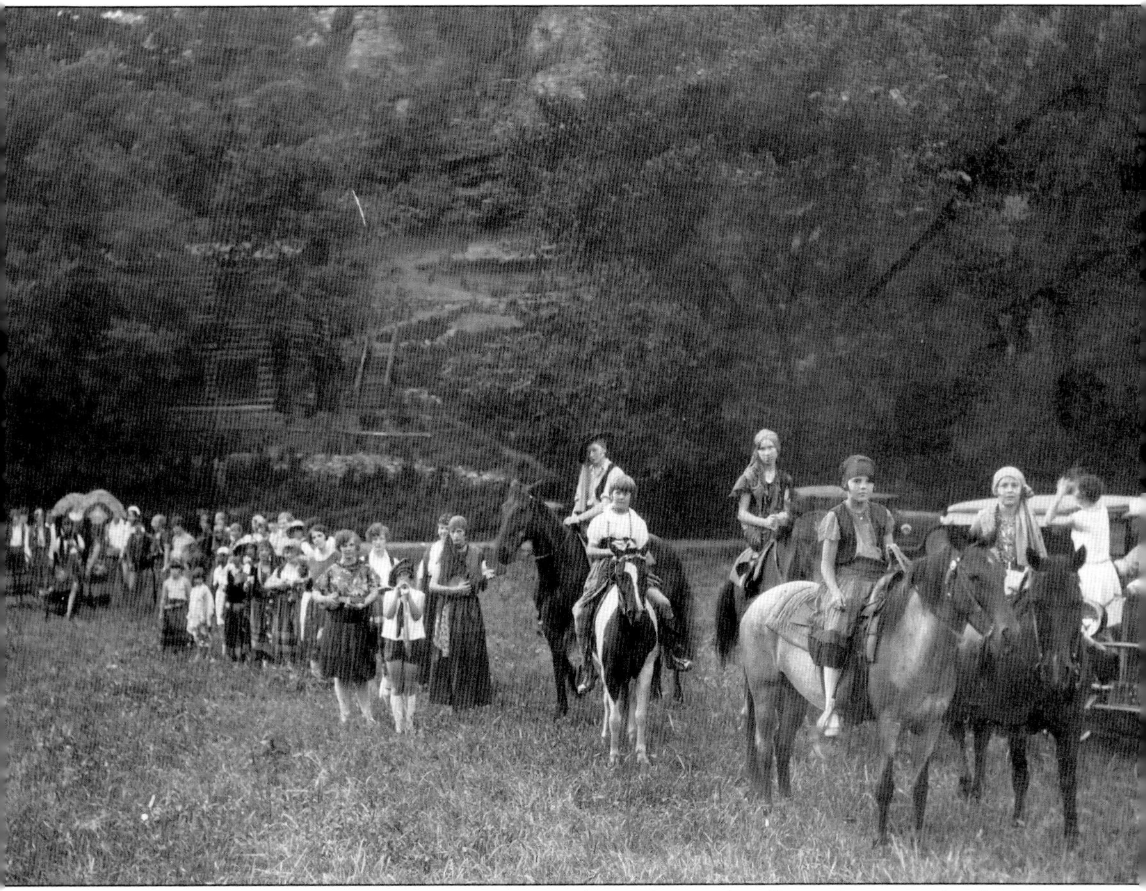

Gypsy Camp was a gypsy-themed camp for girls located near the Illinois River south of Siloam Springs. The camp buildings, some of which are visible in this photograph, were listed as a National Register Historic District in 1988. Camps were held from 1922 to 1978. Campers were told to bring gypsy clothes for activities, like the one in this photograph, and for campfire night, which was Wednesday. Gypsy Camp was owned and operated by three generations. It was first owned by Wessie and John H. "Mr. Mac" McAllister and then by four of John's five children by his first wife (Dave, Tom, Etta, and Bess). Bess married Claude Coe, and their son Bob and his wife, Daisy, ran the camp from 1955 to 1978. The camp was rustic, but was successfully marketed to girls who were used to the finer things in life. One father predicted that his daughter would beg to come home after one week at Gypsy Camp; instead, she became a camper for several years and then a counselor.

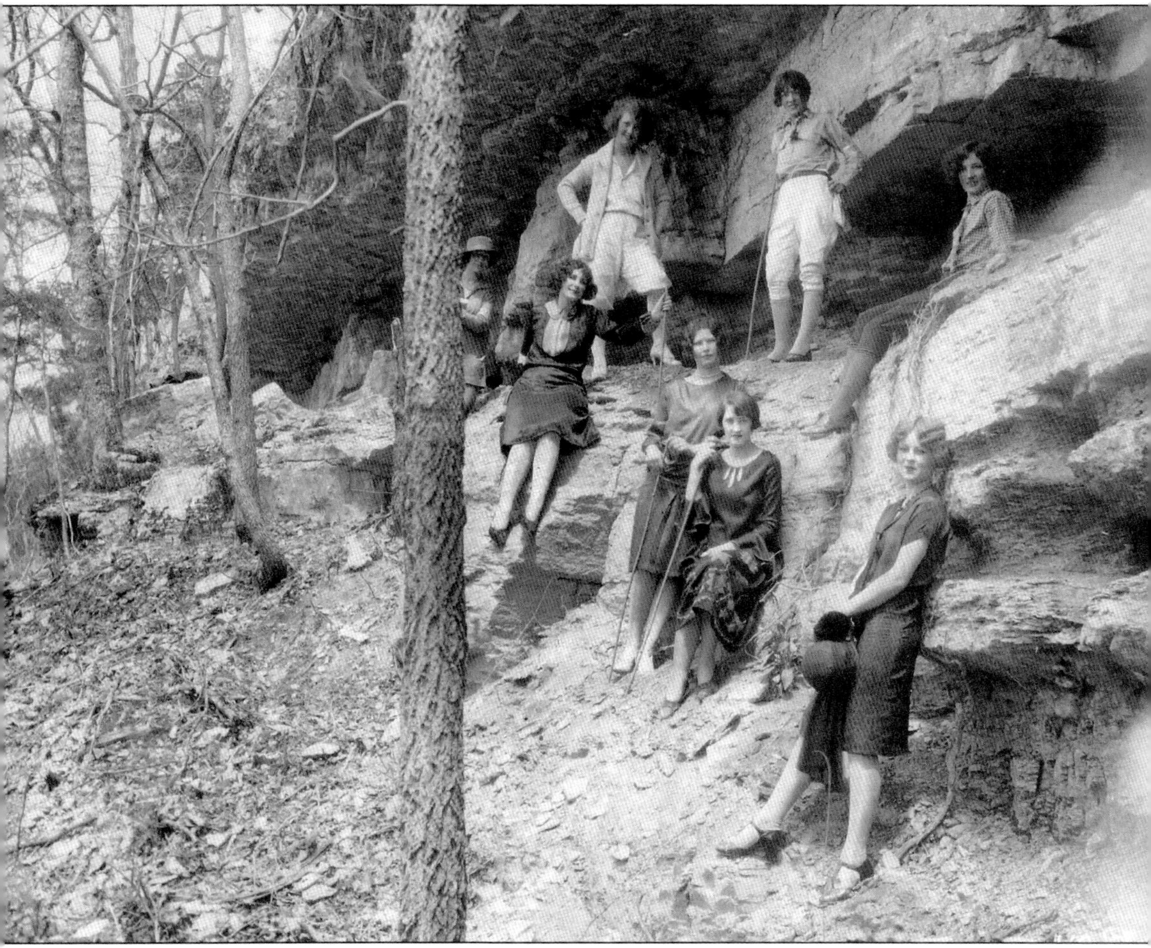

The girls of Gypsy Camp also participated in typical summer camp activities like hiking, swimming, tennis, crafts, and more. The camp kept between six to eight horses, and campers rode for three hours every day. In at least some years, there was a weekly newspaper, which provided camp news and gave the campers a taste of journalism. There were trips to town to use the Laundromat, have lunch out, and see a movie. There were field trips to nearby Civil War sites, parks, and resorts. The camp prided itself on the quality of the food available to campers. The camp buildings could house up to 120 girls, but there were typically 75 to 80 campers. Most came from Arkansas, Oklahoma, Louisiana, and Texas. Camp became a tradition for girls, their sisters, and their friends. They moved up the ranks, and some eventually became counselors.

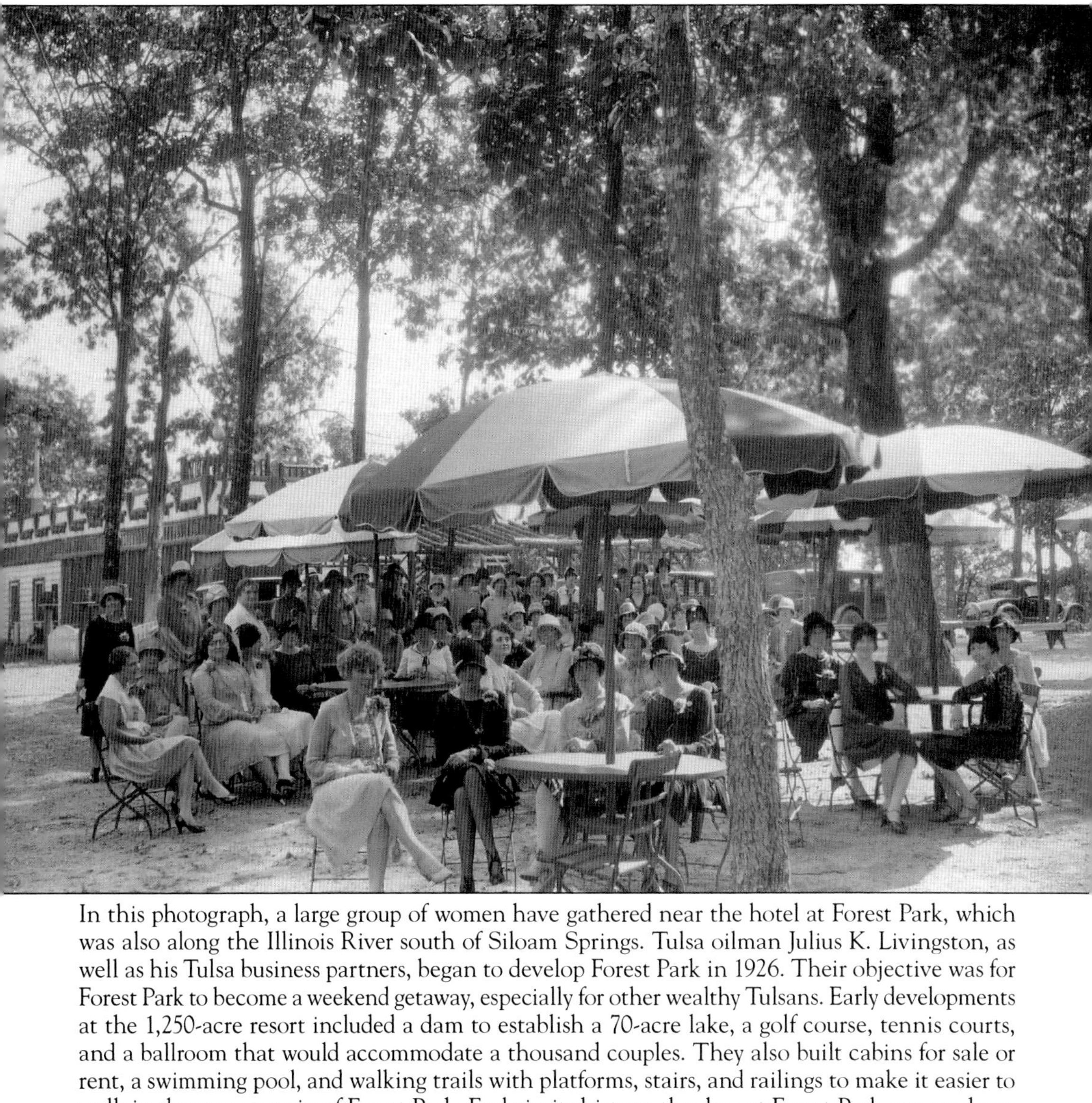

In this photograph, a large group of women have gathered near the hotel at Forest Park, which was also along the Illinois River south of Siloam Springs. Tulsa oilman Julius K. Livingston, as well as his Tulsa business partners, began to develop Forest Park in 1926. Their objective was for Forest Park to become a weekend getaway, especially for other wealthy Tulsans. Early developments at the 1,250-acre resort included a dam to establish a 70-acre lake, a golf course, tennis courts, and a ballroom that would accommodate a thousand couples. They also built cabins for sale or rent, a swimming pool, and walking trails with platforms, stairs, and railings to make it easier to walk in the steep terrain of Forest Park. Early in its history, the dam at Forest Park was used as a hydroelectric-generating facility. The dam was also subject to damage from floods.

Five

The New Deal 1930–1941

The Great Depression was a time of bank failures in Siloam Springs and the devastation that followed. But the town was also able to get several government-sponsored construction projects. There was even a small amount of privately funded construction that took place during the Depression years. Most families in town were poor, but since most of them were just as poor as their friends and neighbors, people who grew up here during that time report that they never really noticed how poor they were.

John E. Brown purchased radio station KUOA to help him get his evangelical and educational programs to a wide audience. The station also became another place that students could complete the work experience portion of their educations. Students also constructed, furnished, and maintained the buildings on campus, grew crops, managed a dairy herd, and made, washed, and repaired clothes. They did some work for area residents and sold extra produce to them.

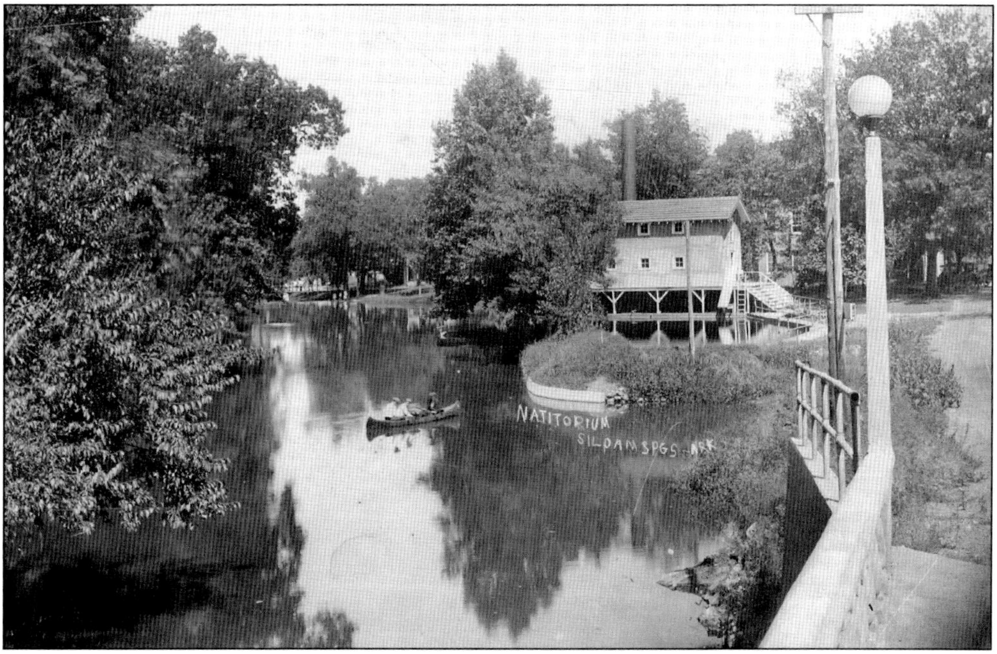

The above photograph is the view from the Mount Olive Street Bridge looking downstream. This concrete bridge was built about 1920. On the right is the Natatorium, which was the city's first swimming pool. The photograph below shows the pool and bathhouse in more detail. This facility was in existence from about 1920 to about 1940 and stood about where the office for parks and recreation is today. At this time, there were also canoes that could be rented for use on this part of Sager Creek. The first floor of the bathhouse contained changing rooms for each gender, and the caretaker and his family lived upstairs during the time the pool was open.

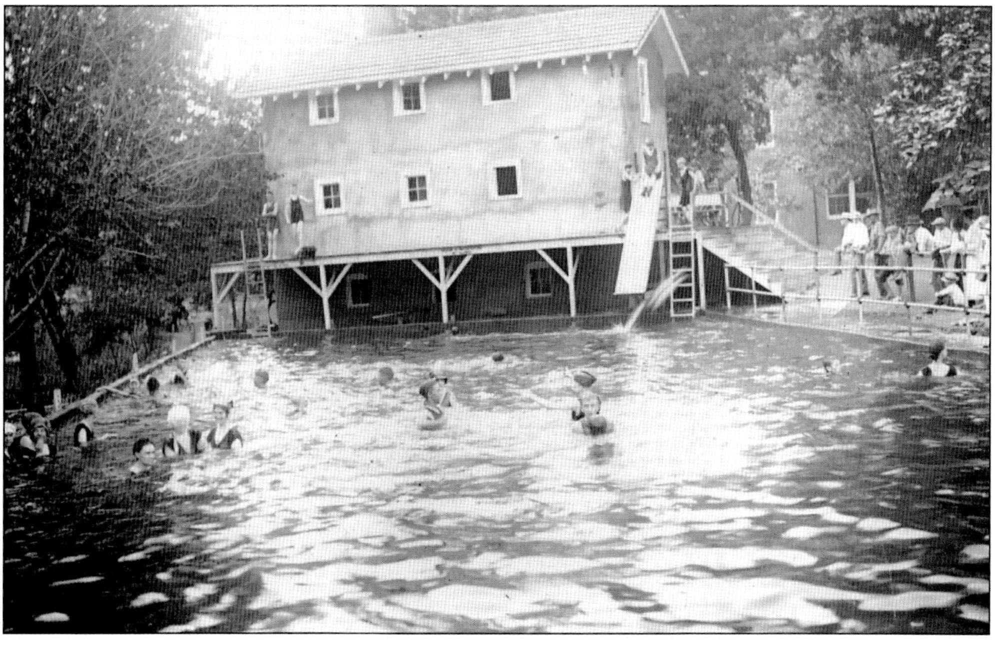

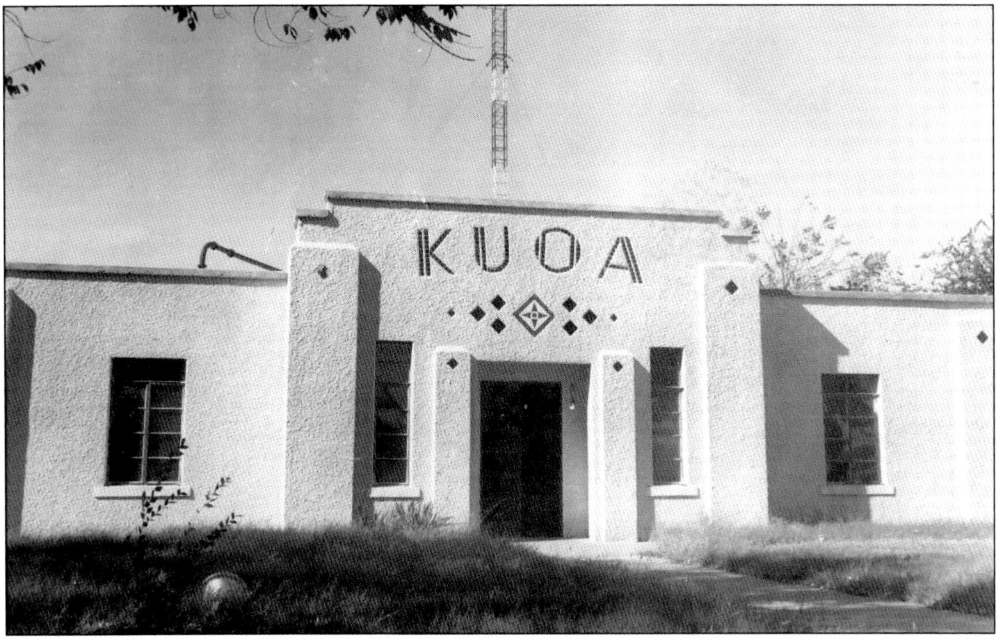

Radio station KUOA started at the University of Arkansas and first used the call letters KUOA in 1926. John E. Brown bought the station from members of the Fulbright family in 1935, but it was over a year before the studio, transmitter, and tower were all on the John Brown University campus, meaning this photograph might have been taken in the late 1930s.

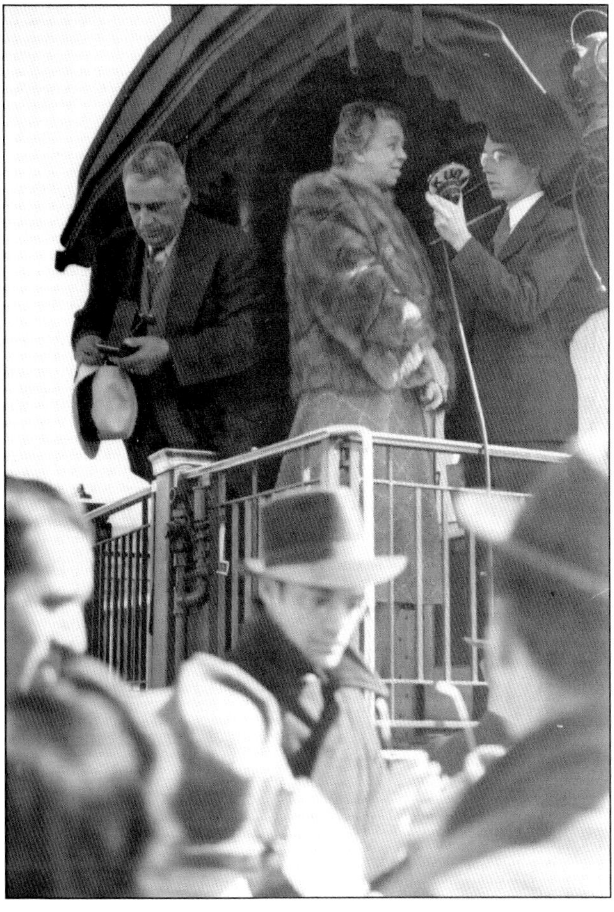

Storm Whaley of KUOA radio interviewed Eleanor Roosevelt at the back of her railcar. Whaley was a recent graduate of JBU and became one of the first employees of KUOA after John E. Brown purchased the station. The date of this photograph is unknown; however, the weather is cool, so it probably was not taken during the Roosevelts' June 1936 trip to the state to launch the state centennial celebration.

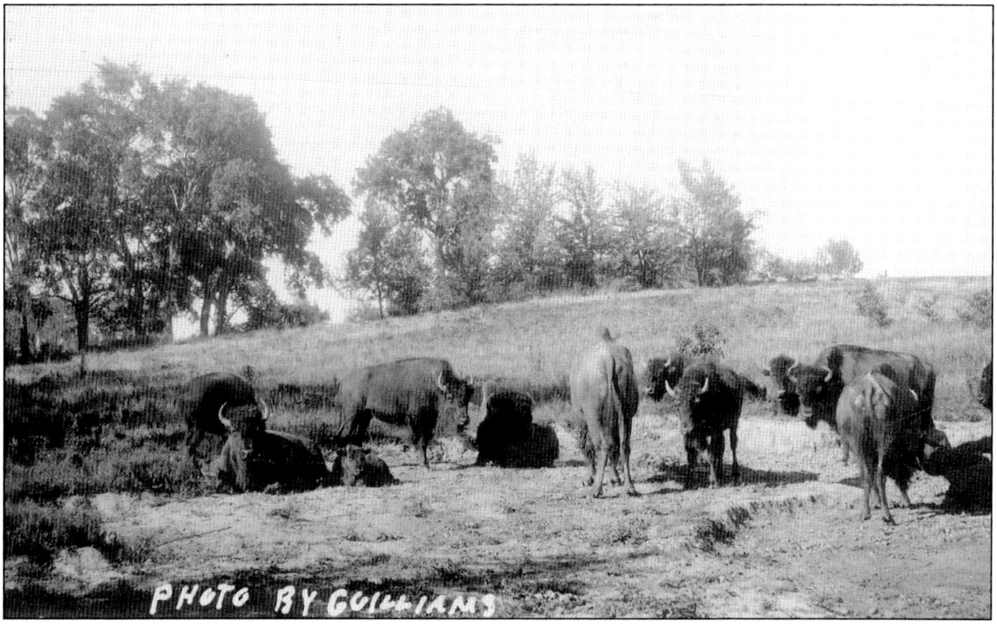

Buffalo Park was at Box Spring, which is now on the Siloam Springs Country Club. Box Spring is the headwaters of Sager Creek and was the city's water source for a while. The photograph below shows Joe Marveggio with the buffalo in the late 1930s. When he started feeding them in 1934, there were nine buffalo, but in 1941, the last two were sold. An article in the May 5, 1938, *Herald and Democrat* accompanying the above photograph declared, "We Siloamians can proudly claim the added unique distinction of owning one of the very few remaining herds of buffalo." They are, of course, much more numerous now, but at that time were quite rare.

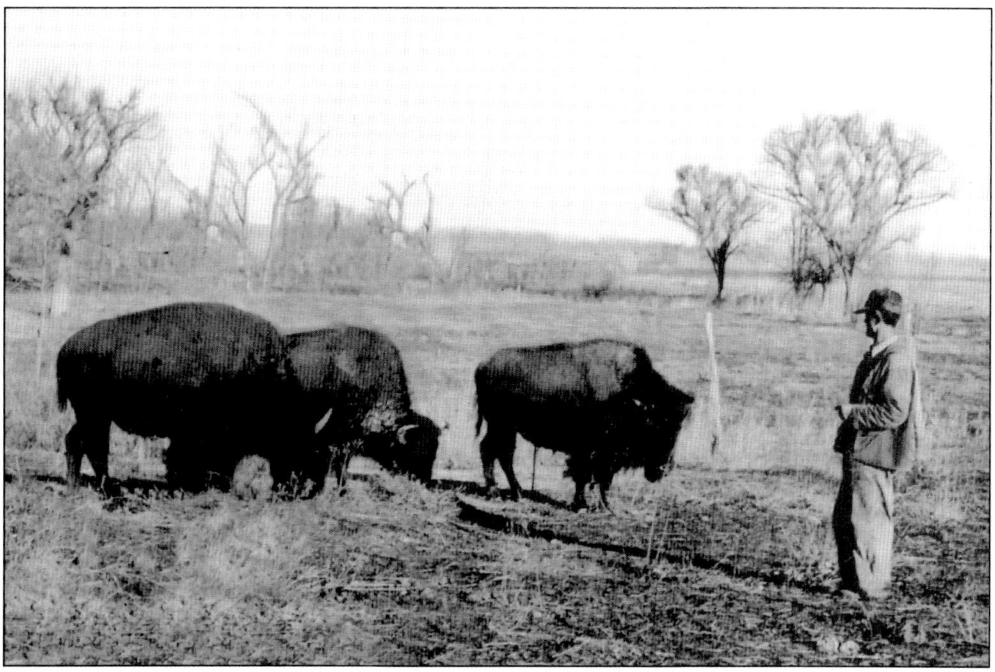

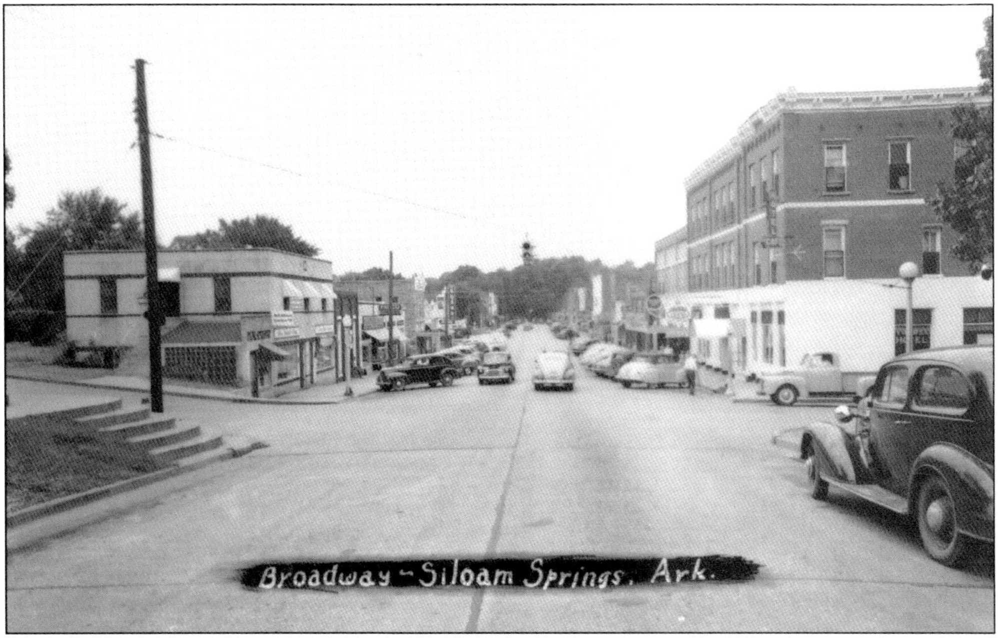

This photograph was taken at the north end of Broadway looking south. The Fenno Building on the left is dated 1941, making it one of the few privately funded construction projects built during the Great Depression. The hotel on the right was built as the Morris Hotel, but by this time, Frank Youree owned it and changed the name. He also removed the balconies, which had probably become unsafe.

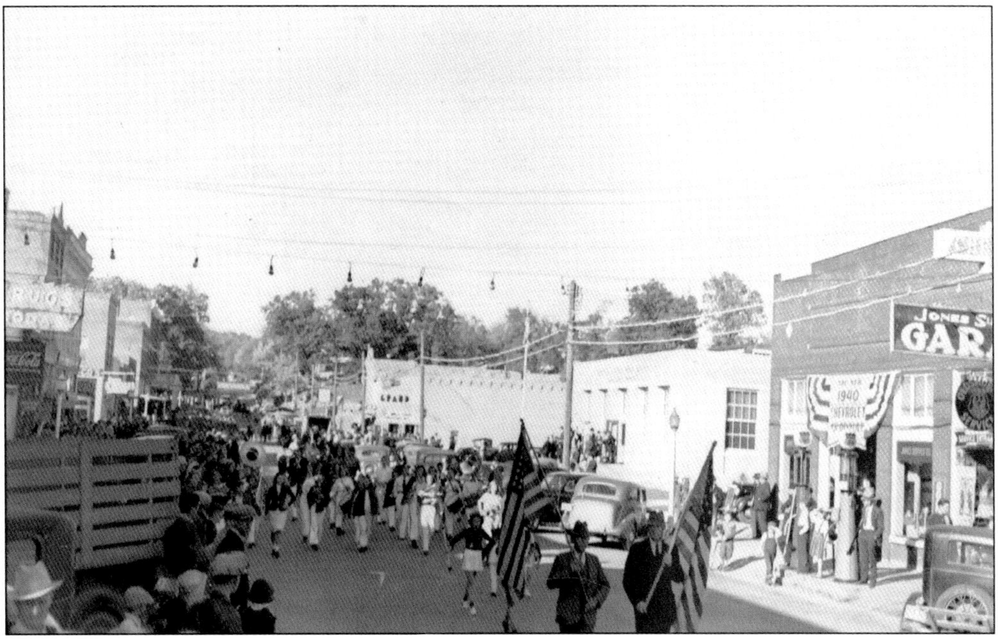

This photograph was taken at the south end of Broadway looking north. At the near right is the Jones Supply Company Garage, which was advertising that the new 1940 Chevrolets were on display. Next are the post office, built in 1937, and the Grand Theater, which was the second movie theater downtown.

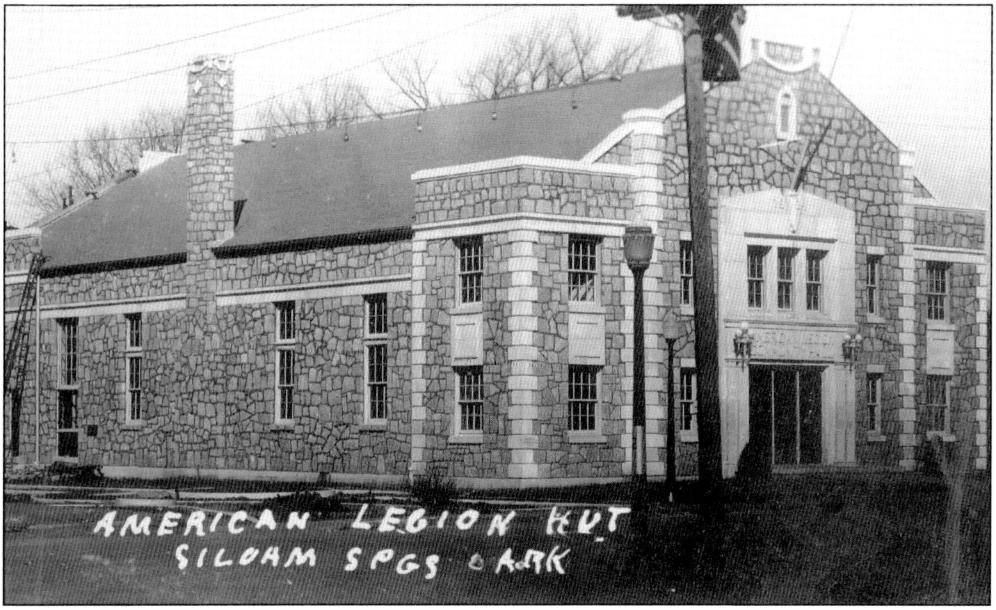

The American Legion Community Hall was built in 1934. The photograph below shows the cornerstone of this building, which tells that Everett Allen, one of the Allen brothers whose work was shown earlier, supervised construction of this building. The American Legion provided major funding toward construction of this building. By 1990, the windows of this building had been boarded up and the building was no longer in use. Main Street Siloam Springs, then directed by Marsha Emanuelson, renovated the windows, installed air conditioning, rewired the building, and returned it to use as the Community Building, which is now in frequent use.

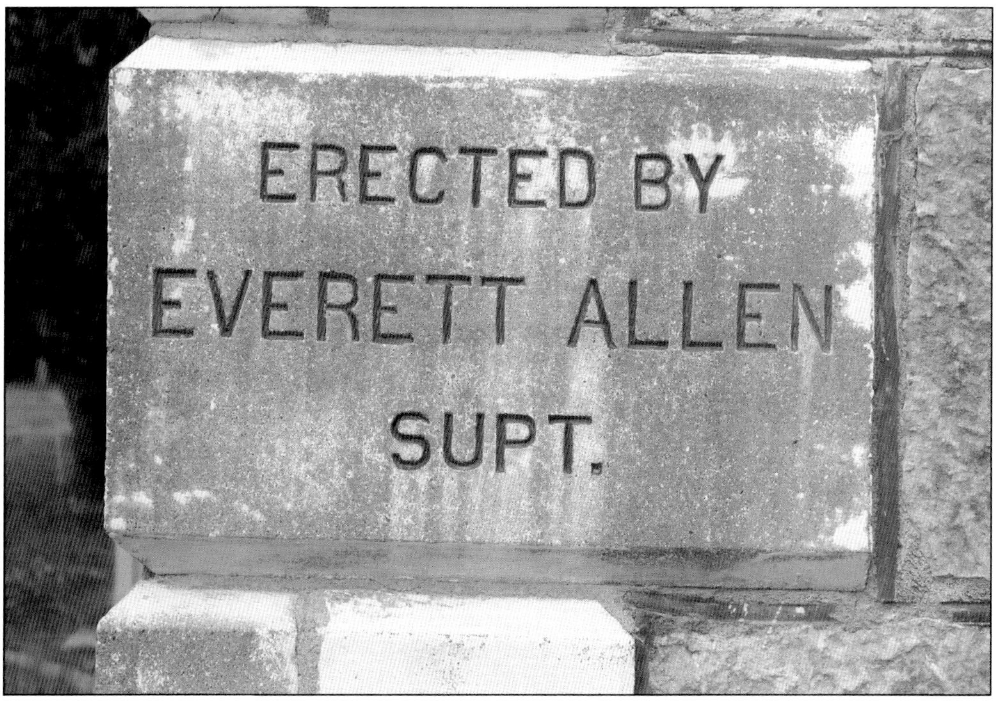

The world's tallest man, Robert Pershing Wadlow (1918–1940), poses with an unidentified woman next to a bench at the back of the Community Building. Also visible behind them is the Chandler Building, which housed Chandler's Drugstore on the ground floor. Upstairs was an opera house that was later divided into offices.

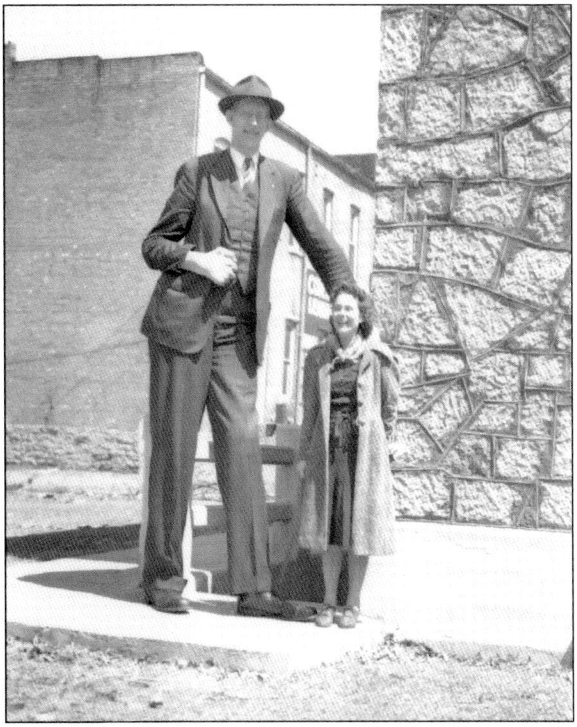

The Siloam Springs police got their first uniforms while Robert LaFollette was police chief, which was from 1931 to 1935. In this photograph, from left to right, are Bill Philpot, Ivan LaFollette, Robert LaFollette, and Joe Sheets. One or both LaFollette brothers went on to serve in the Arkansas State Police.

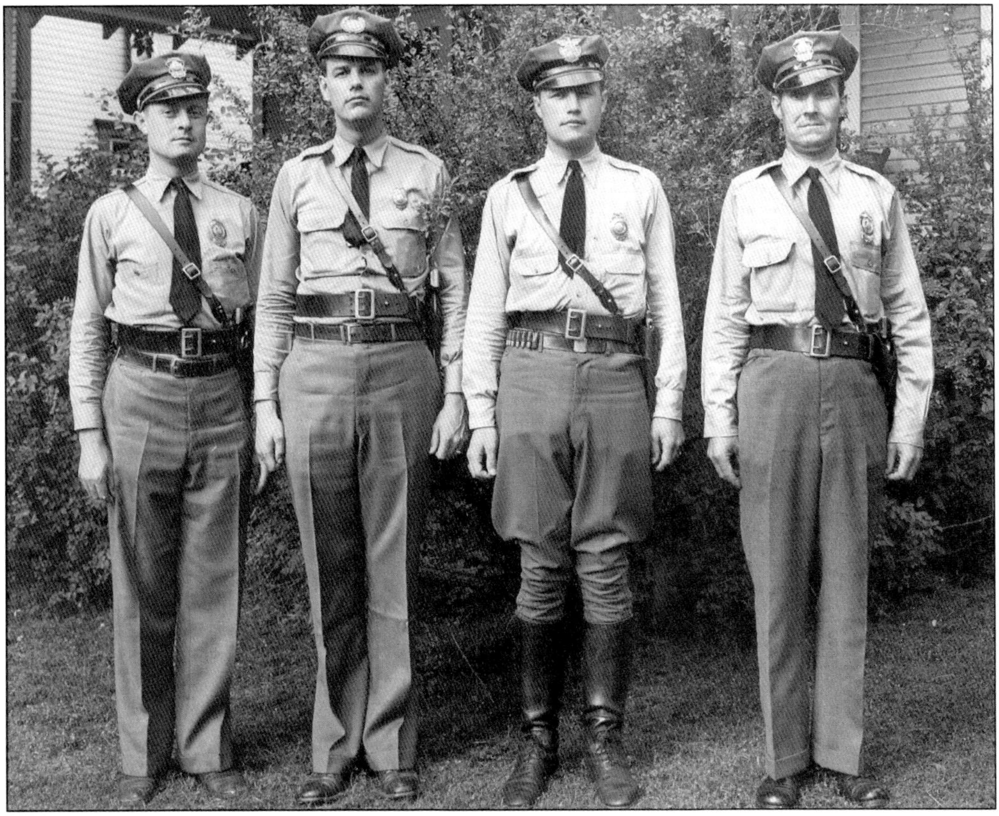

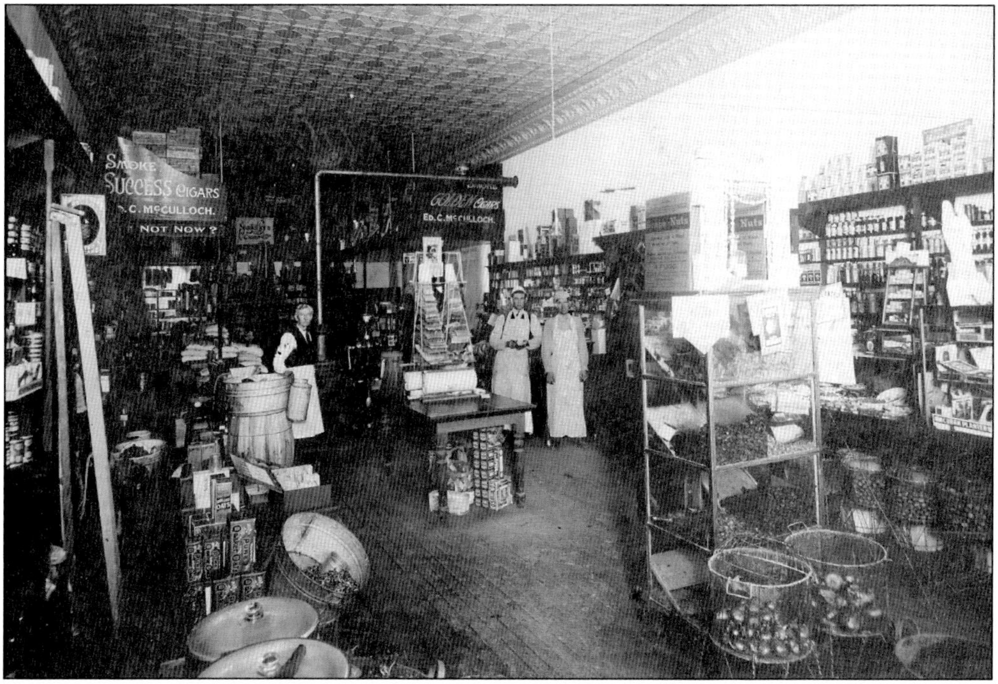

Edwin C. McCulloch (1870–1940) established his grocery store at what is now the corner of Alpine Street and Broadway in 1896. The building standing there today dates from about 1910. Above is a photograph of the interior of this business, and below is a ghost sign for this business, which is on the north wall of the building, along Alpine Street. The large ghost sign for Aristos Flour probably also dates from the time of the grocery. The south part of the McCulloch Building contained the Midway Theater, which was the first movie theater in town. It was later called the Rialto, which burned in 1948 and was never rebuilt.

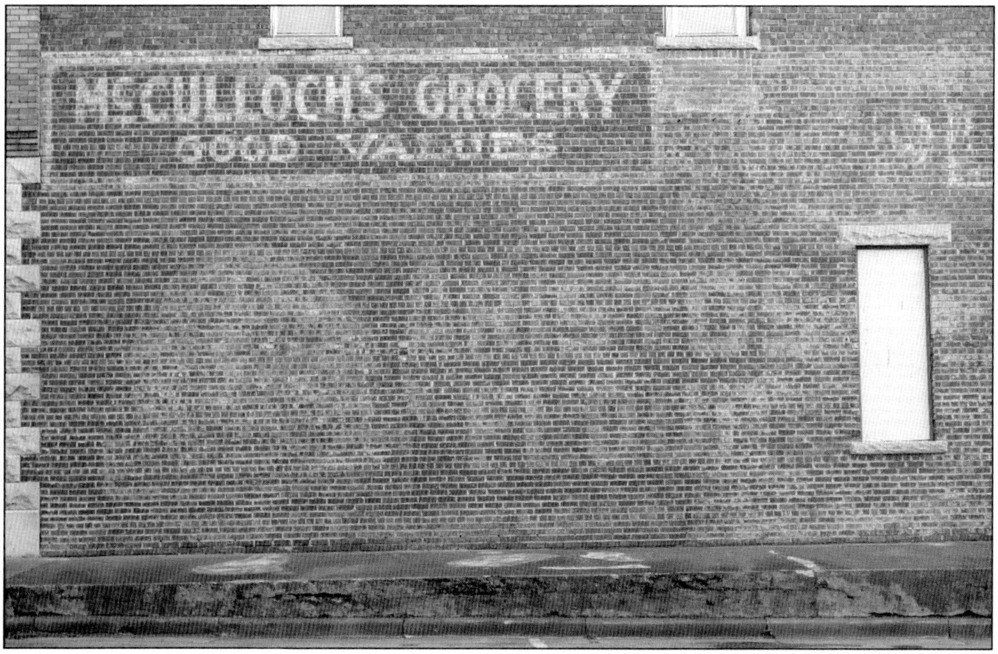

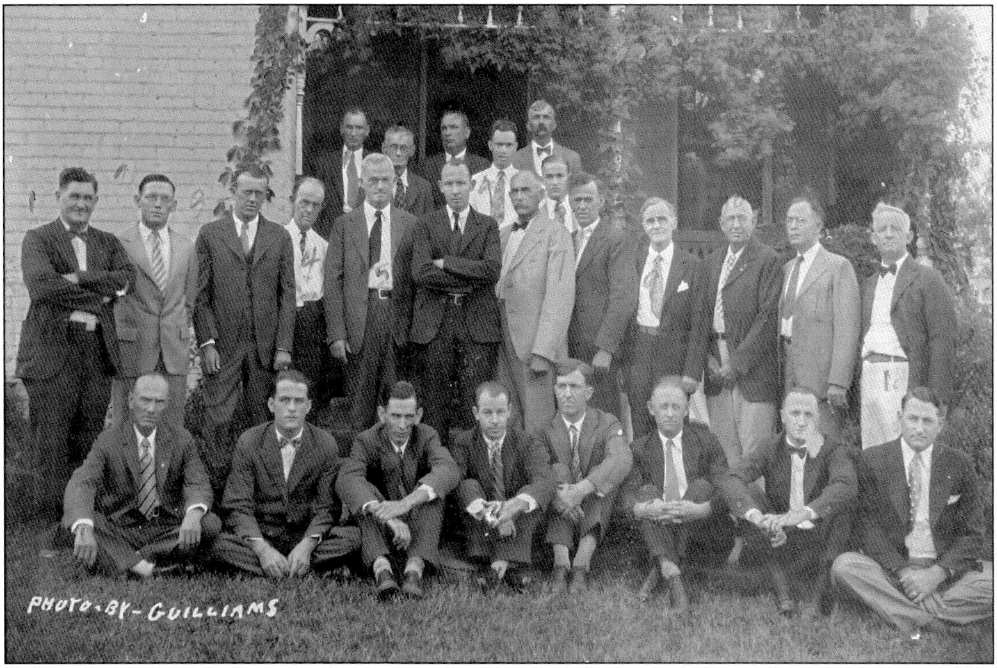

Masons in about 1930 included, from left to right, (first row) W.L. Barns, Earl McNair, Chauncey Darling, Jo Wilson, Ross Cundiff, E.F. Copeland, Ralph Pyeatte, and Earl Hendren; (second row) Frank Howard, O.M. Moore, J. McDonnell, J.R. "Lank" Lancaster, Connelly Harrington, Leon Wasson, E.V. Howard, George Ellis Moss, L.P. Kemper, W.M. Hoslie, A. Lyle Martin, and Tupper Corn; (third row) Henry Mason, William Gilmore, John Chandler, Clarence (Virgil ?) DeWitt, O.D. Mounger, and J.G. Frill.

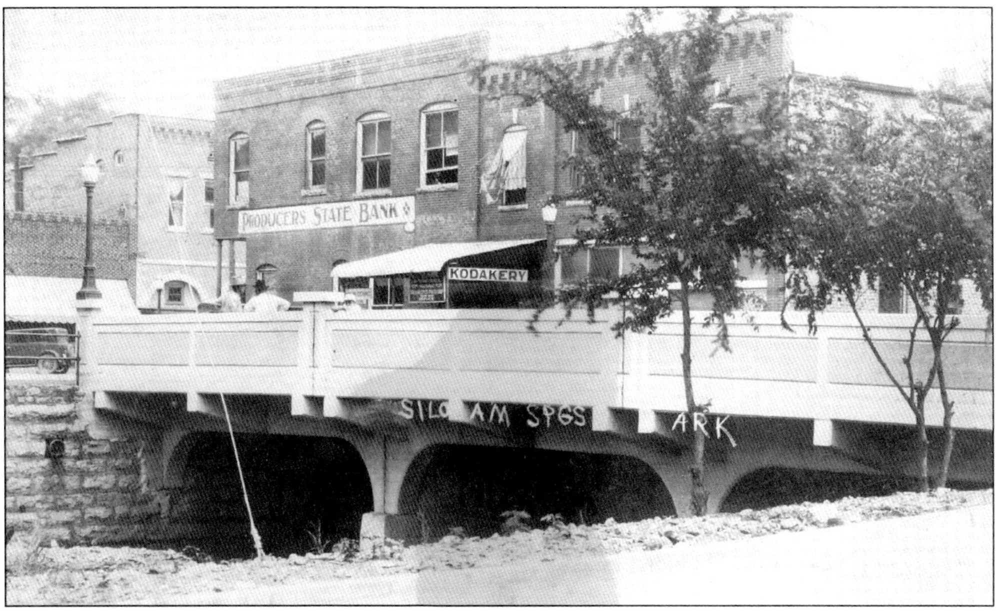

This was probably intended to be a photograph of the East Main Street Bridge, built in 1926 at the beginning of the project to pave the downtown. But also of interest is the Producers State Bank at East Main Street and Broadway. This bank was organized in 1912 and survived until spring 1932.

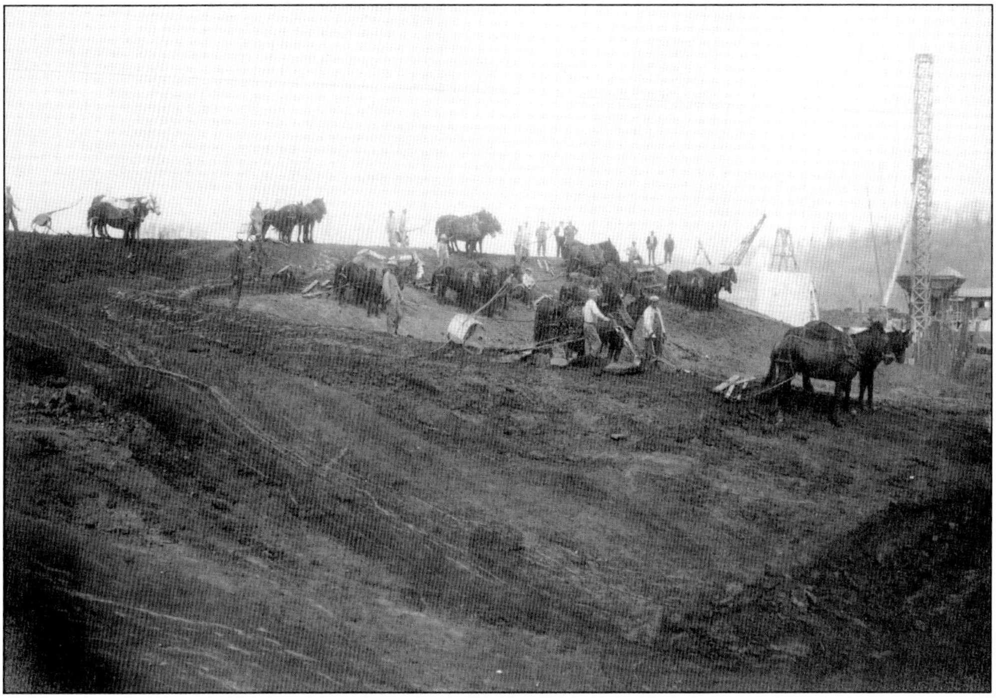

In 1927, James Wallace Sloan gained the controlling interest in Forest Park, which he renamed Lake Frances, after his daughter. In this photograph, workers under the supervision on Caldeen Gunter II are building the Lake Frances dam higher. But before this work was completed, the Great Depression and accompanying local bank failures drove Gunter into bankruptcy. (Courtesy of C.L. "Bub" and Sammye Lou Gunter.)

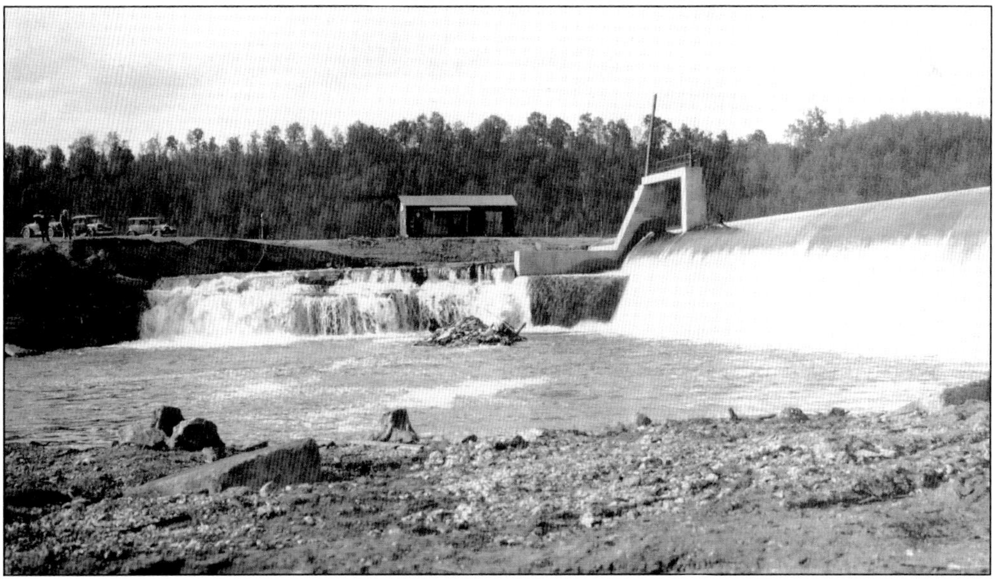

This photograph shows the Lake Frances dam as finished and full of water. Flooding on the Illinois River later damaged this dam, and in 1954, the City of Siloam Springs purchased the lake and rebuilt the dam as a water source and recreational area. By 1989, this dam was damaged, so the lake was drained to avoid a catastrophic break that would cause damage downstream.

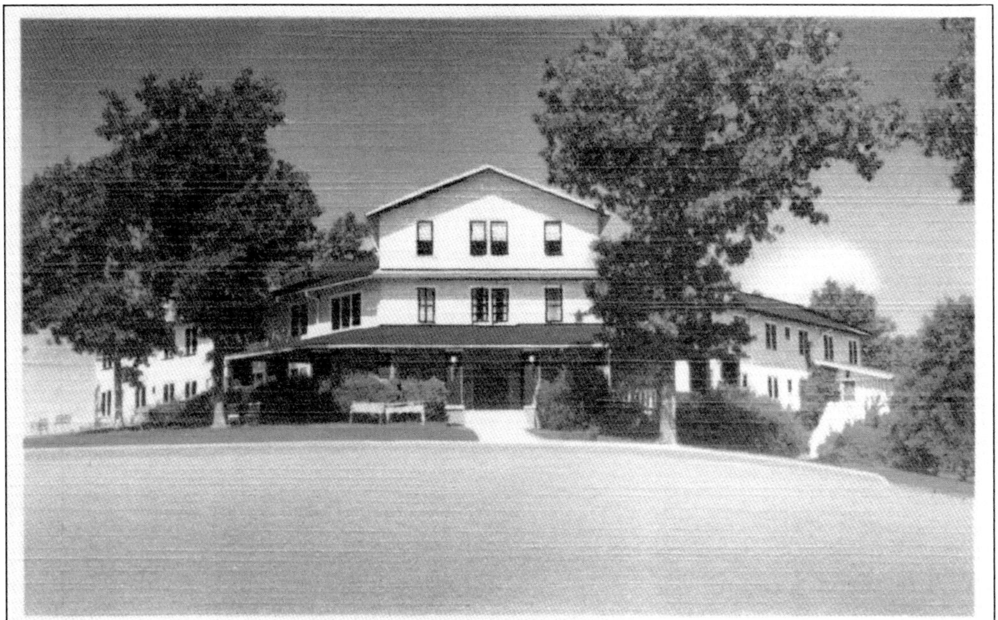

LAKE FRANCES HOTEL, Siloam Springs, Arkansas

The image above shows the Lake Frances Hotel, which was a 60-room lodge on the plateau seen in the photograph below. Near the hotel were the ballroom, swimming pool, and tennis courts. Water for the resort was stored in a water tower near the hotel and ballroom. The golf course was along Highway 59. Cabins throughout the resort were available for rent or purchase, or one could buy a lot and build a cabin. This resort was promoted as a weekend getaway, especially for Tulsans with oil money. People from Siloam Springs went there for an evening's entertainment or a day of golf, fishing, and tennis.

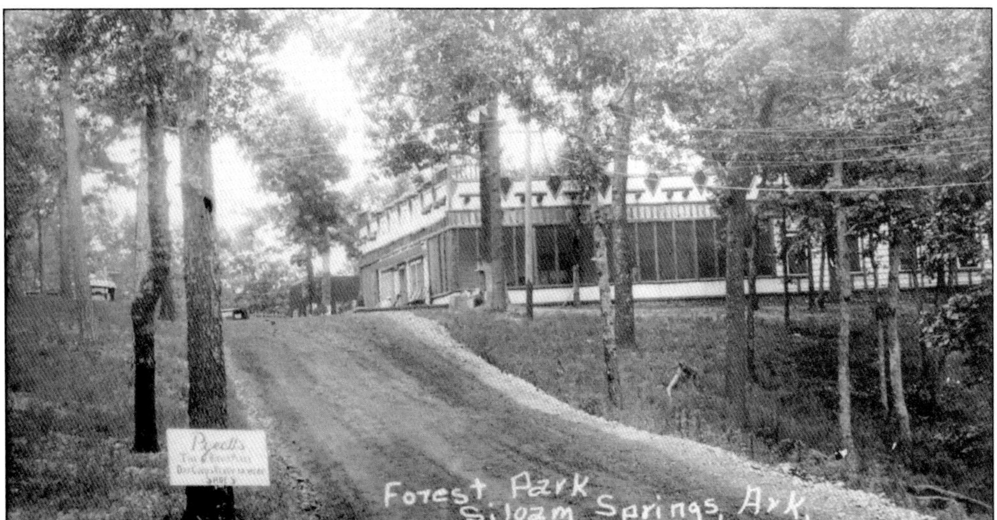

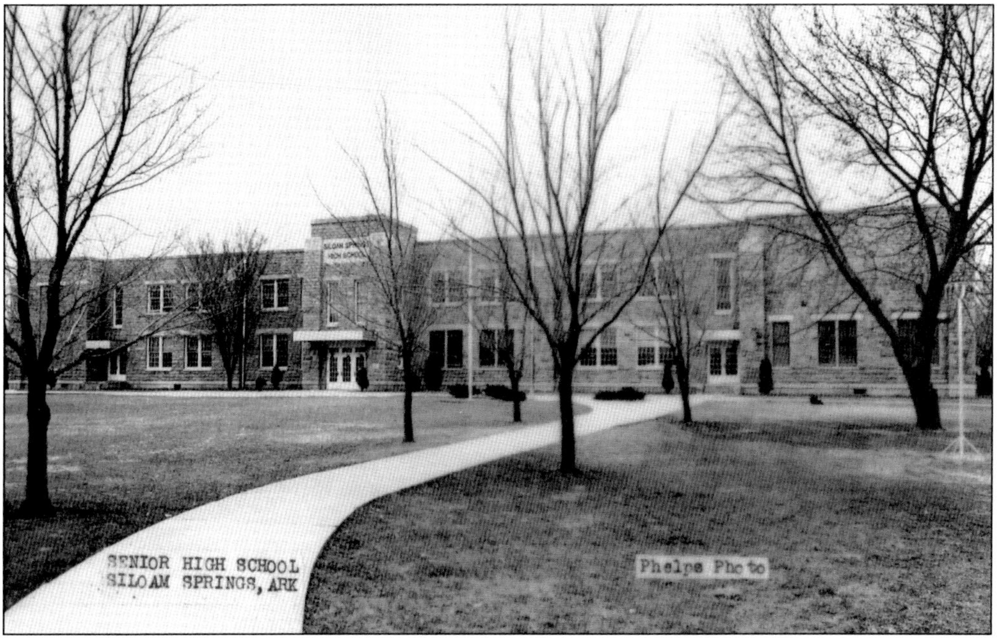

The photograph above shows the 1940 high school as completed, and the photograph below shows the monument to this building today. The Works Project Administration logo was originally beside the front door of this building to show that it was built as part of this New Deal program. Also visible here are the names of the graduates from this school, by year, engraved on bricks. These names were once pressed into the wet concrete of the sidewalks in front of the building. The 1940 high school was torn down in 1994 as part of the expansion of Southside Elementary.

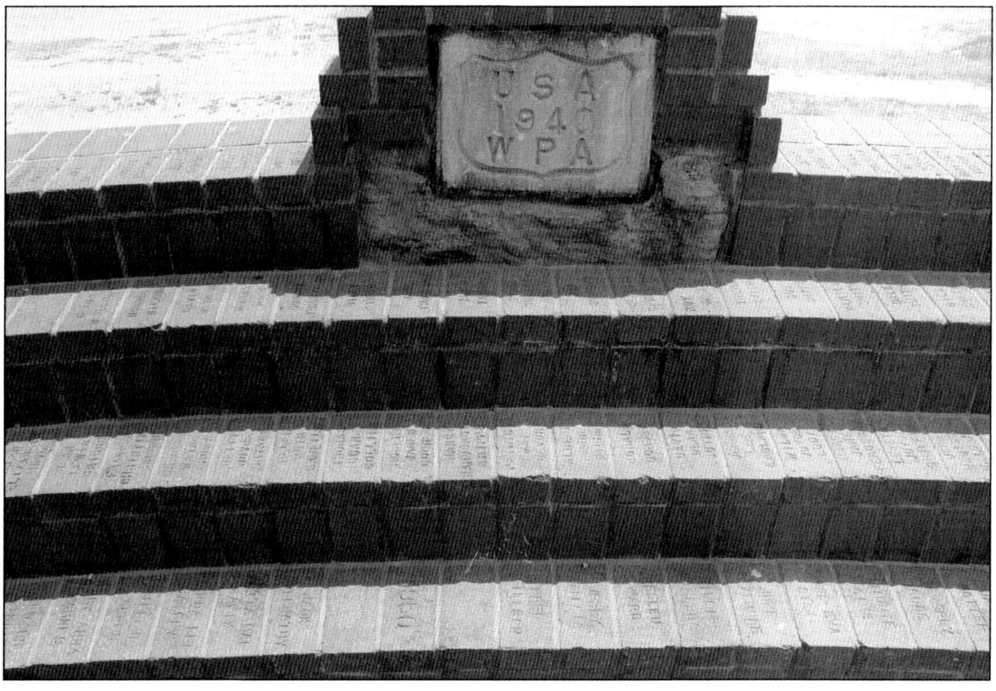

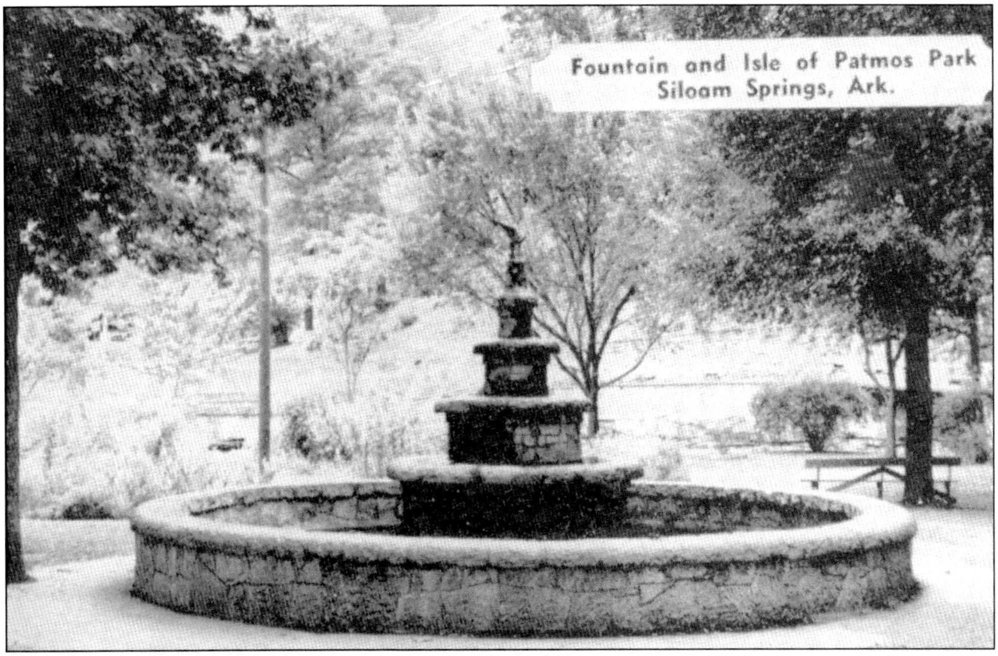

The National Youth Administration (NYA) built this fountain in Twin Springs Park in 1936. The NYA was a New Deal program intended to help youth stay in school by providing summer work and requiring that they return to school in the fall. The fountain at this location today is modeled on the 1936 fountain.

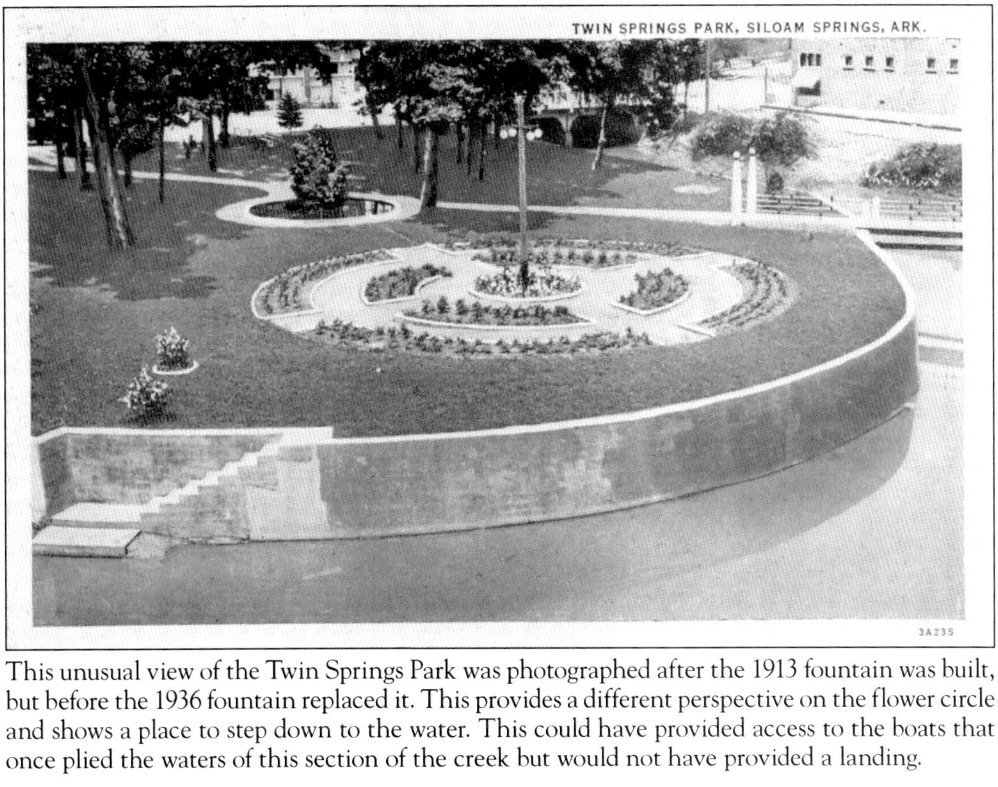

This unusual view of the Twin Springs Park was photographed after the 1913 fountain was built, but before the 1936 fountain replaced it. This provides a different perspective on the flower circle and shows a place to step down to the water. This could have provided access to the boats that once plied the waters of this section of the creek but would not have provided a landing.

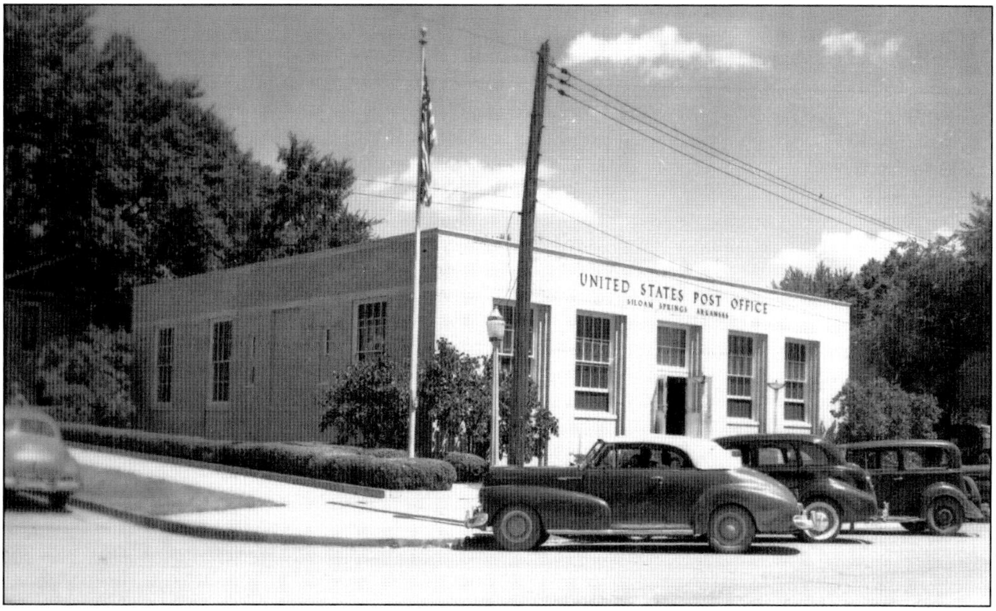

The 1937 post office was another government-funded construction project in town. It features a government-funded mural, which is above the postmaster's office door. In 1965, an addition was built at the back of the building. This addition included a surveillance catwalk from which inspectors could keep an eye on postal employees. This building is the future home of the Siloam Springs Museum.

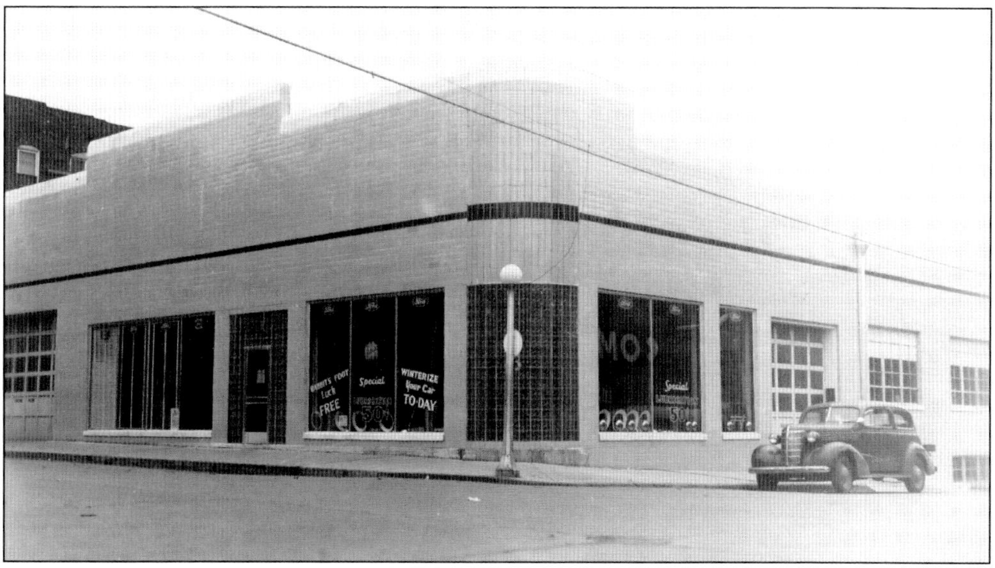

The Crain Building was built as a Ford dealership at the corner of Mount Olive and University Streets in 1935. It has a full basement that was once a fallout shelter. The tile exterior has now been covered with stucco, but the glass bricks have been retained. It is now the location of 28 Springs restaurant.

Six

From World War II to the Bypass 1942–1962

Prior to 1962, virtually anything a person needed, from birth to death, could be found in downtown Siloam Springs. There were doctors from general practitioners to dentists, and for a while, there were two hospitals. There were stores from dry goods to groceries. There were offices of real estate agents, lawyers, and undertakers. For a while, there were three movie theaters and a pool hall.

During World War II, of course, everyone was concentrating on the war effort. But once the war was over and postwar shortages resolved, businessmen in town began to consider how to grow the town again. One group decided that a town with ambition needed street names that reflected ambition, and so, in 1947, St. Nicholas Avenue became Broadway, St. John Avenue became University Street, and so on. A few streets, like Tahlequah and East Main, kept their names, but most changed. Streets on a north-south or east-west line were given the same name on both sides of Sager Creek, even if they may never connect.

At about the same time, a new house numbering system was adopted, with north and south parts of each street divided at Central Street and east and west divided at Mount Olive Street. The sequence of house numbers is now much more uniform than it was before.

In memory of locals who died in World War II and the Gold Star Mothers, the entire town worked together to build and open Memorial Hospital in 1950. Two years later, the town worked together again to plan and carry out the Silver Strike Jubilee, which was a segment on a Universal-International newsreel. The chamber of commerce used footage of the Silver Strike in their promotional film, "A Future to Share."

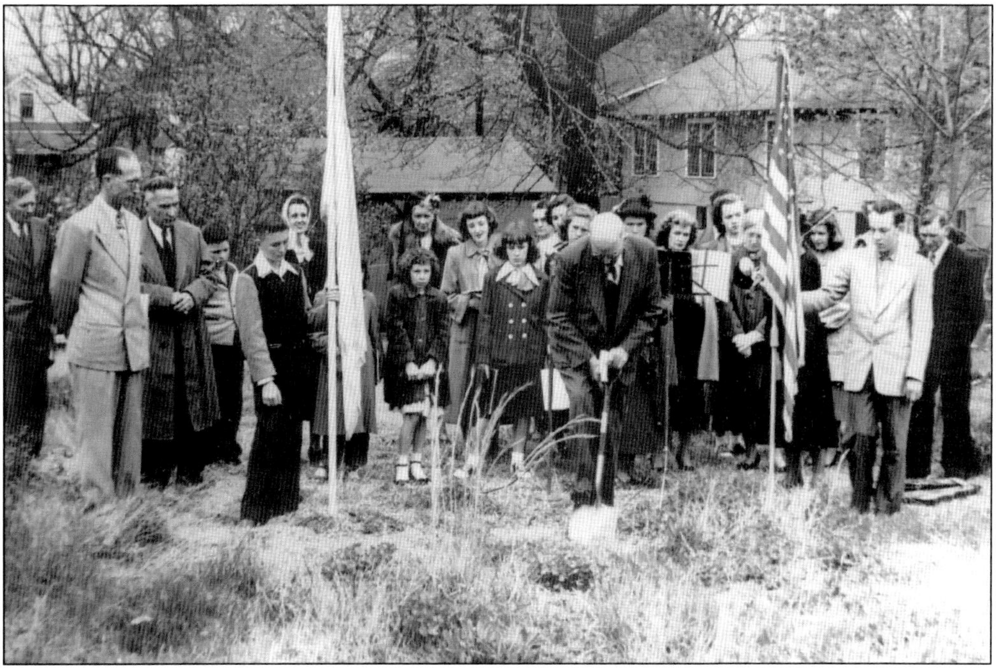

The ground breaking for the current First Presbyterian Church building on Maxwell Street was on April 10, 1949. The following are identified as being in this photograph: Arthur Sebastian, Leslie M. and Gertrude Greene, Leah Hoke, Jerry Rank, Barbara Phillips, Ann Darling, Margarette Elrod, Reverend Kornfield, Betty Nell Hastings, Dorothy Bast, Charles W. Brown, Robert Stephens, and Charles Hoke with the shovel. Below is an interesting photograph of that building in snow. The building contains some pieces of stained-glass art designed and built by Beatrice Stebbing. In 2002, she became the first artist named by the Arkansas Arts Council as an Arkansas Living Treasure.

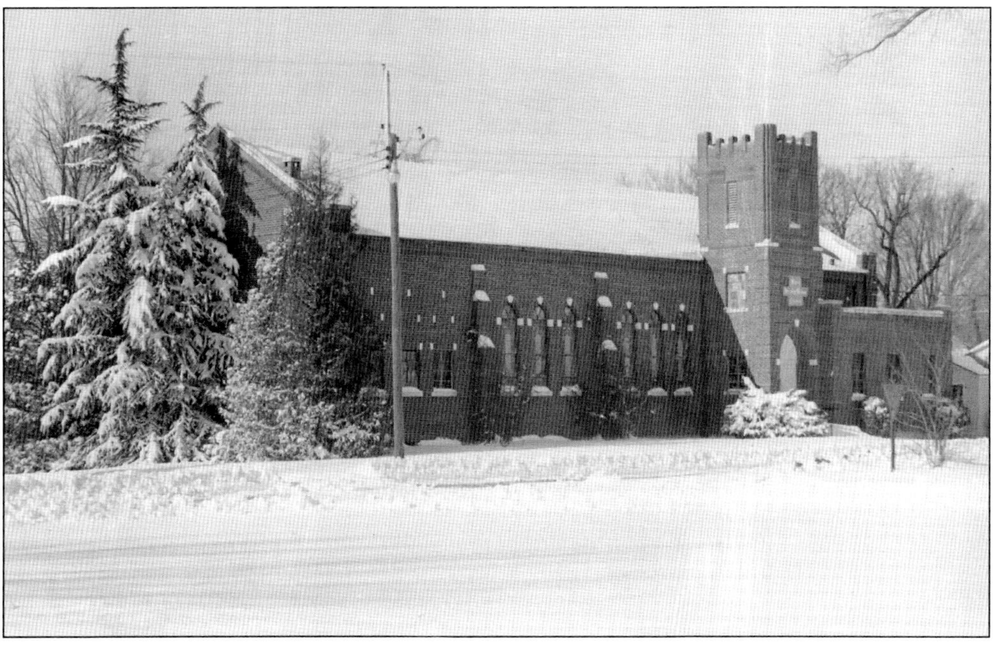

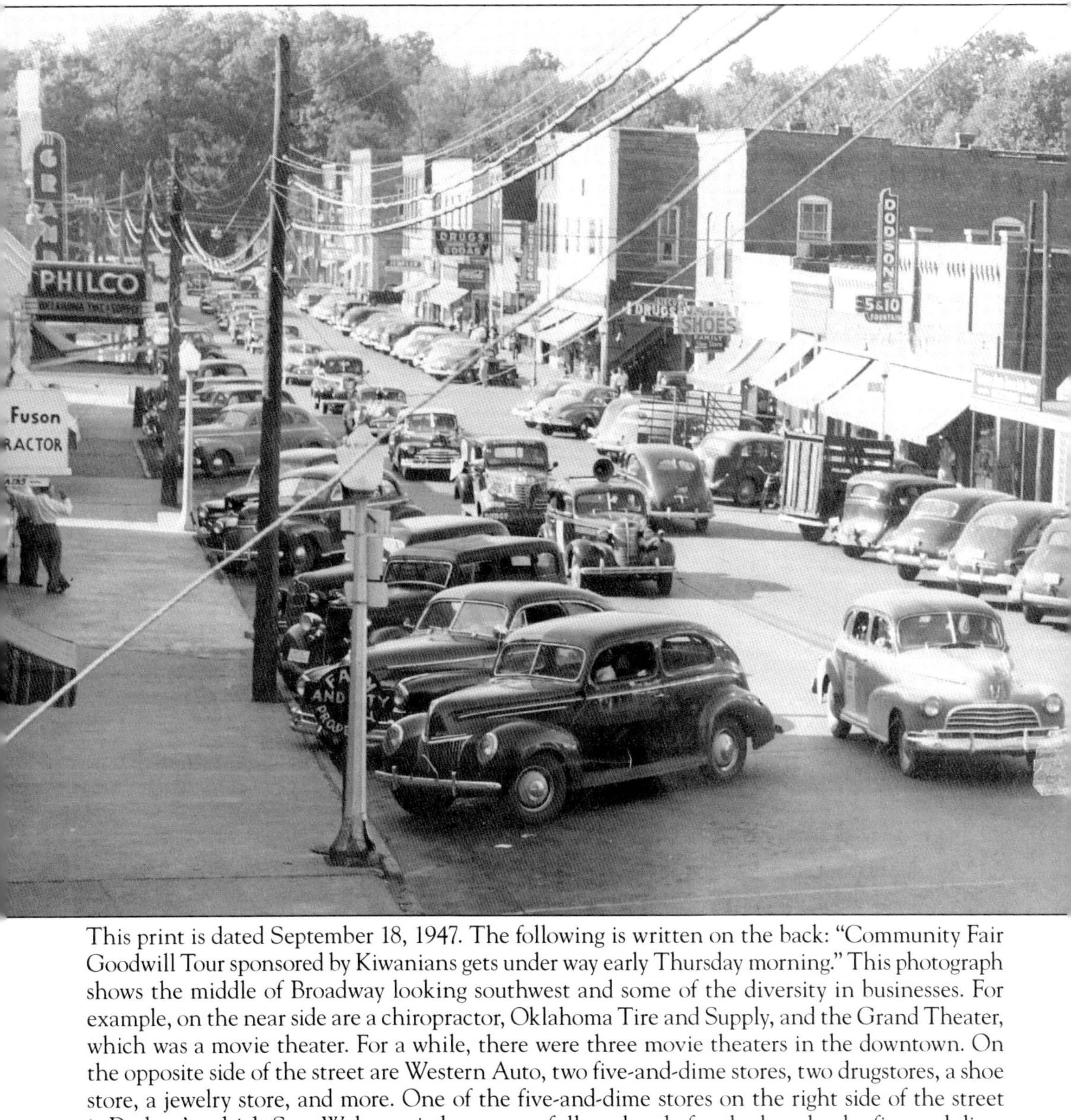

This print is dated September 18, 1947. The following is written on the back: "Community Fair Goodwill Tour sponsored by Kiwanians gets under way early Thursday morning." This photograph shows the middle of Broadway looking southwest and some of the diversity in businesses. For example, on the near side are a chiropractor, Oklahoma Tire and Supply, and the Grand Theater, which was a movie theater. For a while, there were three movie theaters in the downtown. On the opposite side of the street are Western Auto, two five-and-dime stores, two drugstores, a shoe store, a jewelry store, and more. One of the five-and-dime stores on the right side of the street is Dodson's, which Sam Walton tried unsuccessfully to buy before he bought the five-and-dime on the Bentonville square from which he launched Walmart. Locals still speculate about how different this town's history might have been if Dodson's had sold to Walton.

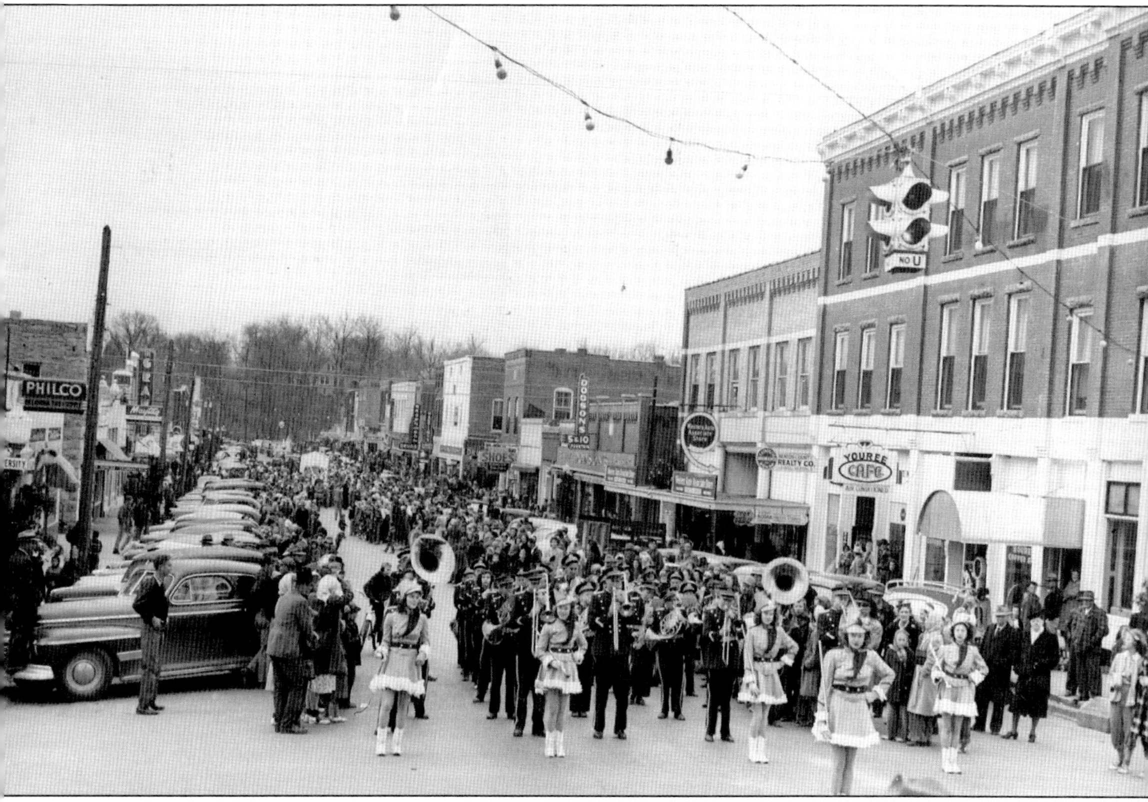

The 1949 Christmas parade reaches the north end of Broadway. The majorettes are, from left to right, Jettie Marveggio, Dorothy Kirkpatrick, Helen Zoe Coates Nitz, drum major Sally Gorum, and Tommye Garrett Strassheim. In honor of the season, they have white fleece on their cuffs and hems. Today, the Christmas parade is held in the evening of the first Saturday in December. The Heritage League organizes the parade and establishes a theme for each year. Floats are lighted, and riders on horseback have battery-powered lights on their reins. Another change from this photograph is that the traffic lights downtown have been replaced with stop signs. Similar lights provide light along the sidewalks today. The businesses downtown are now entirely different from those seen in this photograph.

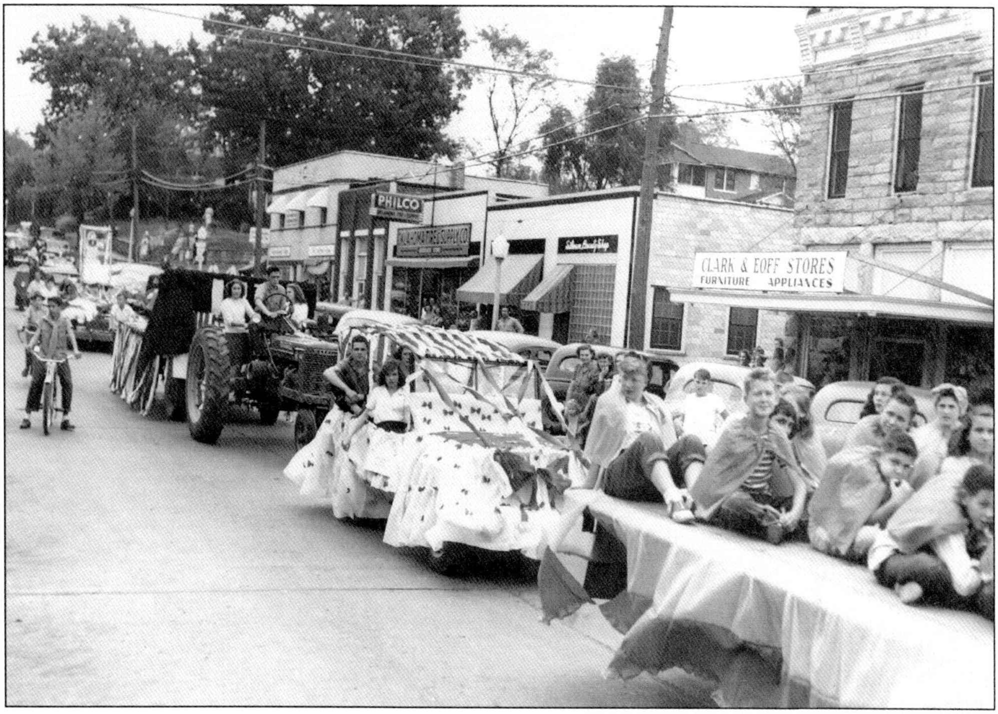

A 1947 parade at the north end of Broadway is going south. The photograph was taken looking north. The bow tie–covered vehicle is labeled "Freshman Class," so this might be a homecoming parade. The building that was then occupied by the Clark and Eoff Stores was built in 1894 and represents the boom in stone-and-brick construction after the arrival of the railroad at the end of 1893.

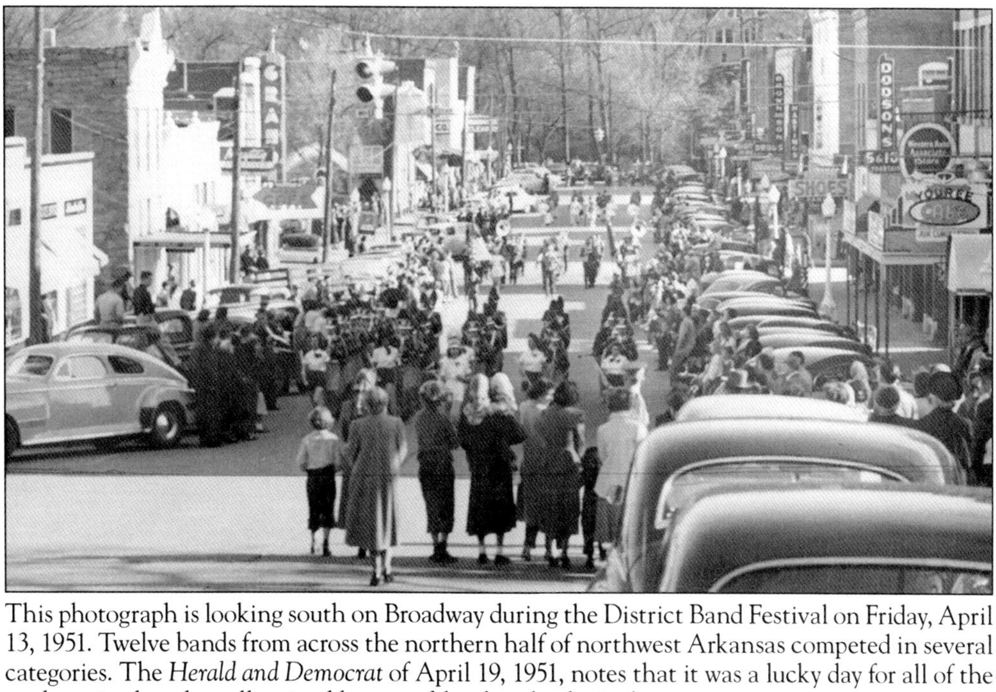

This photograph is looking south on Broadway during the District Band Festival on Friday, April 13, 1951. Twelve bands from across the northern half of northwest Arkansas competed in several categories. The *Herald and Democrat* of April 19, 1951, notes that it was a lucky day for all of the students in that they all arrived home safely after the festival.

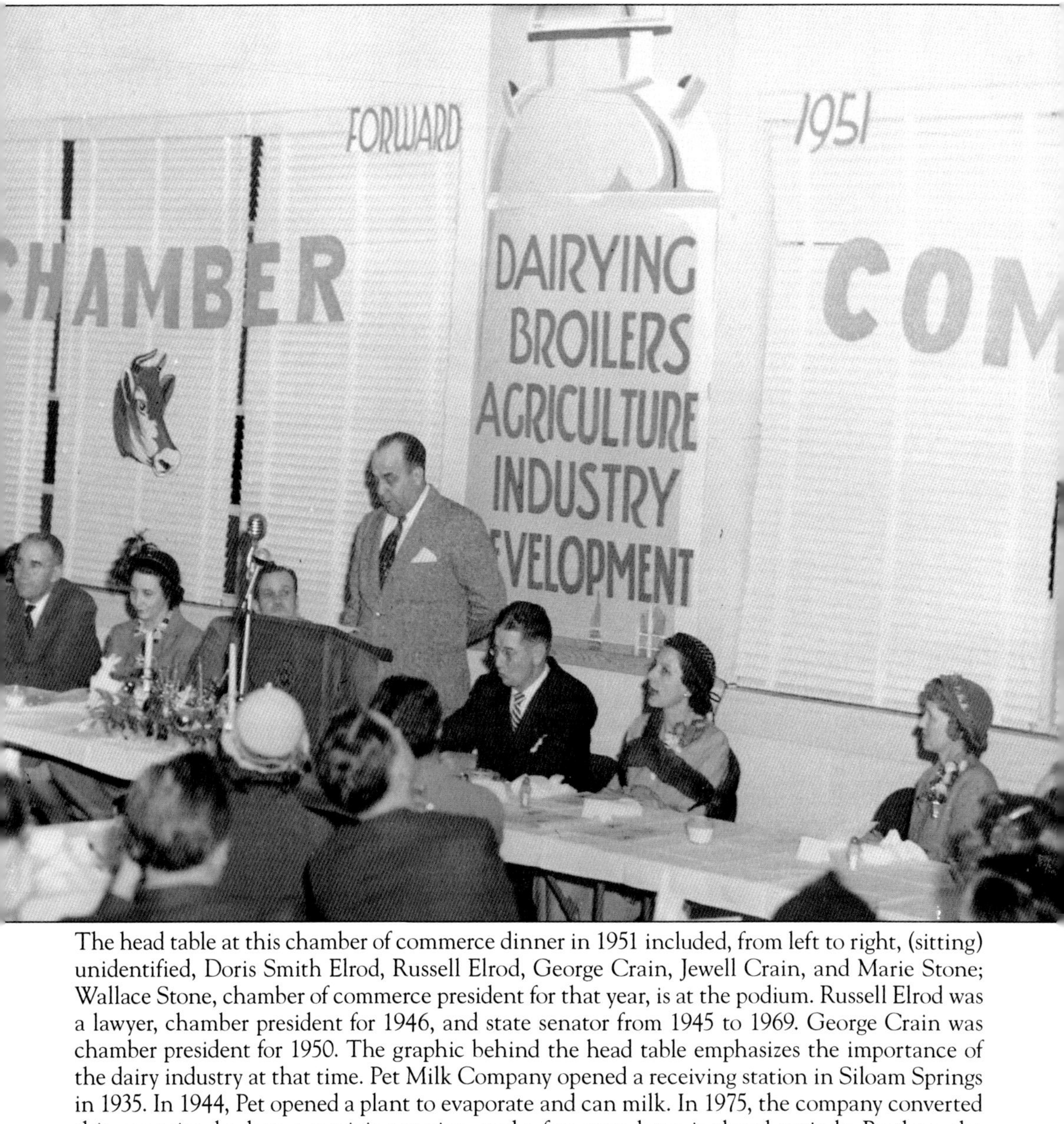

The head table at this chamber of commerce dinner in 1951 included, from left to right, (sitting) unidentified, Doris Smith Elrod, Russell Elrod, George Crain, Jewell Crain, and Marie Stone; Wallace Stone, chamber of commerce president for that year, is at the podium. Russell Elrod was a lawyer, chamber president for 1946, and state senator from 1945 to 1969. George Crain was chamber president for 1950. The graphic behind the head table emphasizes the importance of the dairy industry at that time. Pet Milk Company opened a receiving station in Siloam Springs in 1935. In 1944, Pet opened a plant to evaporate and can milk. In 1975, the company converted this operation back to a receiving station, and a few years later, it closed entirely. By then, the company was Pet, Inc., with diverse business interests. Broilers are still an important part of the economy of northwest Arkansas. Local agriculture also includes beef cattle, hay, and some row crops. Siloam Springs still has a diverse group of industries.

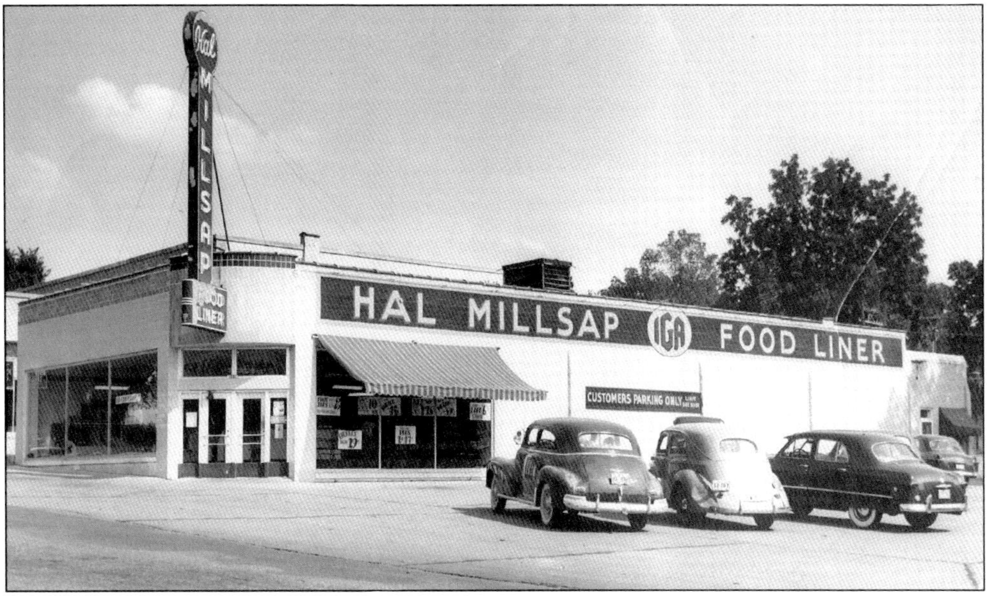

Hal Milsap's IGA was at East Main and Washington Streets from August 3, 1946, to March 1, 1963. This was the first grocery in the area with self-service meat counters. Milsap opened his first store in 1931 at Mount Olive and University Streets and then moved to a location on Broadway before moving to the East Main location. The store later moved to Mount Olive and West Tulsa Streets.

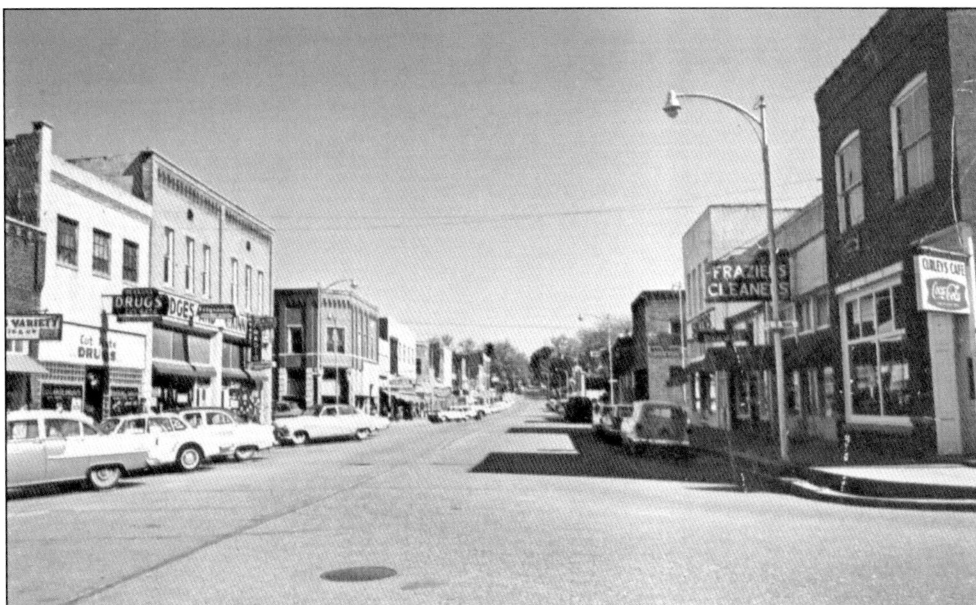

Modern streetlights line Broadway in this photograph, taken at the south end looking north, around 1956. The photograph shows the variety of businesses that were in the downtown at that time. There were variety stores, at least two drugstores, two hardware stores, a jewelry store, a furniture store, a laundry, and cafés.

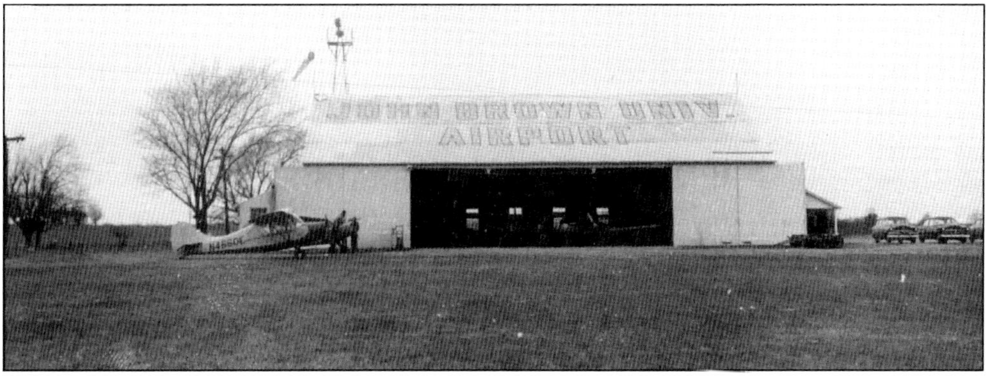

This John Brown University Airport was just across the state line in Oklahoma and was dedicated in 1940 by World War I flying ace Eddie Rickenbacker. The first JBU airport was a smaller facility immediately south of campus. The school's aviation program taught several pilots and aviation mechanics for service in World War II.

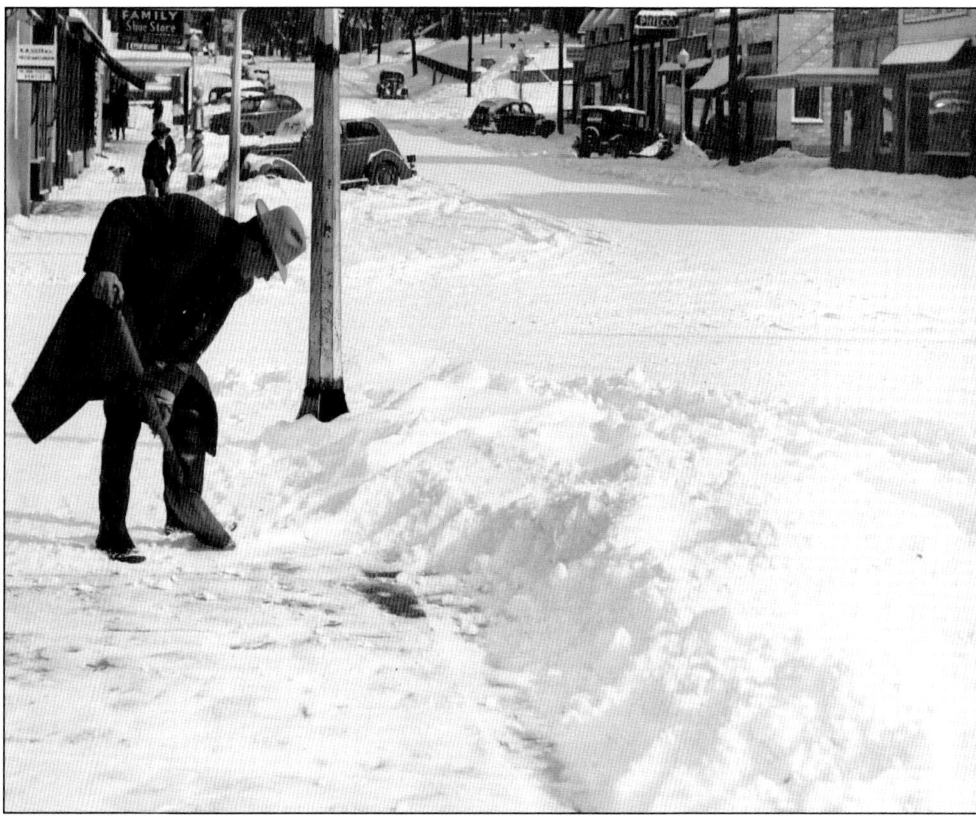

In March 1948, Dale Robinson shovels the walk in front of the variety store owned and operated by three generations of his family at Broadway and Central Street. Fading signs from this business are still visible on the north wall. The label on the back of the photograph notes, "Merchants faced mountains of snow on their walks Friday morning—traffic almost at a standstill—reports of many cars in the ditch."

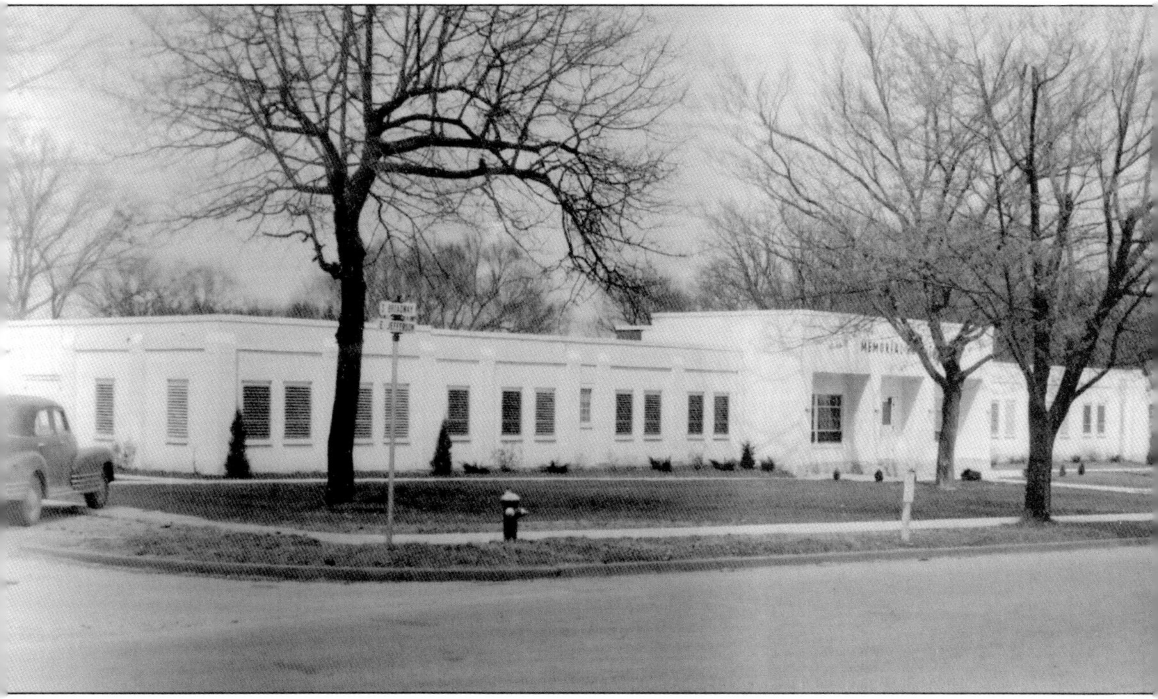

Memorial Hospital opened on Jefferson Street between Maxwell Street and Broadway, which was previously the Chautauqua grounds, in December 1950. The community came together to build, fund, and supply this 33-bed facility without federal money. It was named in honor of those who died in World War II and their Gold Star Mothers. Cash was raised in many different ways including a pie sale, coffee day at the Youree Café, and a benefit ball game. Some of the labor to build the hospital was donated, and items like linens were also donated. Total cash needed for the hospital was $125,000, of which $75,000 came from a bond issue. There was one large ($10,000) donation from F.M. Dye, but the remaining $40,000 came from a large number of small donations. Memorial Hospital has now been replaced by Siloam Springs Regional Hospital (see page 103).

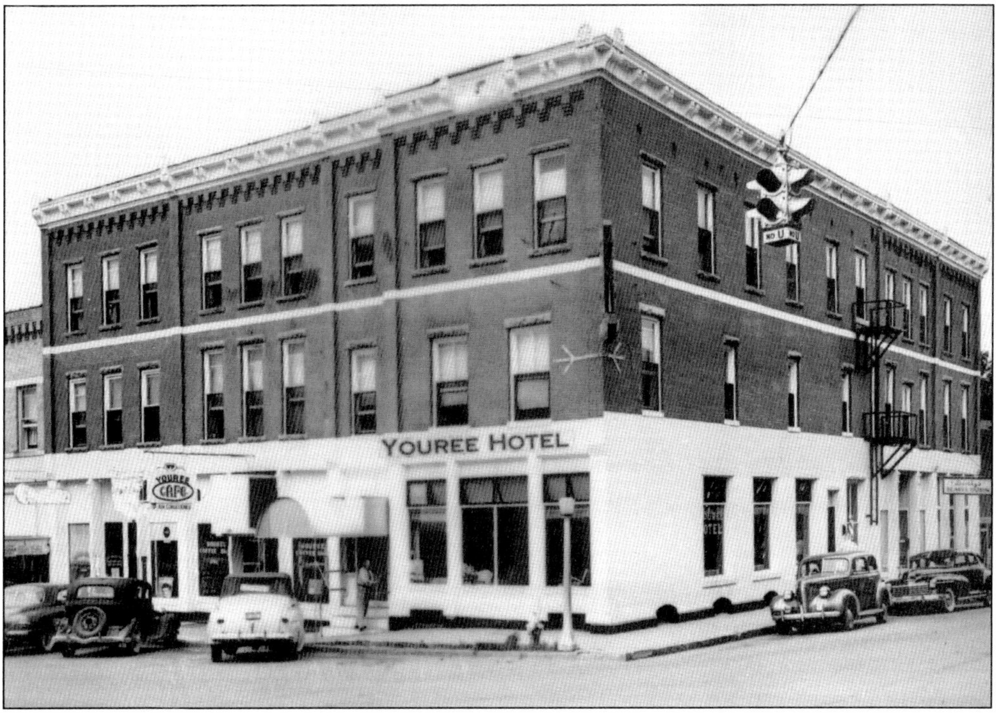

Frank Youree bought the former Morris Hotel and lent his name to the hotel and café. He removed the balconies when they became unstable but continued to keep businesses on the first floor and hotel rooms above. Note also the traffic light. Today, there are stop signs at the intersections downtown.

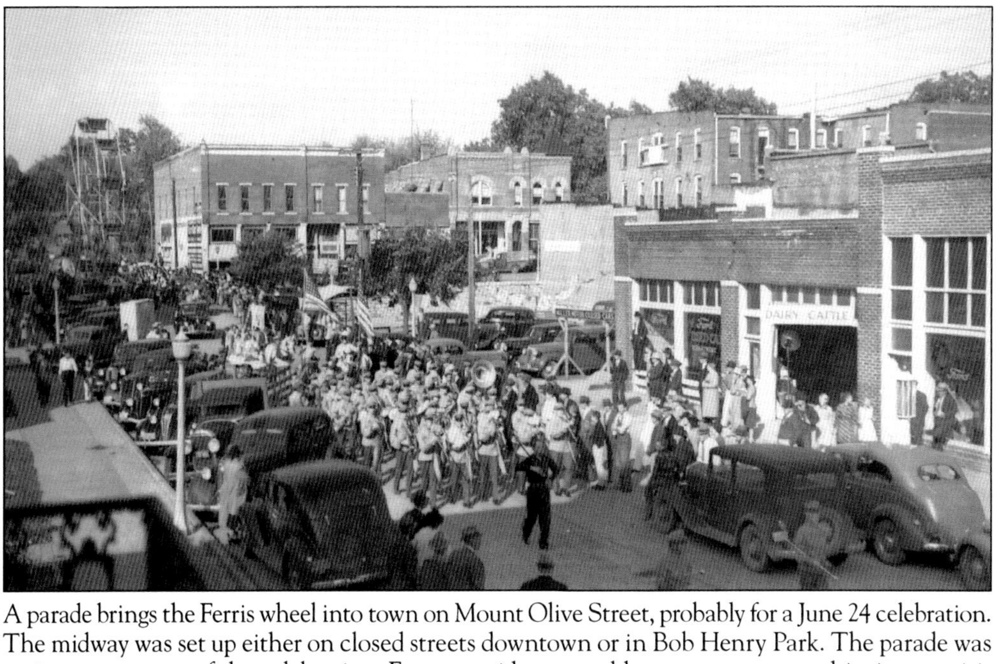

A parade brings the Ferris wheel into town on Mount Olive Street, probably for a June 24 celebration. The midway was set up either on closed streets downtown or in Bob Henry Park. The parade was an important part of the celebration. Former residents would return to town at this time to visit familiar people and places, and many families would come to the parks for a picnic.

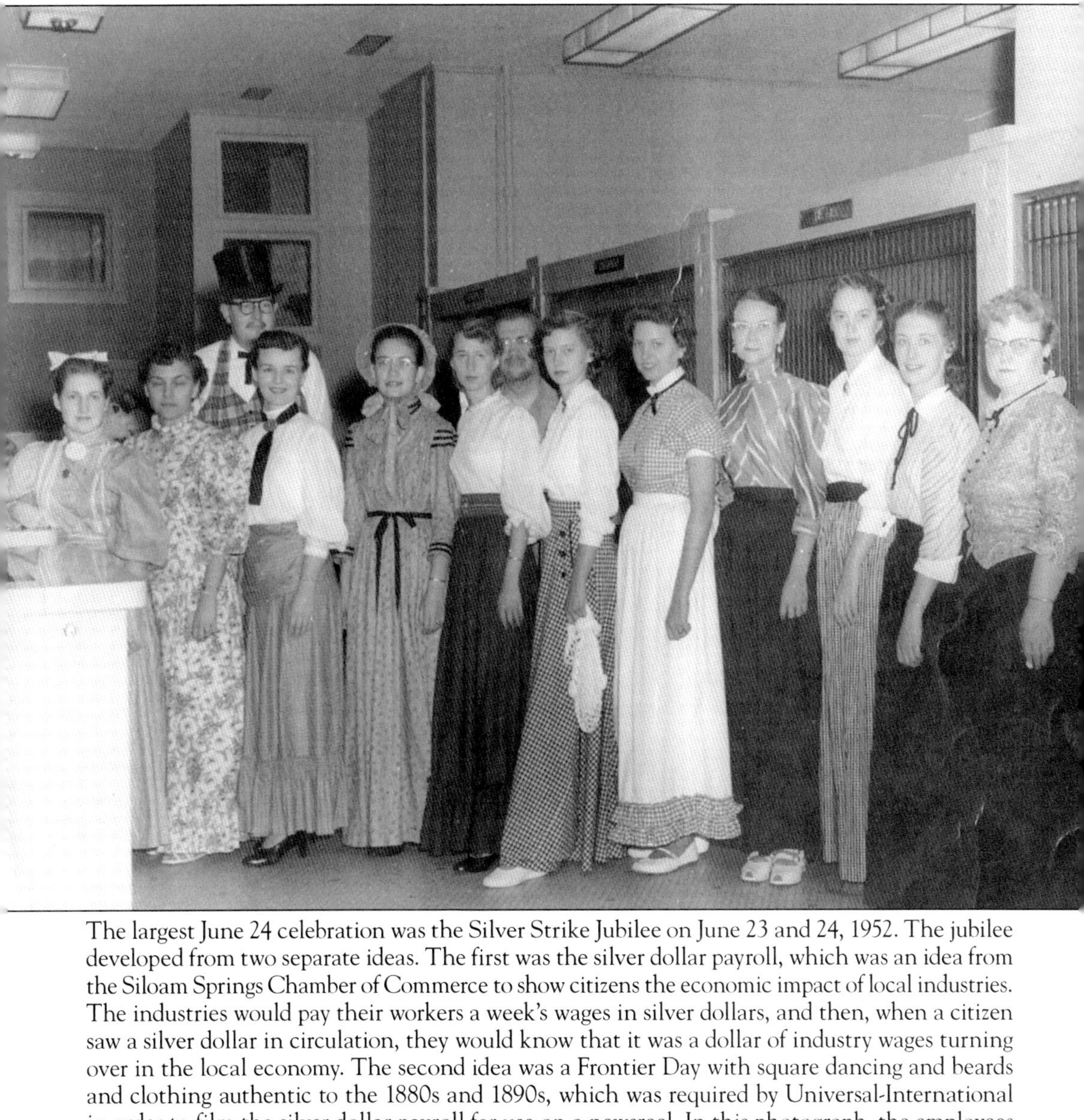

The largest June 24 celebration was the Silver Strike Jubilee on June 23 and 24, 1952. The jubilee developed from two separate ideas. The first was the silver dollar payroll, which was an idea from the Siloam Springs Chamber of Commerce to show citizens the economic impact of local industries. The industries would pay their workers a week's wages in silver dollars, and then, when a citizen saw a silver dollar in circulation, they would know that it was a dollar of industry wages turning over in the local economy. The second idea was a Frontier Day with square dancing and beards and clothing authentic to the 1880s and 1890s, which was required by Universal-International in order to film the silver dollar payroll for use on a newsreel. In this photograph, the employees of the Bratt-Wasson Bank pose in their frontier clothes. They are, from left to right, Elizabeth Wilson Walker, unidentified, ? West, Art Melson, Wanda Anderson Robinson, Sue Nelson, Tom Whiteside, Carol Dowdy Whiteside, Anita Barney Ray, Lillian Barney Ford Cartwright, Martha Moss Newton, Patsy Walker Eudy Pyeatte, and Elsie Sumner.

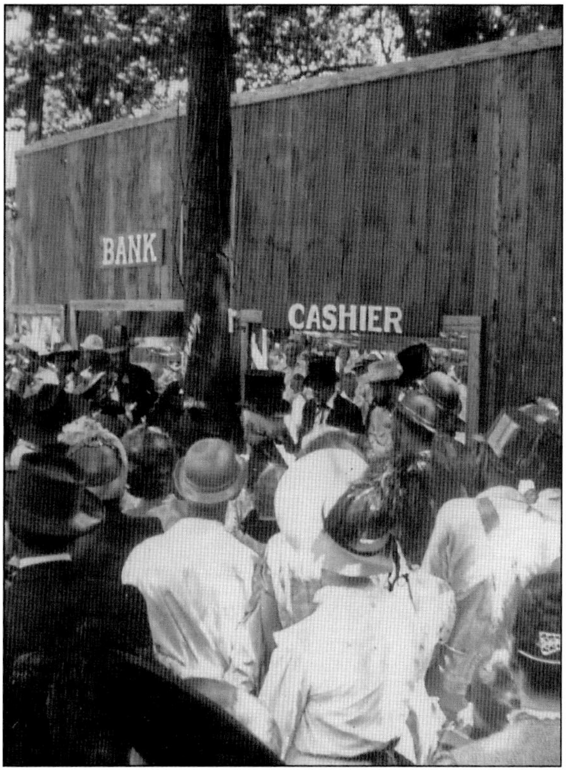

Pictured here are the front (left) and back (below) of the false-front town that was built at the north edge of Twin Springs Park during the Silver Strike Jubilee in 1952. For the newsreel and movie, a Wells Fargo stage with a rifle-toting guard pulled up to unload a chest full of silver dollars for the cashier's window, and several employees received their silver dollar payroll at this window. Home movies recorded this action, and some footage is included in the chamber of commerce movie "A Future to Share." Unfortunately, the Universal-International newsreel does not seem to have survived.

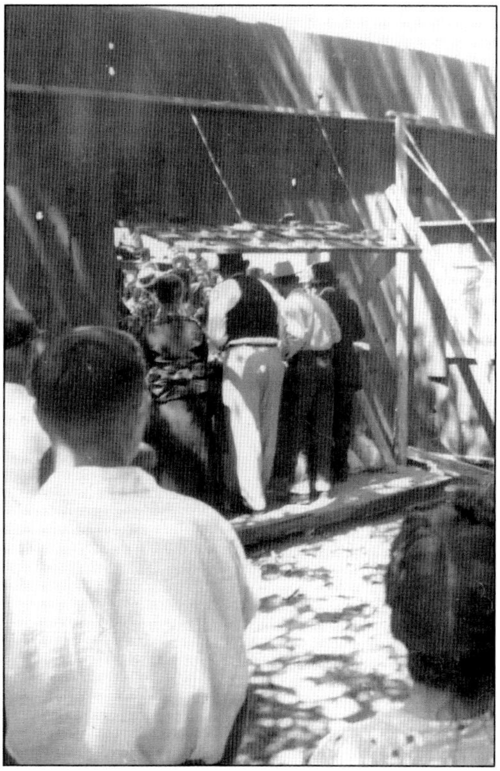

Mules pull a rig south on North Wright Street for the parade during the Silver Strike Jubilee in 1952. Everyone who was in the parade was required to wear frontier-style clothes. No advertising was allowed, and no mechanized equipment. The parade included 600 horsemen, representing 25 riding clubs from Ozark to Shawnee, and over 25 stagecoaches. A total of 1,280 square dancers participated as well as Native American dancers.

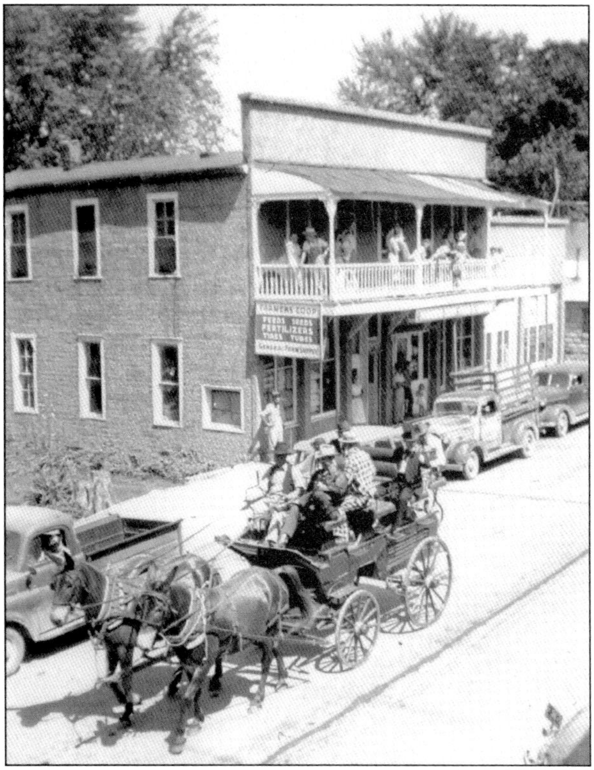

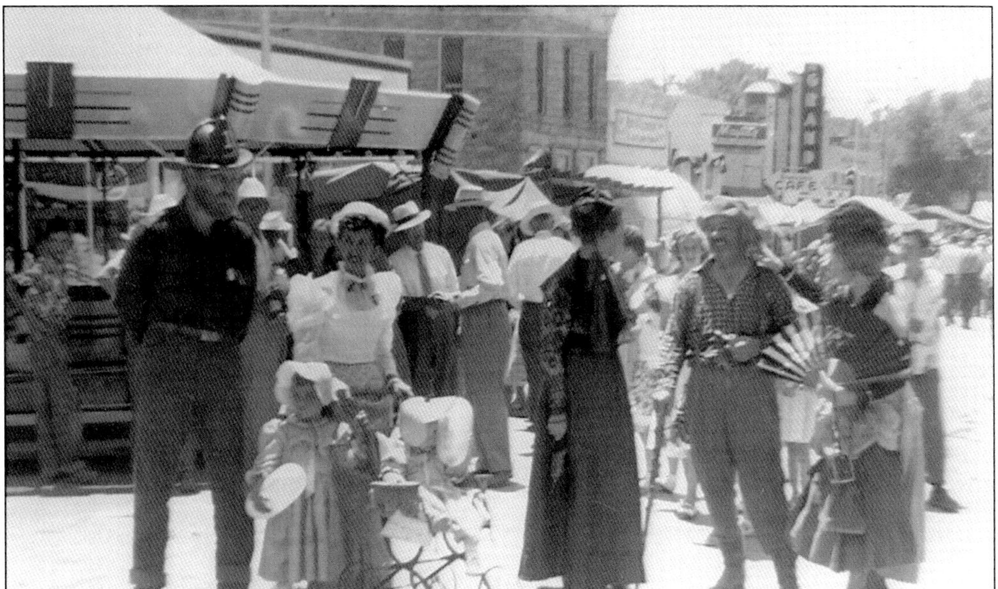

During the Silver Strike Jubilee, downtown streets were closed to traffic and the midway spread out along Broadway and adjoining side streets. At the south end of Broadway was space for special events like square dancing with over 1,000 participants and Plains Indian war dances. In the foreground of this photograph are, from left to right, Rex Robrahn, Jeannie Robrahn, Rex's wife Jerryann, possibly Eleanor Fenno, Buck Fenno, and unidentified.

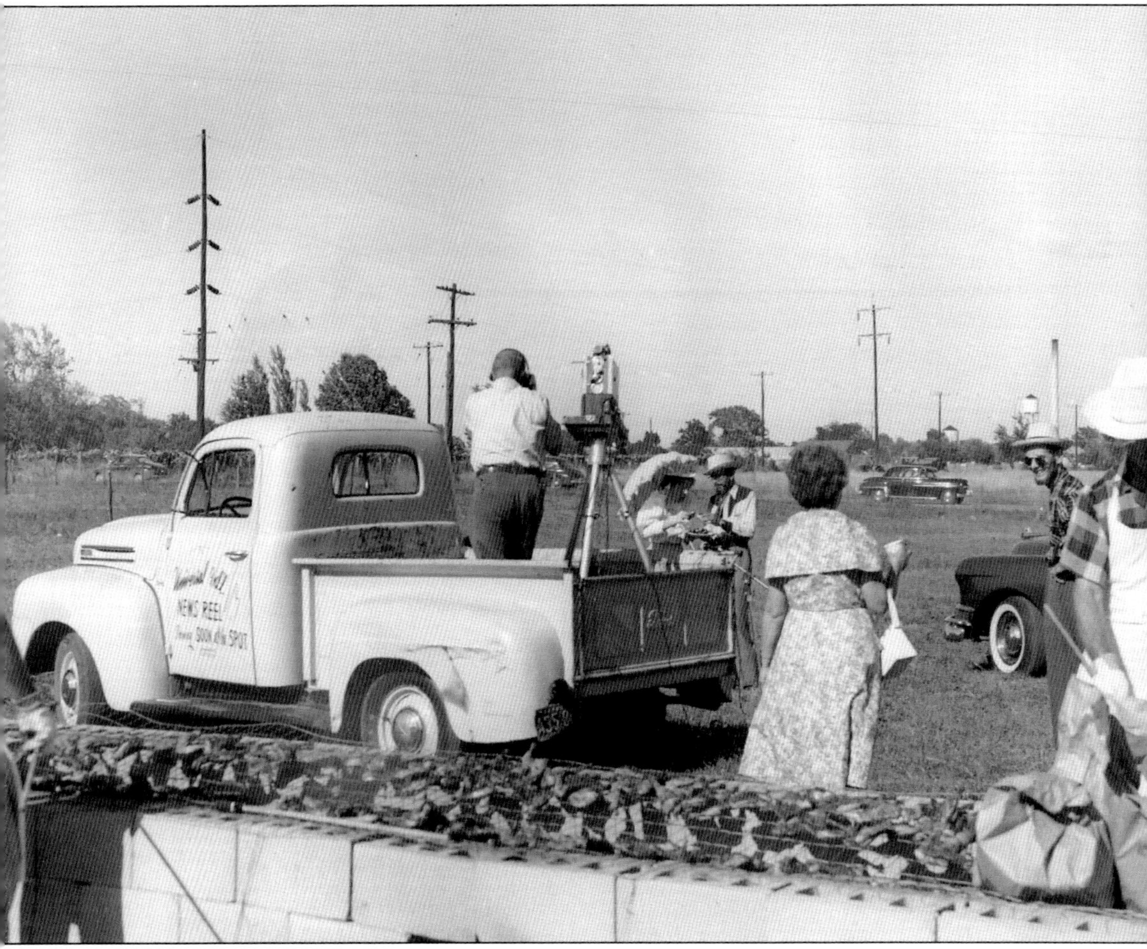

In 1952, Bill Simmons moved the Pluss Poultry plant and offices from Decatur to Siloam Springs. Chamber manager Rufus Brown decided to carry out his silver dollar payroll plan as soon as Pluss Poultry was in full operation. At that time, one week's payroll for the local industries was $30,000. When Brown considered the weight of that many silver dollars (nearly 2,000 pounds—literally a ton of silver), he realized that this was an event that could be of national interest. Universal-International agreed to film the silver dollar payroll for a newsreel, but only if the town also held a frontier day to include in the footage. This left the town with less than six months to plan the silver dollar payroll and frontier day. The chamber of commerce formed 18 organizing committees. The finance committee set a budget of $3,000. The entire town pulled together to make this event a success. This photograph shows a Universal-International photographer filming a couple eating during one of the barbecues at Pluss Poultry.

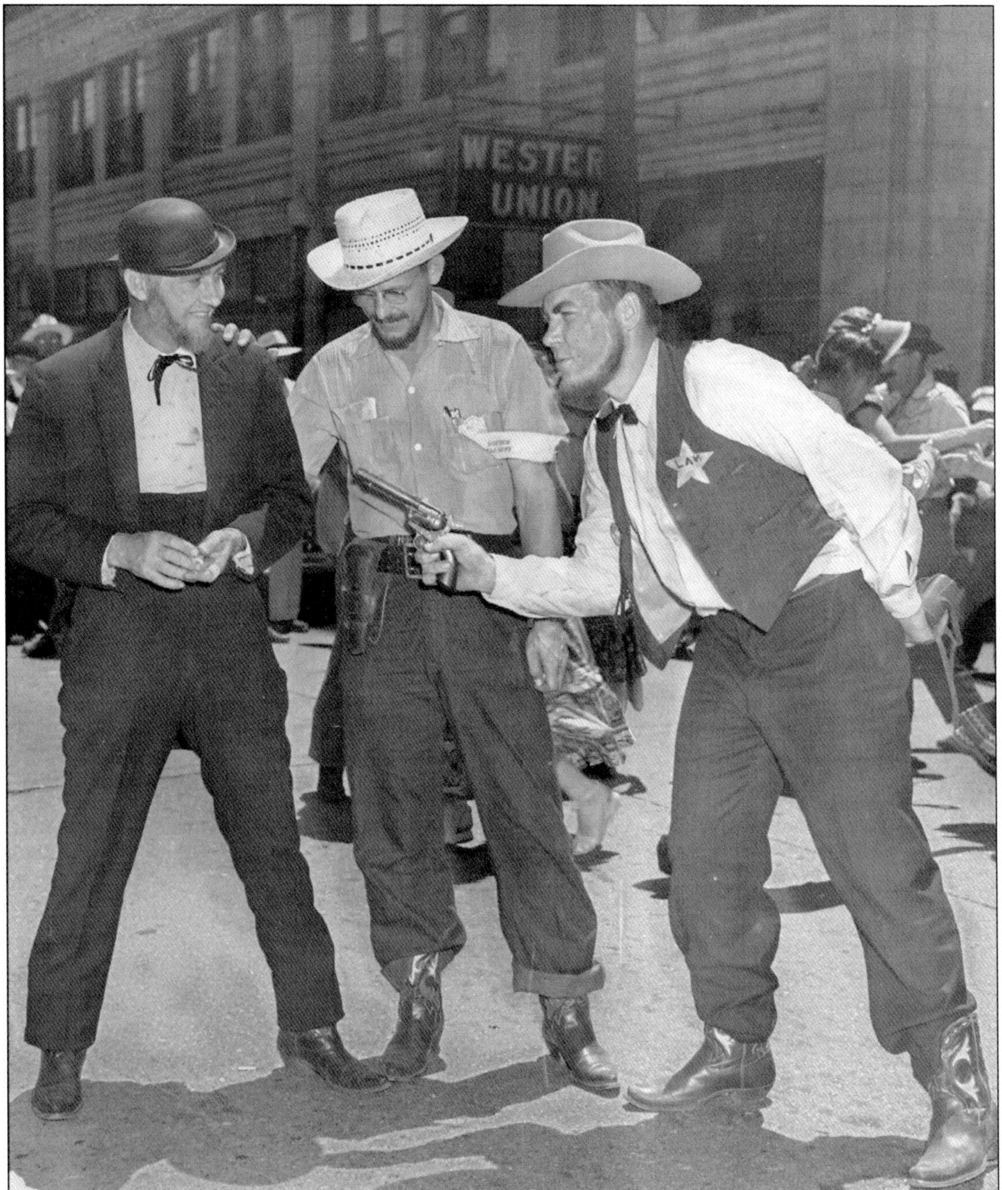

As June 24, 1952, neared, caravans of square dancers and characters in frontier clothing promoted the event with 10-to-20-minute programs in every town within a day's drive, from Fort Smith to Joplin and from Tulsa to Fayetteville. They used silver dollars to pay for their meals and other expenses. This photograph was taken during the program in Joplin. Square dancers are visible in the background while Ronald Robrahn (on right), Wilson Ford (middle) and Roy Jameson build drama and excitement. For the three months leading up to the jubilee, there were signs in town to explain why the men were growing beards and to encourage visitors to come back to town to see the jubilee. A chance to appear in a Universal-International newsreel helped to inspire many of the participants in the jubilee. Universal-International capitalized on this, too, by selling single frames of film.

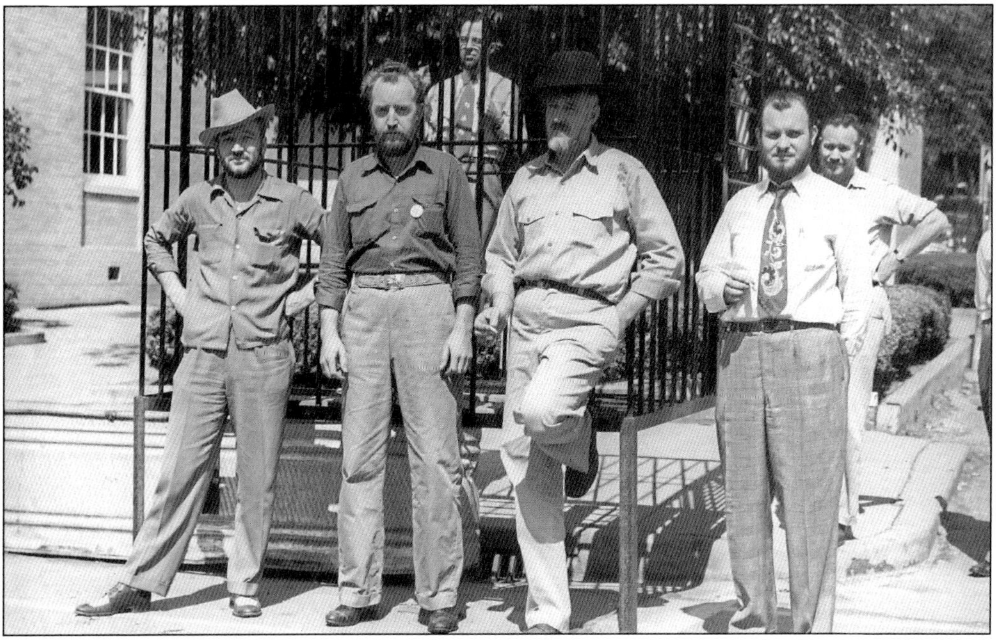

At a time when almost all men were clean-shaven, for three months in 1952, leading up to the Silver Strike Jubilee, Siloam Springs held a compulsory beard-growing contest for the men in town. Ron and Rex Robrahn built a "Bare Cage" (above) for barefaced men who had not purchased a shaving permit from the excuse committee. This cage and tank were placed in front of the post office downtown, and once a man was locked in, his only escape was to go through the tank of water. Below, Brian Grower goes through the tank while Ron Robrahn and a large crowd cheer him on.

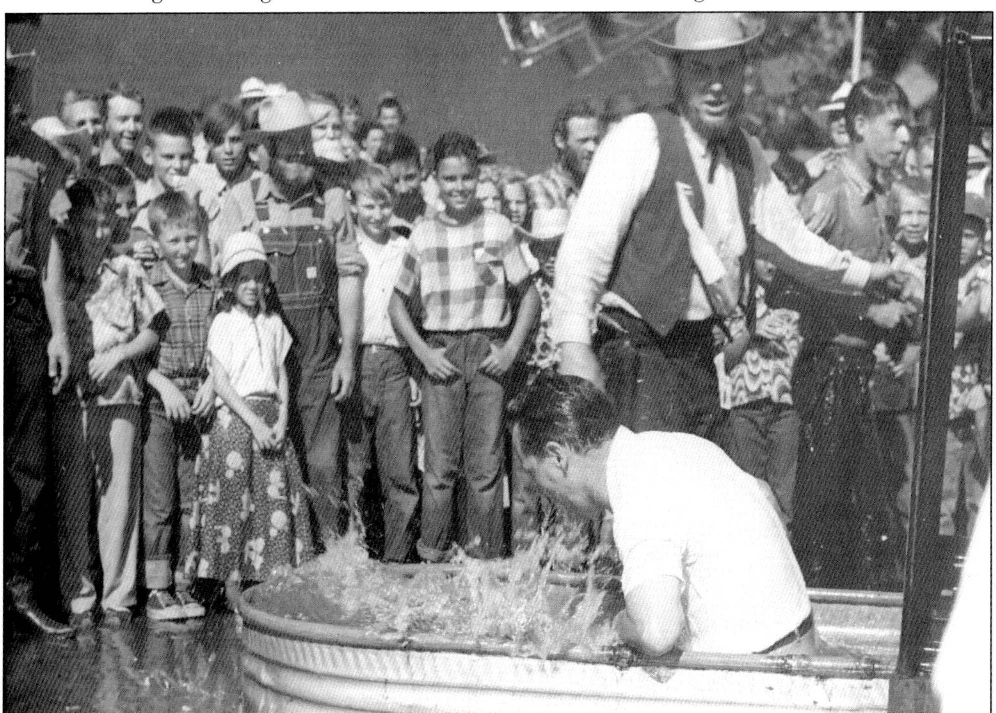

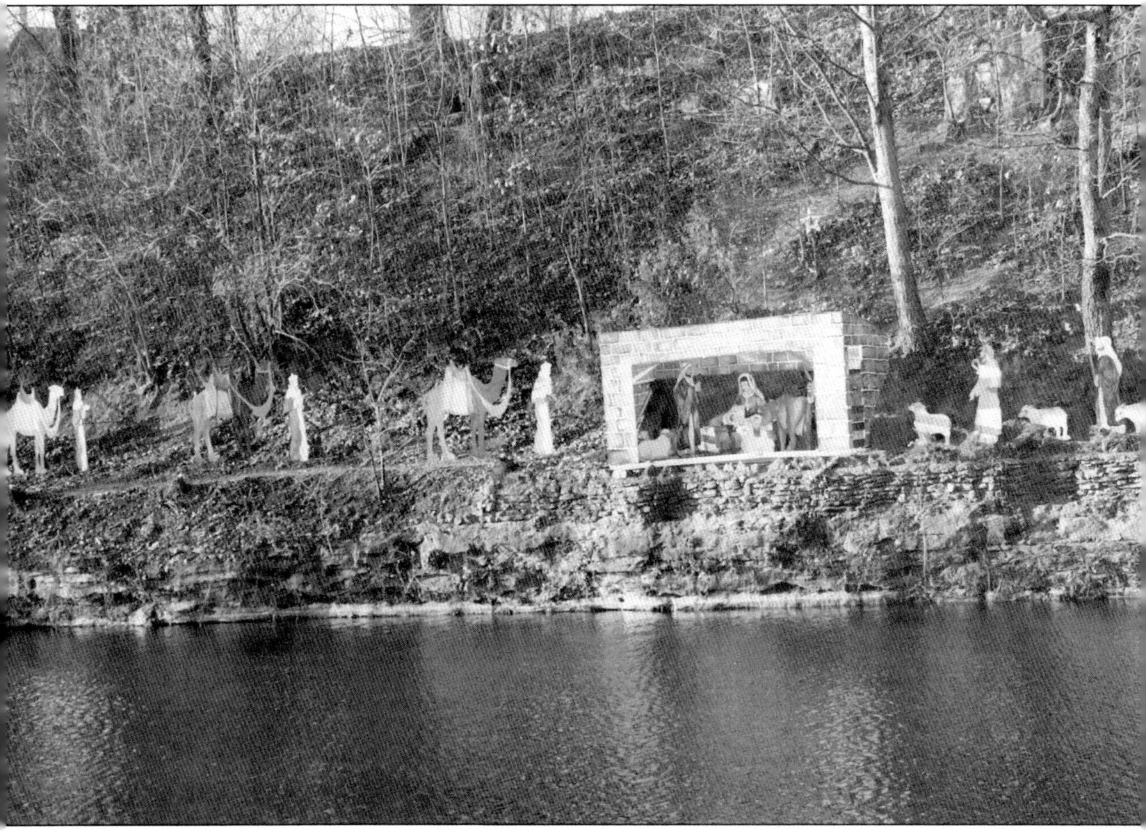

In 1955, an editorial by newspaperman R.S. Knowlson presented the idea of placing scenes from the life of Christ on the bank of Sager Creek at Christmas time. This photograph shows the Pool of Siloam in 1956, in the first phase of the display. At this time, the display was a life-sized nativity scene built by Burtice Woody. Over the next few years, Woody built more scenes, and eventually, the display included scenes from the entire life of Christ from birth to resurrection. One scene floated on Sager Creek and portrayed the healing at the Pool of Siloam from which this town got its name. Scenes would be lit in turn, accompanied by music provided by the John Brown University choirs, and narrated by Storm Whaley. Vandalism eventually ended this program. It was revived in the 1980s, but vandalism again took its toll, and the program was ended.

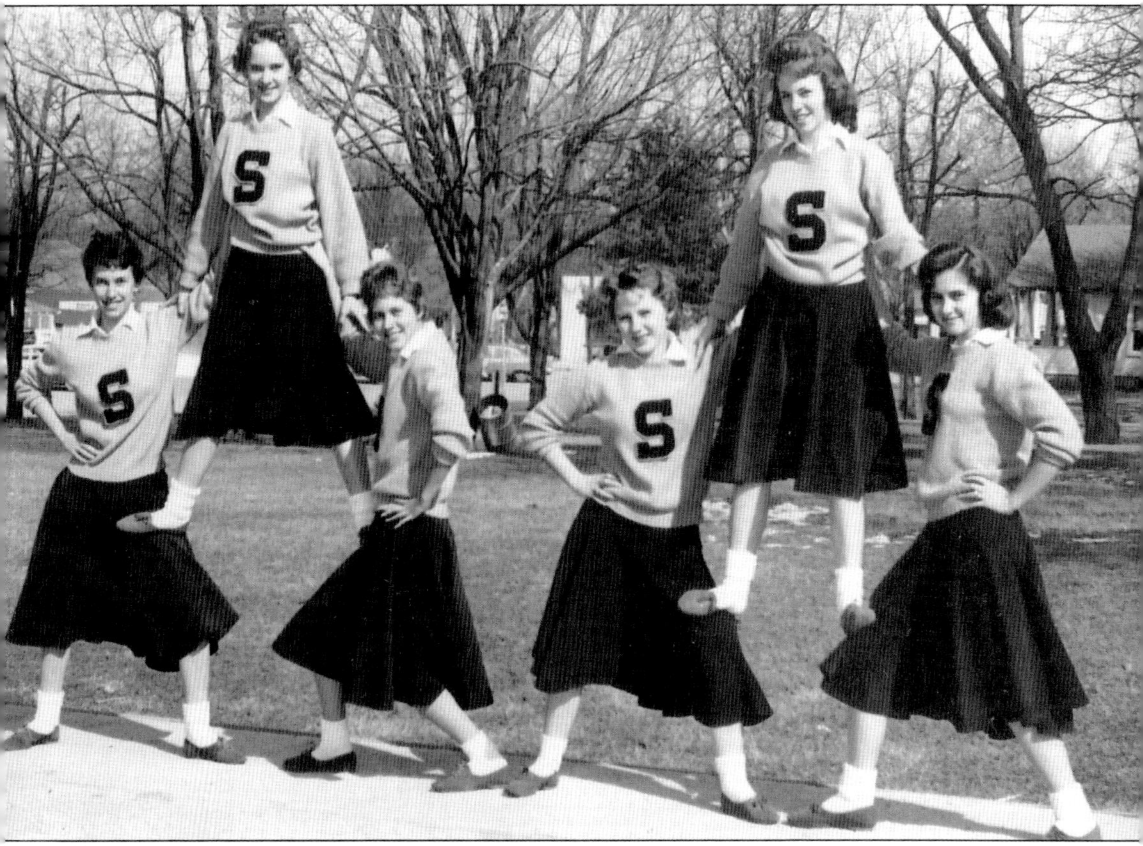

The junior high school cheerleaders in 1960 were, from left to right, Paula Barnes, Karen Dodson, Nancy Pittman, Marilyn Younger, Candy Jones, and Fern Buchanan. Three of these students were in eighth grade, and the other three were in ninth. There was also an older group of cheerleaders, called senior high cheerleaders, which included two seniors, two juniors, and two sophomores. These squads, joined by several other students, worked together as the Pepperettes. The 1940 high school building was in use at this time and seems to have housed grades eight through twelve. The grades from first through seventh were considered the elementary grades. The elementary school buildings standing in town at this time were Central Elementary for the first through fifth grades and Junior High Elementary for grades six and seven. Cincinnati Elementary was standing in the town south of Siloam Springs in Washington County. There was also a Vocational Agriculture Building.

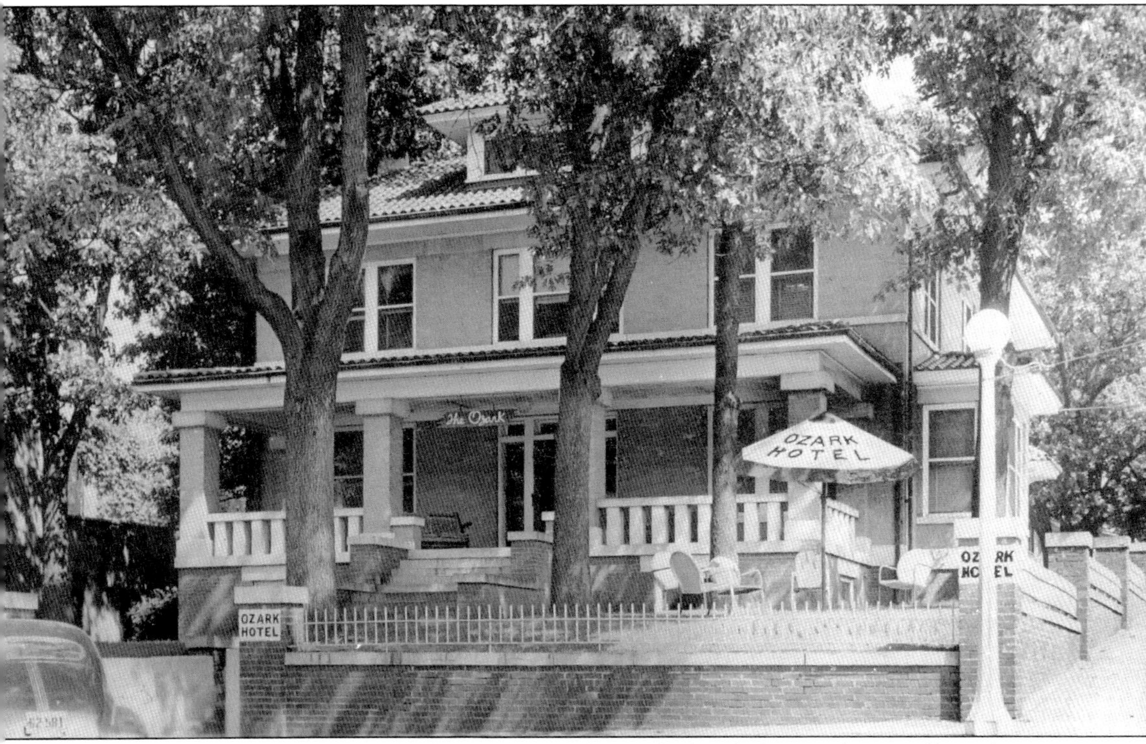

The house seen here was built about 1920 as the single-family home of Connelly and Minnie Harrington. After they both died in 1935, John Brown University purchased it to use as a hospital that was open to the general public until 1948. It was then the Ozark Hotel, and apartments are for rent today. It was listed in the National Register of Historic Places in 1988. First National Bank donated it to the chamber of commerce in 1989. The chamber of commerce offices were on the main floor, and the rest of the building was rental space. Then, the chamber of commerce sold it in 2007 to Drake Renovation and Construction. Later, one of the renters accidentally caused a fire on January 10, 2012. Repair of that damage was just the second project in town that took advantage of the federal Rehabilitation Tax Credit.

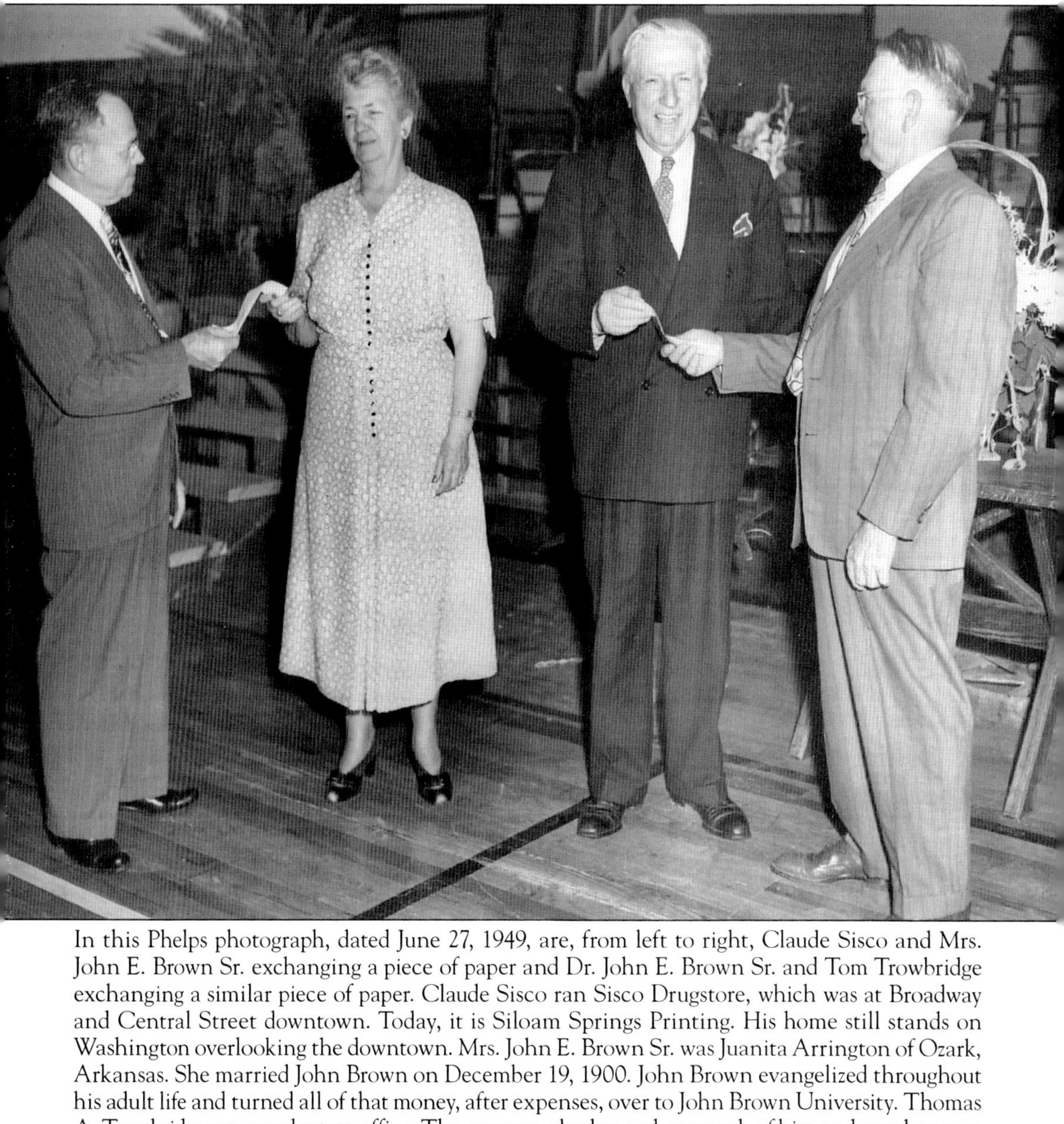

In this Phelps photograph, dated June 27, 1949, are, from left to right, Claude Sisco and Mrs. John E. Brown Sr. exchanging a piece of paper and Dr. John E. Brown Sr. and Tom Trowbridge exchanging a similar piece of paper. Claude Sisco ran Sisco Drugstore, which was at Broadway and Central Street downtown. Today, it is Siloam Springs Printing. His home still stands on Washington overlooking the downtown. Mrs. John E. Brown Sr. was Juanita Arrington of Ozark, Arkansas. She married John Brown on December 19, 1900. John Brown evangelized throughout his adult life and turned all of that money, after expenses, over to John Brown University. Thomas A. Trowbridge ran a real estate office. The museum also has a photograph of him and another man after a successful duck hunt in the 1920s. He was also one of several prominent businessmen who participated in the Womanless Wedding fundraiser held in Twin Springs Christian Church in the 1910s. Audience members paid to see several of the town's merchants, physicians, newspapermen, and more dressed as women.

Seven

Downtown versus the Bypass 1963–Present

"The bypass," now US Highway 412, was built as a two-lane east-west road through fields south of town. But before long, businesses saw this road as a more direct route for their out-of-town customers, and buildings began to spring up on the land along the bypass. Today, there is very little vacant land along 412, and many visitors to town think that 412 is the town. With increased traffic volume and the combination of local traffic and through traffic, there has been an increased risk of accidents, to the point that some people talked in recent years about the need to bypass the bypass. In the end, the conclusion was to reconfigure 412 to make it safer. For part of the road, there are three lanes in each direction, and a median to limit left turns and u-turns to intersections.

For a while, the growth along 412 came at the expense of the downtown. By the 1990s, there were professional offices downtown, a few retailers, and several vacant buildings. That has gradually changed, and now, there is a much healthier mix of offices, retail, restaurants, and apartments. Much of the credit for this improvement goes to the Main Street program, which is now part of the Arkansas Main Street system.

Siloam Springs still has a diverse mix of industries, and part of the celebration of the golden anniversary of the Silver Strike Jubilee was a celebration of industries.

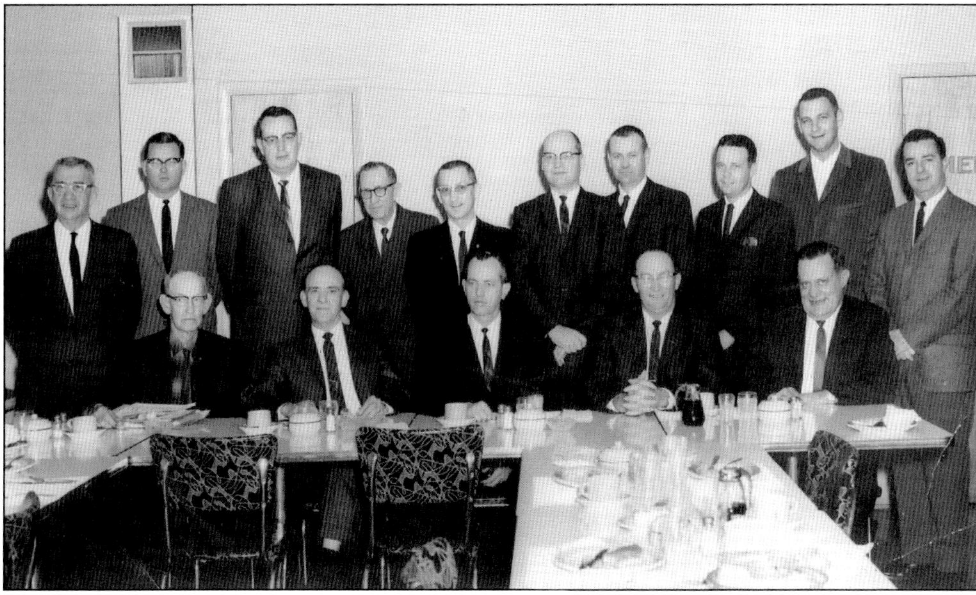

The chamber of commerce board in 1965 included, from left to right, (sitting) Ray Henry, Graydon Comstock, Carl Bonner, Grant Layne, and Dr. John Stockton; (standing) Tom Whiteside, Field Wasson, Art Melson, Jean Trahin, Marion Snider, Maurice Derdeyn, O.A.Yancy, Bernard Jones, Preston Bynum, and John Brown Jr.

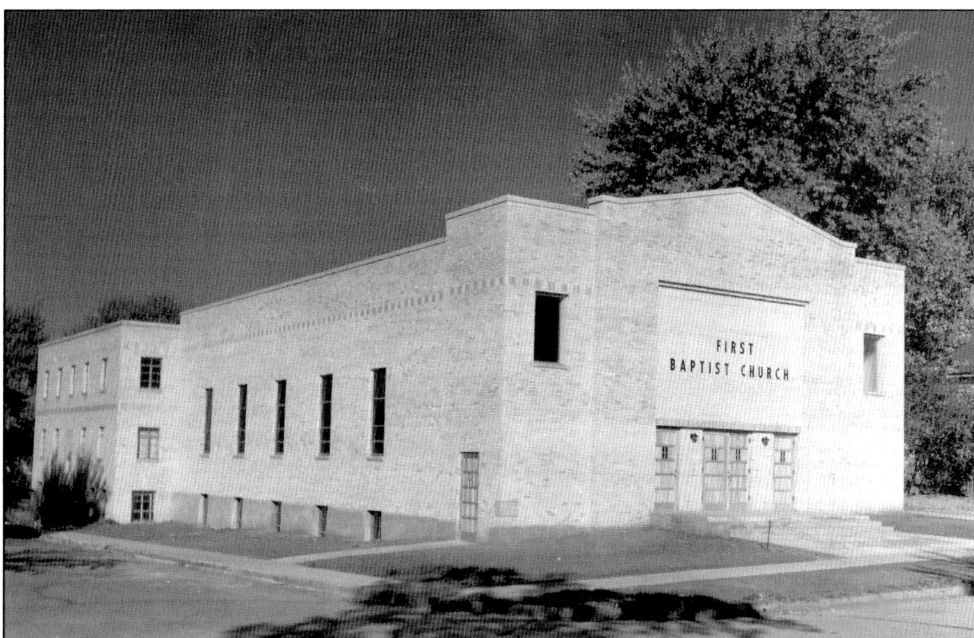

This First Baptist Church building stood between Broadway and Mount Olive Street, north of Ashley Street, which is where city hall is today. In 1903, the congregation moved into its new building on this lot, and in 1948, the building seen in this photograph was constructed, with the older building being removed later.

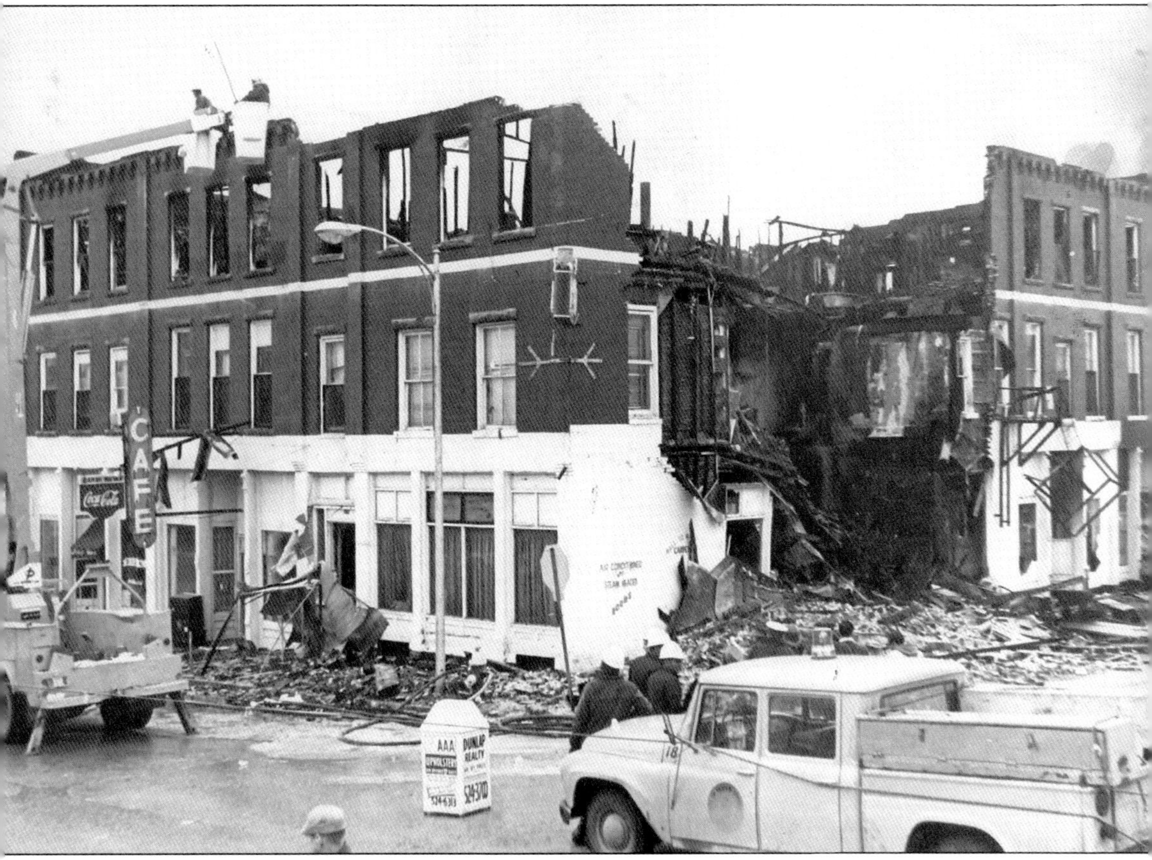

In 1970, the Youree Hotel suffered a major fire. As a result, the top floor was removed, and the roof was built at the second floor. The northeast corner of the building was completely rebuilt, and today, it is the City Barbershop. In other parts of the exterior, the bricks from the Morris Hotel can still be seen. The Morris Hotel was built in 1899 for $12,000. The top two floors were hotel rooms, and the ground floor and basement were businesses. The top two floors originally had verandas that provided a good vantage point for watching parades. Robert S. Morris's bank, the Bank of Siloam, was also in this building until it failed in 1910. Morris had been involved in promoting and developing the town. Frank Youree later purchased the building, and the name changed. The verandas were removed when they became unsafe.

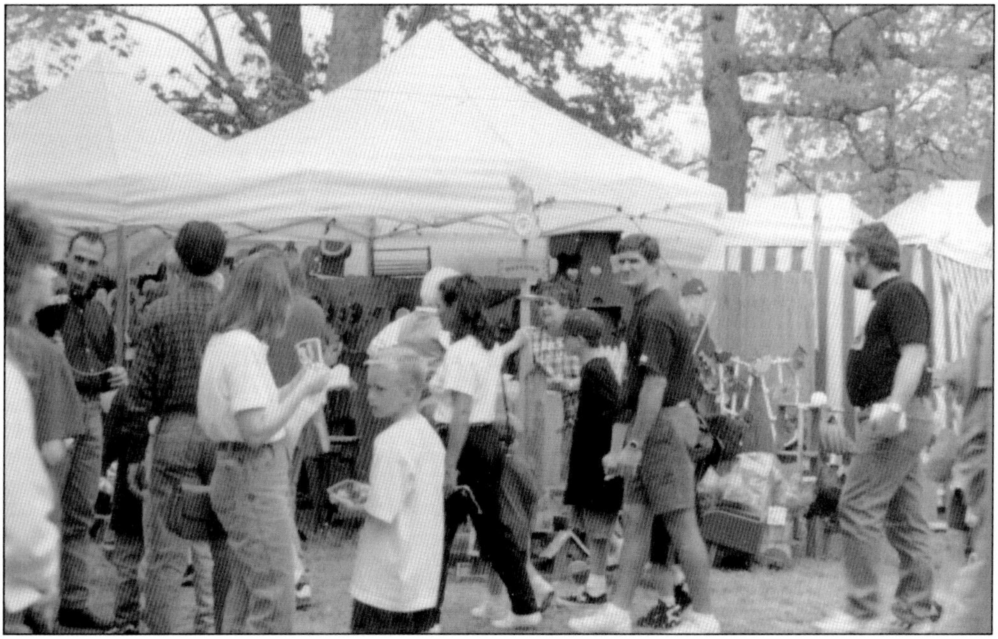

The chamber of commerce organizes the Dogwood Festival for the last full weekend in April. At the first Dogwood Festival in 1974, an estimated 7,000 visitors toured 60 to 70 arts-and-crafts booths. The Dogwood Festival now draws more than 30,000 visitors to over 200 booths during the three days of the festival, which has expanded geographically to include not only the Community Building and surrounding park but also to the middle of Bob Henry Park to the west. The chamber of commerce and Main Street Siloam Springs are now also trying to draw attention to downtown businesses, where sidewalk sales and specials are offered to draw in customers.

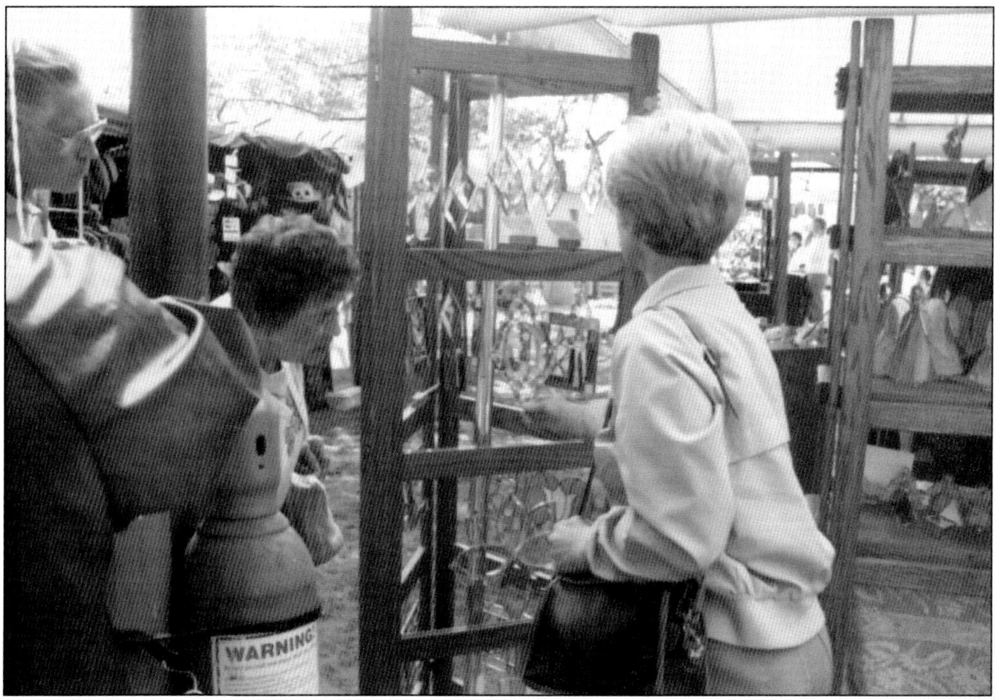

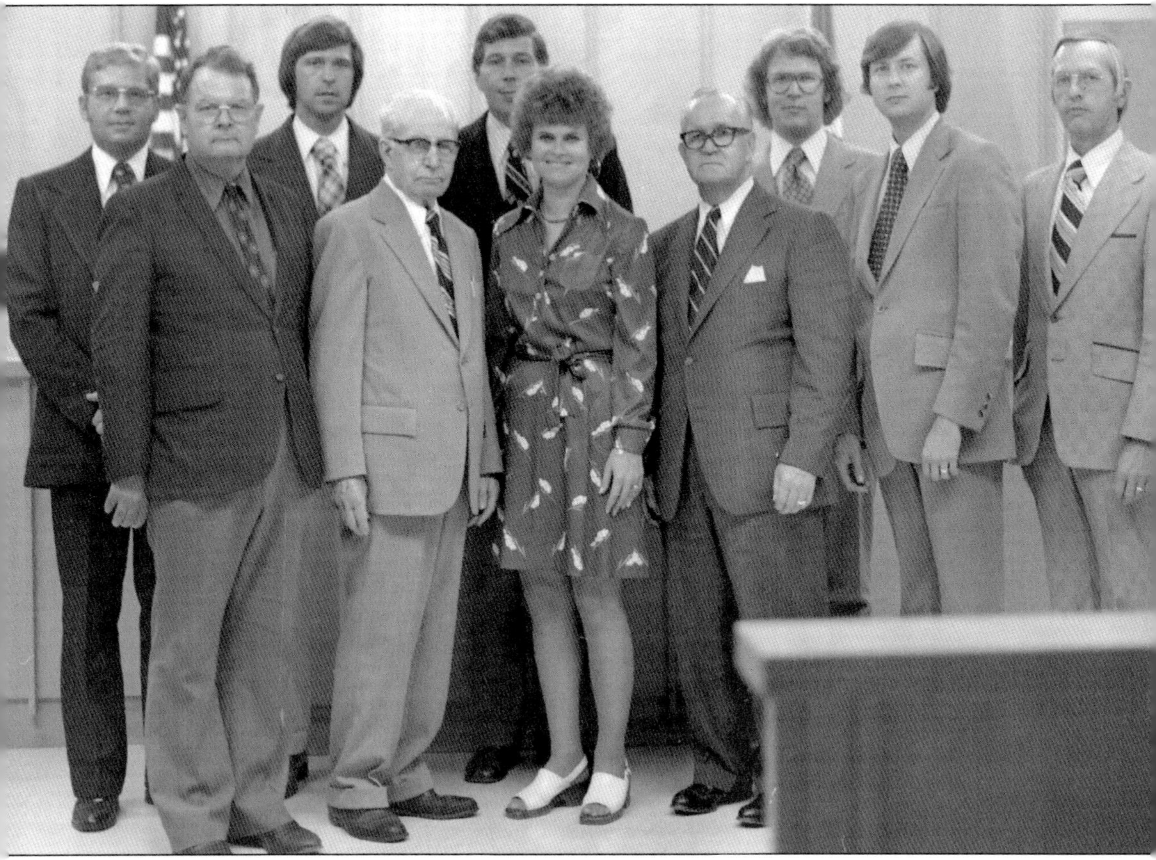

Practicing attorneys in Siloam Springs in 1975 were, from left to right, Don Killebrew, Powell Woods, Michael E. Moss, Kent Watson, Nicholas Bierwirth, Georgia Elrod, Russell Elrod, John Elrod, John Terry Lee, and Carl Bonner. The Goodspeed *History of Benton County* shows that there were just three practicing attorneys in Siloam Springs in 1889. The arrival of the railroad in 1893 brought an increase in population and an increase in business activity, which should have led to an increased need for attorneys, but the 1908 city directory shows just three, all different from the 1889 list. Georgia Elrod researched the growth of the legal profession in Siloam Springs and found that, in the teens, three attorneys opened offices in Siloam Springs. They all went on to practice here for many years, as did some of their family members. Today, there are eight attorneys based in Siloam Springs.

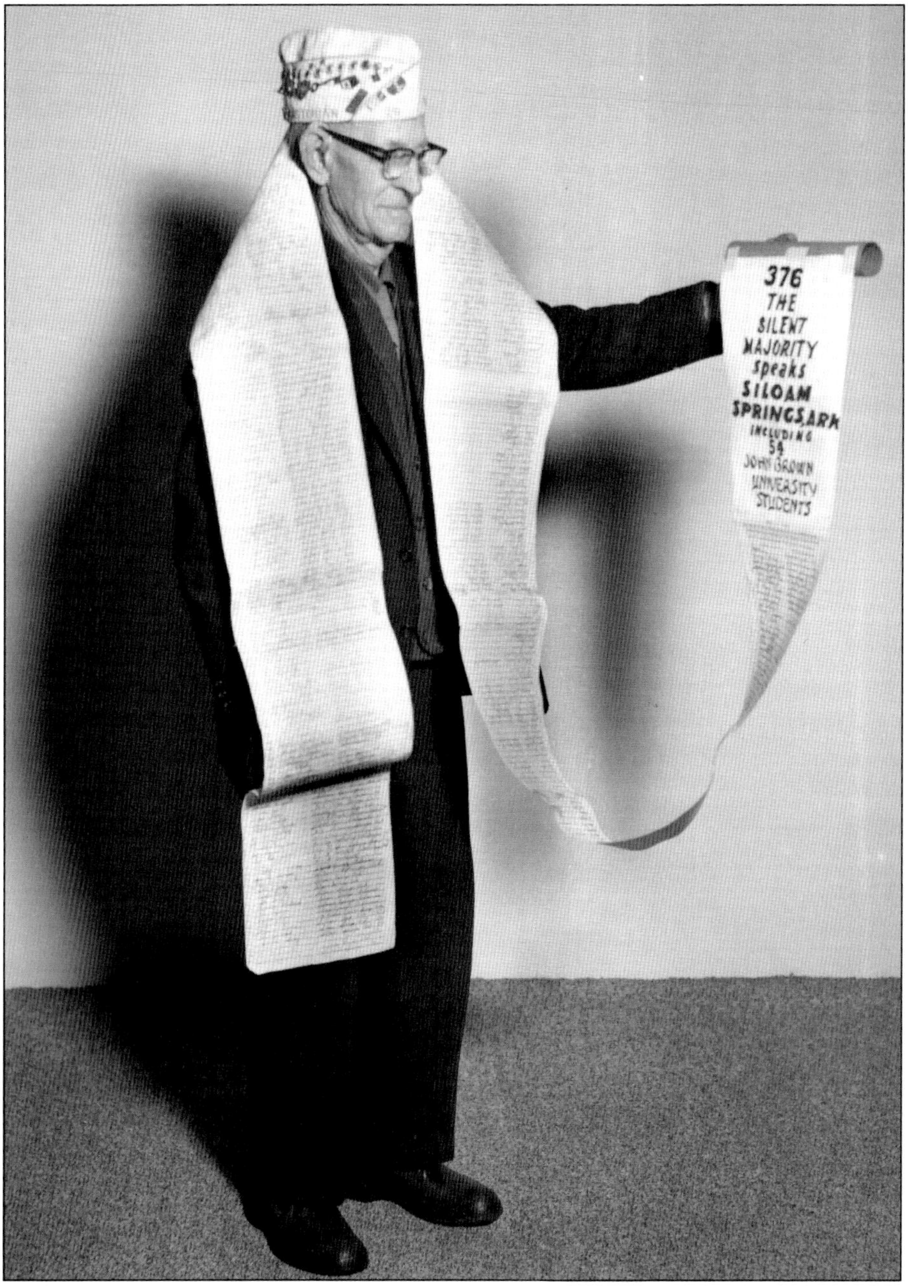

Ray Henry is seen with a petition signed by 376 people, including 54 John Brown University students. He labeled them the silent majority who supported the Vietnam War and sent this petition to Pres. Richard Nixon. On November 5, 1969, the president sent him a preprinted postcard to thank him for his support of the administration's effort to end the war through "peace with honor." Ray Henry was department historian of the American Legion and wrote a book, titled *Arkansas History of the American Legion*. He served in the Army from 1904 to 1919 and rose from sergeant to captain. He later held several different jobs with railroads, including the Kansas City Southern, then moved to Siloam Springs about 1953 and worked as secretary-manager of the chamber of commerce. He was still working at the chamber at the time of his 80th birthday in 1963.

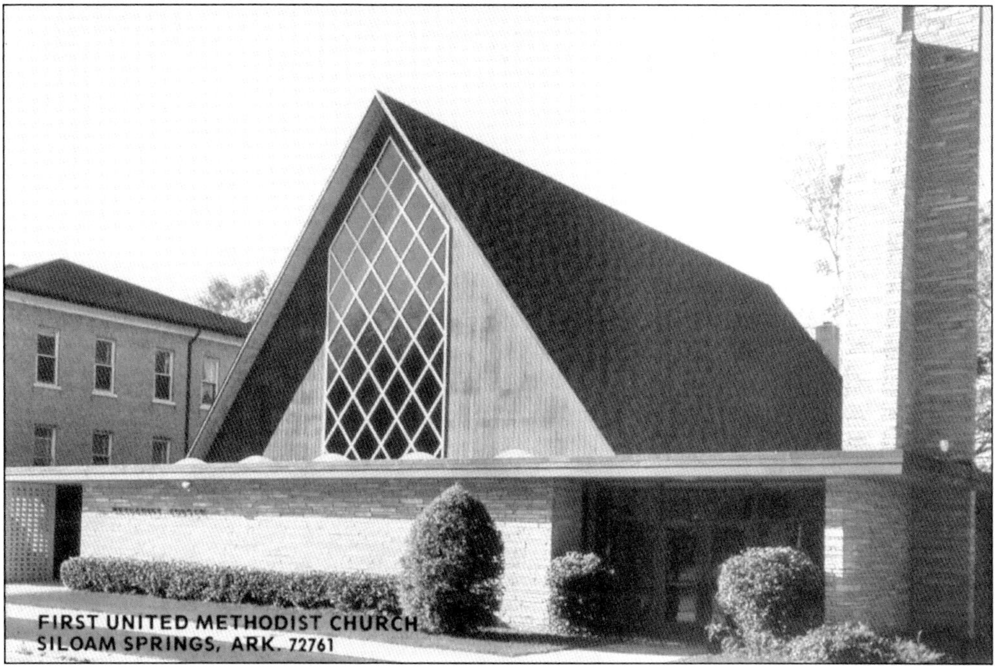

The first Methodist services in what is now Siloam Springs were held at Sager Cabin. A church for the Methodist Episcopal Church South was later built in Hico, and the first Methodist church built after Siloam Springs was established was Methodist Episcopal Church North. Over the years, various Methodist Episcopal Church South buildings were built in town, and the last one was built in 1920. It is visible in these photographs to the left (west) of the present building. The photograph above shows the present building as it looked from 1958 until the latest renovations. The photograph below shows some of the renovations, which expanded the entryway and improved security in the children's classrooms, among other improvements.

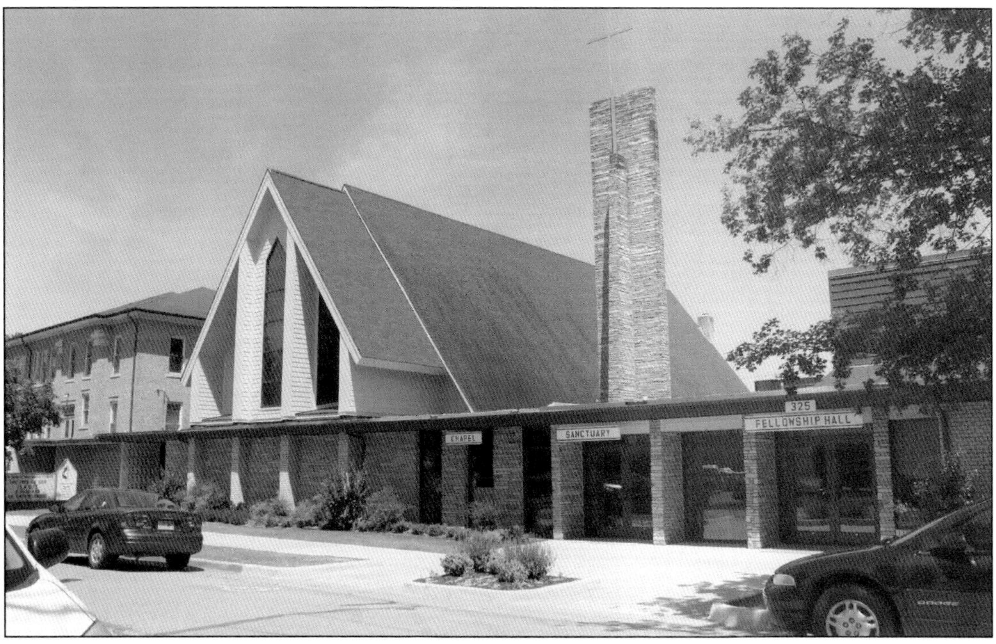

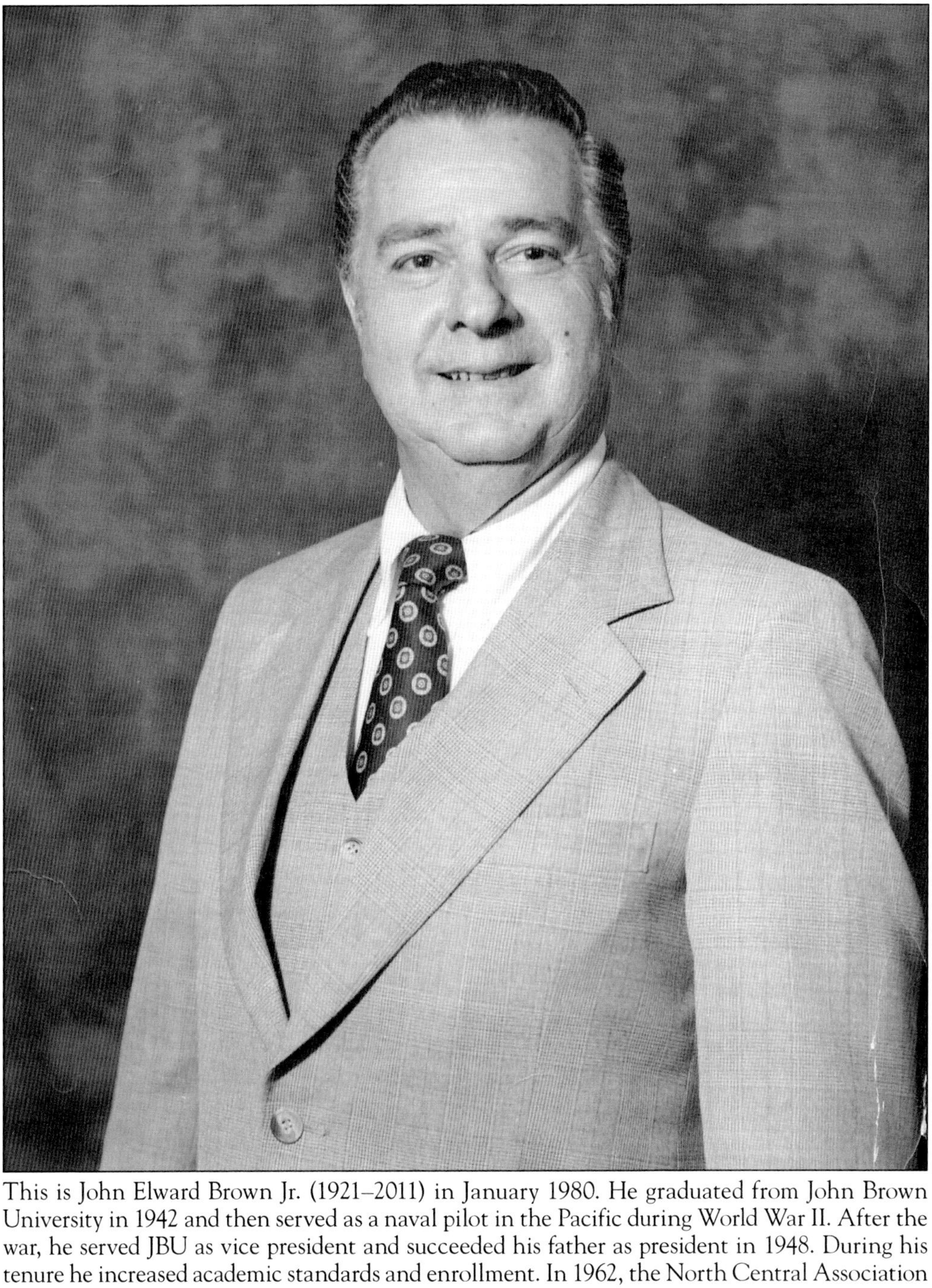

This is John Elward Brown Jr. (1921–2011) in January 1980. He graduated from John Brown University in 1942 and then served as a naval pilot in the Pacific during World War II. After the war, he served JBU as vice president and succeeded his father as president in 1948. During his tenure he increased academic standards and enrollment. In 1962, the North Central Association of Colleges and Schools accredited JBU. Brown started the intercollegiate athletics program at JBU. He took a great interest in the school's radio stations: KUOA in Siloam Springs and KGER in Long Beach, California. At this time, the school also operated a military academy in Long Beach, and John Brown III remembers many family trips to California. Brown Jr. is remembered as someone who loved people, was quick with a joke, and had a warm smile. He served as JBU president until 1979, when his son John Elward Brown III became president.

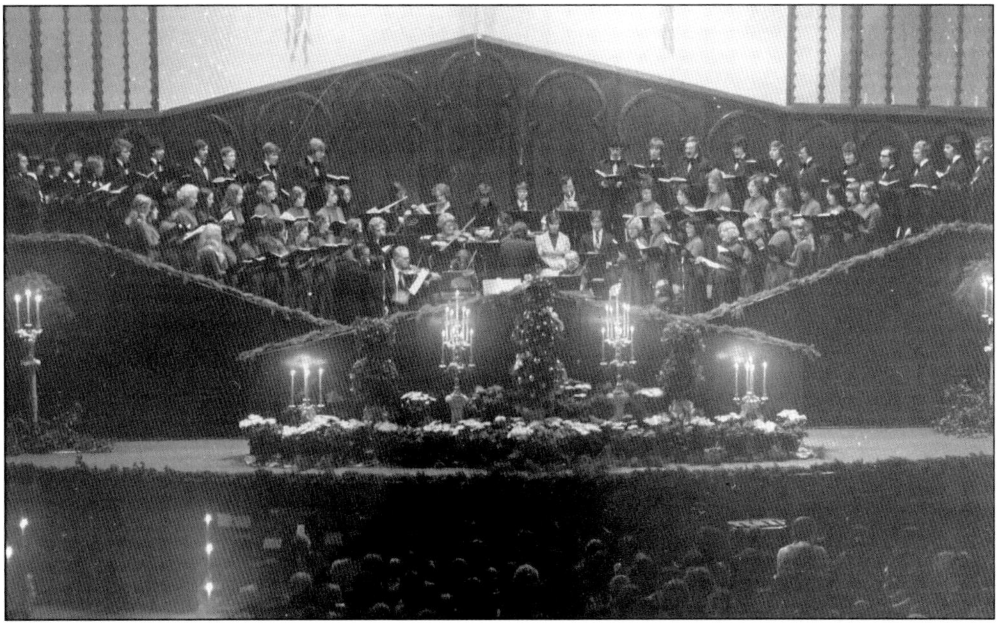

The candlelight services in John Brown University's Cathedral of the Ozarks have been a popular Christmas tradition since 1943 and include the Cathedral Choir, Chamber Choir, Woman's Chorus, and Chamber Orchestra and inspirational readings by JBU faculty, staff, and students. John Brown Sr. was a firm believer in the power of music to present the Christian message, and this Christmas program reflects the continued strength of the JBU music program.

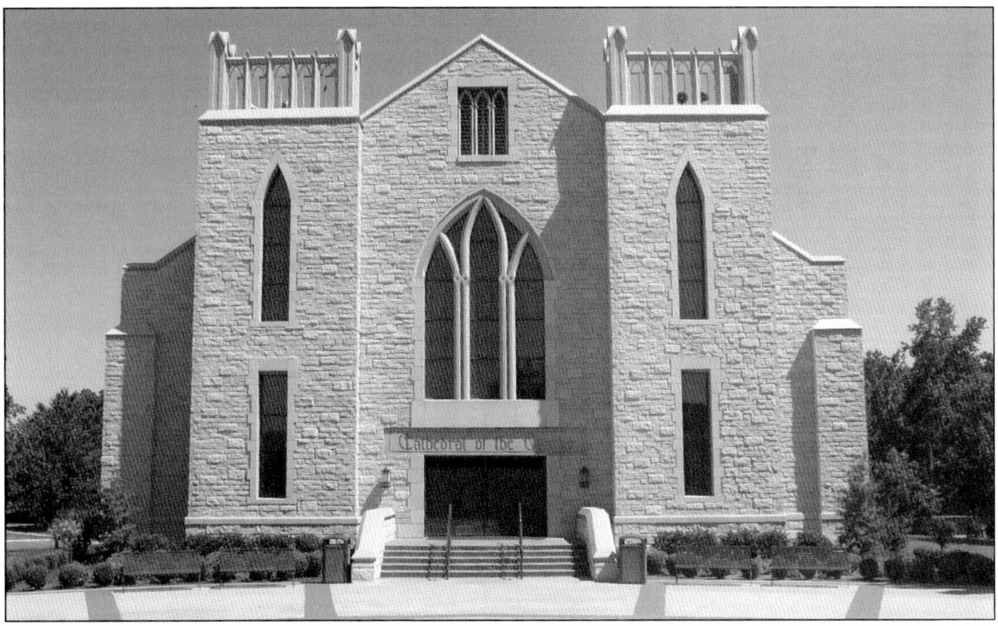

The Cathedral of the Ozarks stood on the John Brown University campus for many years with a block exterior; the rock facade, seen here, was added in 2008. The sanctuary was completed in 1957 and was dedicated on April 28 of that year. Ground breaking was in 1945, in memory of JBU students and faculty who lost their lives in World War II. Construction was divided into several phases.

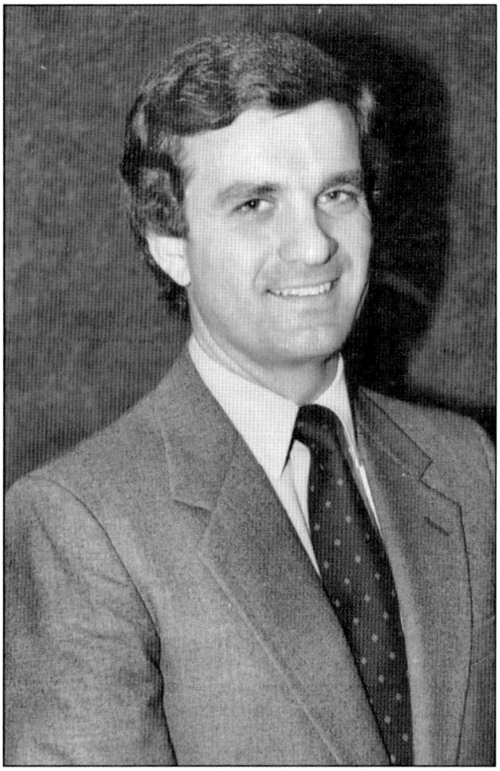

John Elward Brown III was born at Siloam Springs on July 1, 1949. He earned his bachelor's degree from JBU in 1971 and then commuted to the University of Arkansas Law School, which he completed in 1974. He was president of JBU from 1979 to 1993 and then became director of Wingate Foundation. He served as a state senator from 1995 to 2002.

John Brown University students performed operas even before the Berry Performing Arts Building was built. This photograph shows a dress rehearsal of their production of *The Marriage of Figaro*. Karla Schantz, left, tries to win the affection of the countess, played by Susan Agan, while Susanna, played by Tamara Hicks, looks on.

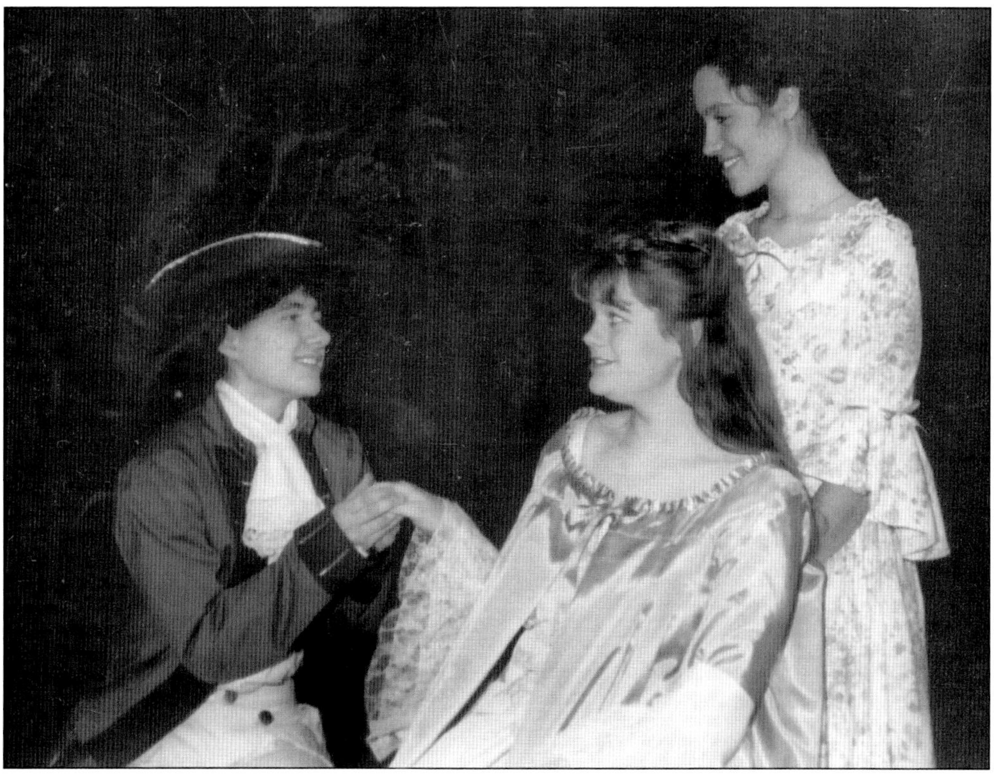

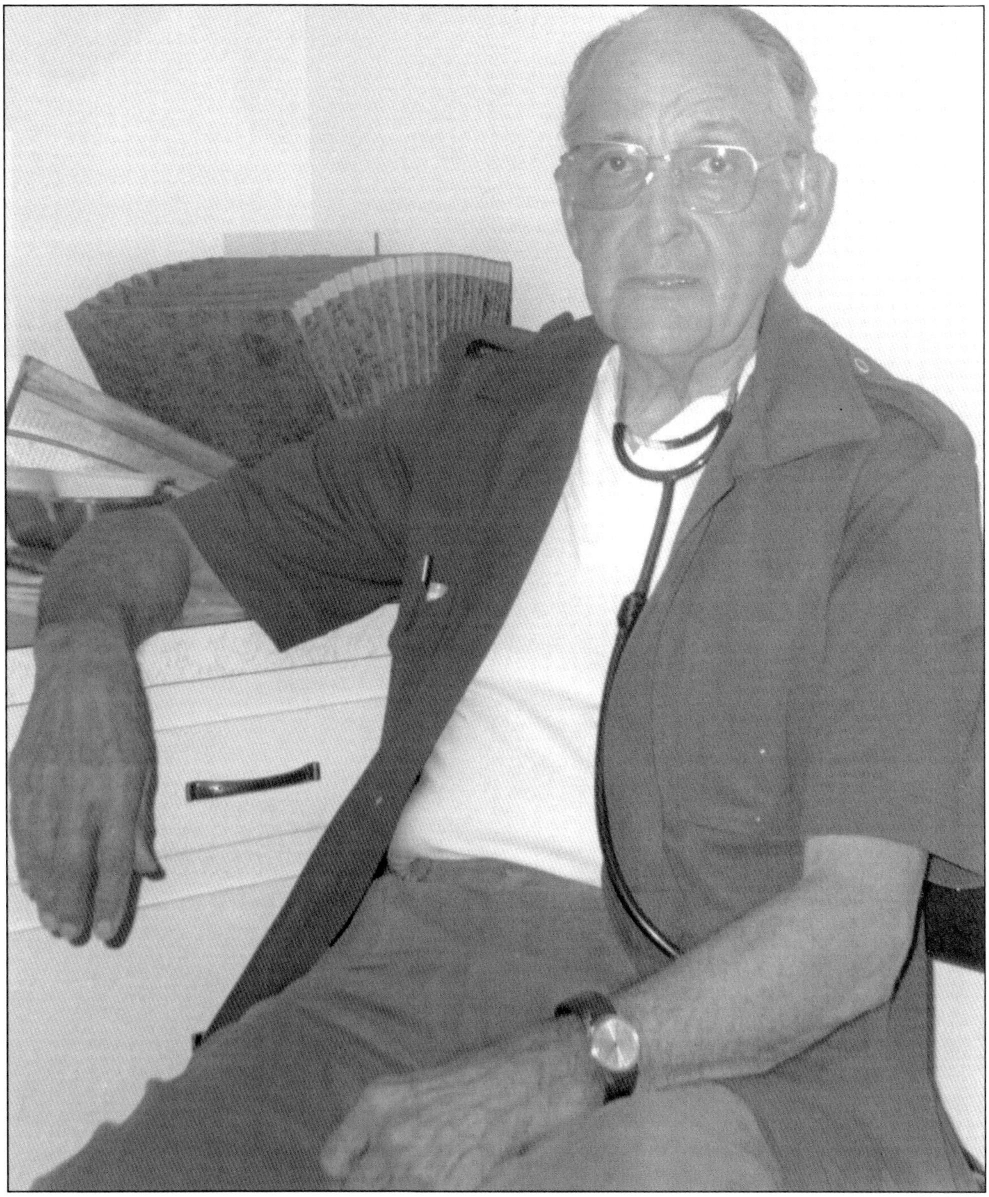

Dr. James D. Huskins (1915–2004) first came to Siloam Springs in 1939, just after completing his medical training, and learned more about surgery by working with Dr. G.A. Hughes at city hospital. In the next year, he was called into the military, and then the United States entered World War II; he served in the medical corps in Europe until 1945. He then returned to Siloam Springs and continued to practice, but by then, many of the older doctors in town had retired, so he had a great deal more to do, and in those days, they still made house calls. In 1956, he and Dr. Caldeen Gunter III started the medical center down the hill from Memorial Hospital, along Maxwell Street at the end of Twin Springs Street. Over the next few years, other doctors joined this facility. He retired in 1995, but still saw some of his long-established patients.

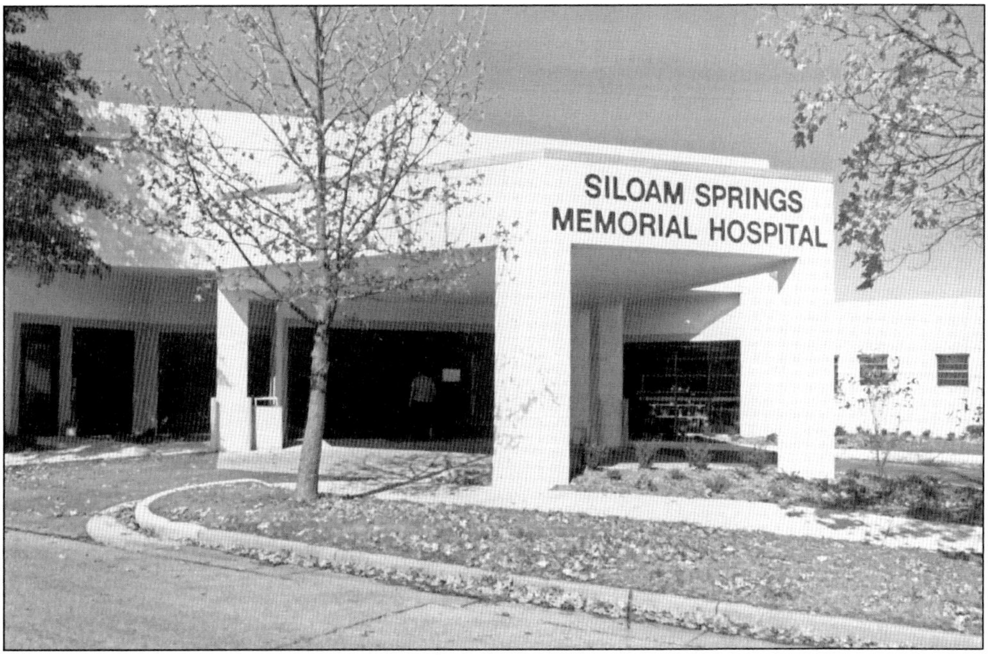

In 1989, Memorial Hospital underwent a $2.9 million expansion and renovation project which resulted in the entryway seen in this photograph. The expansion also included larger emergency room and surgery areas and a new 31-bed wing. This work was dedicated in 1990, and a donor tree preserves the names of those who donated to this project.

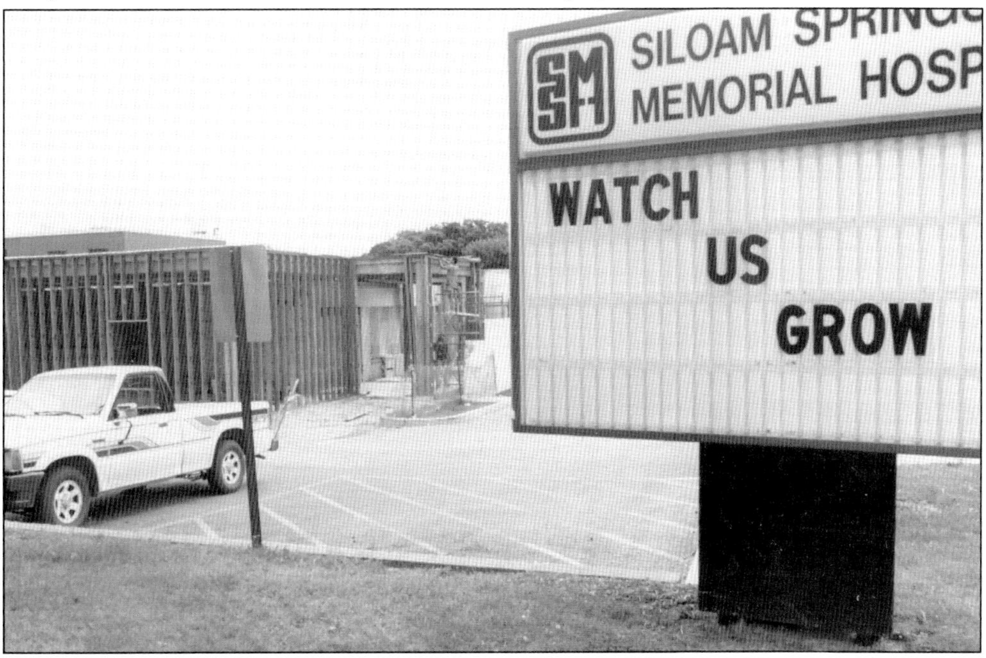

Construction on the west side of Memorial Hospital in 1994 added two large surgical suites and three obstetric areas. The new birthing rooms were built to have a home-like atmosphere with comfortable furniture for the mother and her family, but there was also room for machines to be brought in in case of problems.

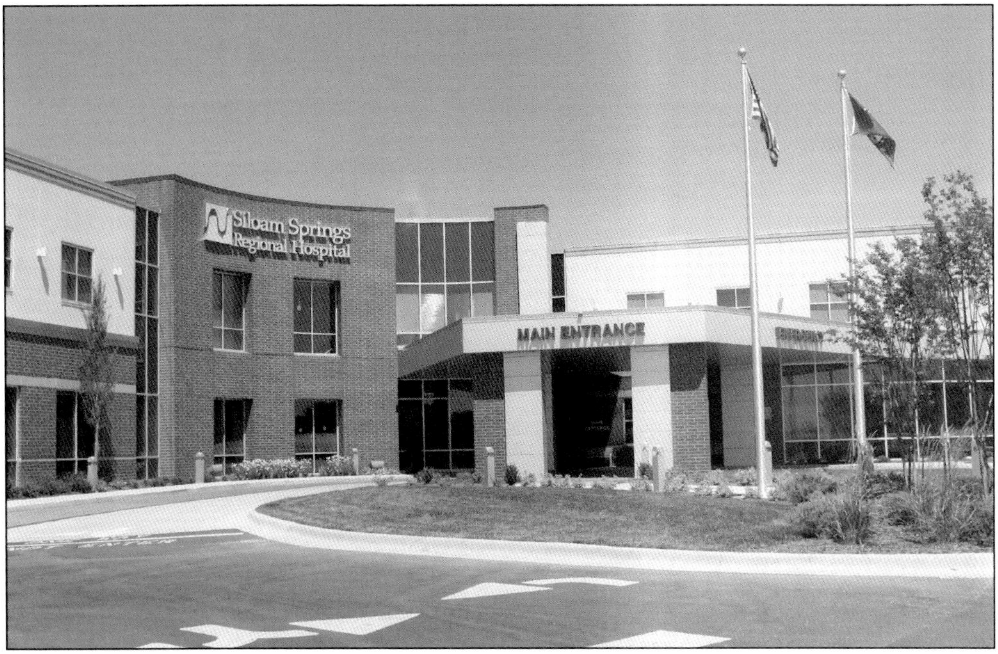

The new hospital on Progress Avenue, Siloam Springs Regional Hospital, opened April 28, 2012. It is a $40 million, 92,188-square-foot facility that is designed for the efficient movement of patients from private rooms to scanning machines, operating rooms, or the helicopter pad. It is envisioned as a regional hospital serving a four-county area with an estimated population of 50,000.

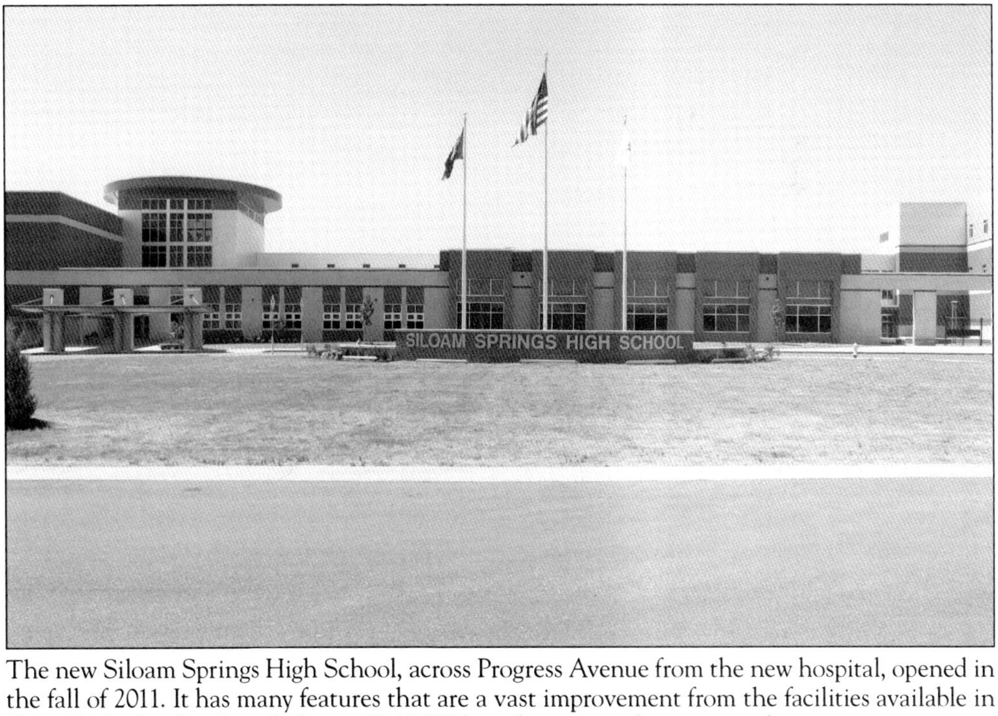

The new Siloam Springs High School, across Progress Avenue from the new hospital, opened in the fall of 2011. It has many features that are a vast improvement from the facilities available in the 1963 high school, including a SMART board in every classroom with projector, computer, and document camera; better science laboratory facilities; and better drama facilities.

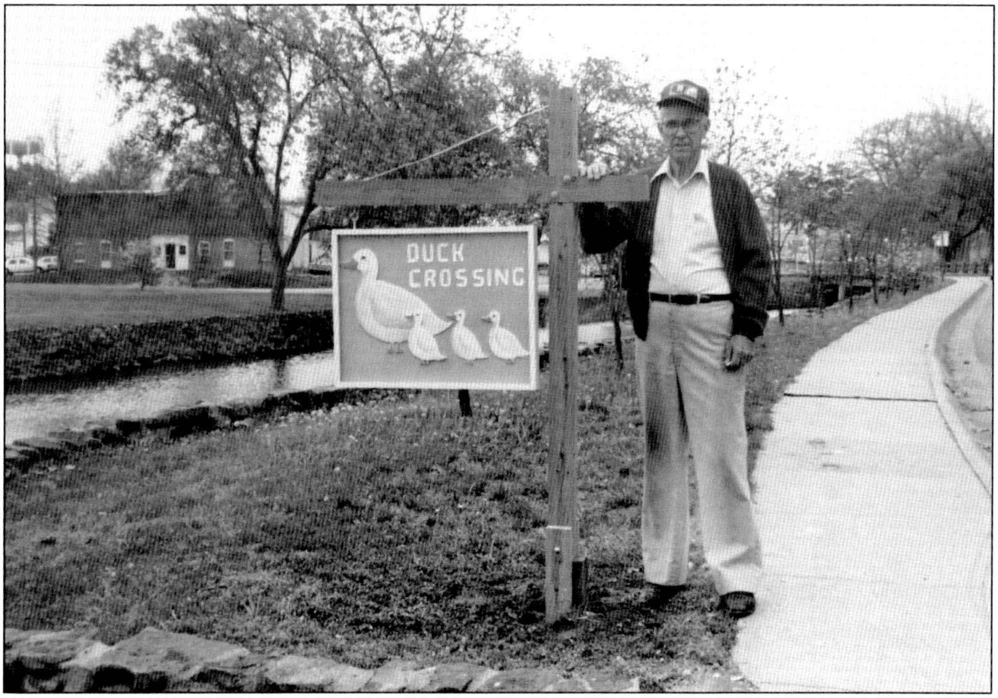

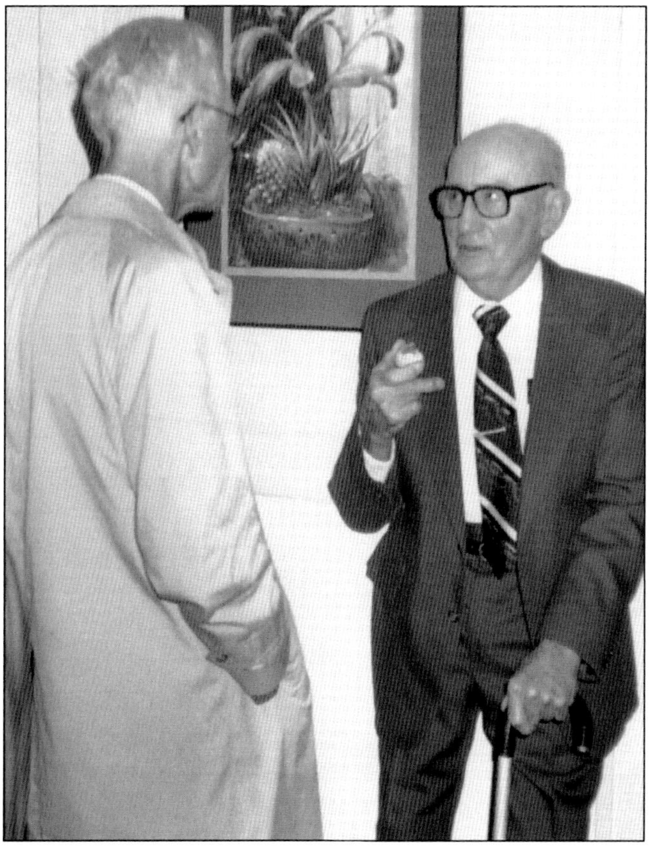

Eldon Robb was one of the men who tended the duck feeders downtown for a few years after his retirement. But vandalism eventually made it too expensive to continue the project. A veteran of World War II, Robb later worked as a field man for Pet Milk Company. He died in May 2008 at the age of 88.

Kenneth Lynch (right) talks to Ralph Kennedy at the opening of an exhibit of Lynch's work in the Sager Creek Arts Center (SCAC). SCAC opened in 1985 in the 1920 Methodist Episcopal Church South, which is still owned by First United Methodist Church of Siloam Springs. At one time, SCAC offered plays, art displays, classes, and much more. Financial problems have forced a return to all volunteer staffing and reduced programming.

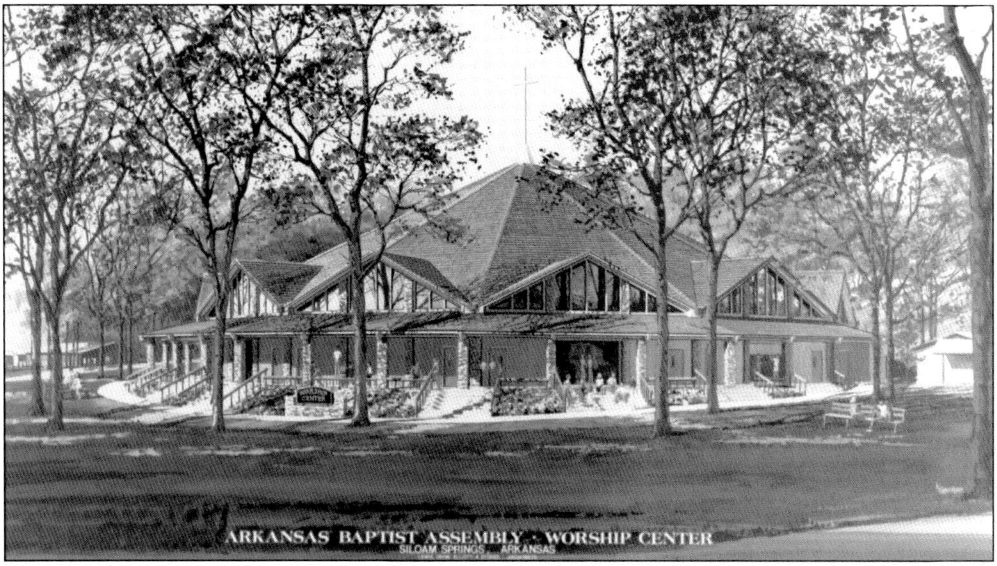

From 1926, the Arkansas Baptist State Convention operated Arkansas Baptist Assembly (ABA) as a 188-acre youth summer camp, located near the Illinois River south of Siloam Springs. In 2005, refugees of Hurricane Katrina stayed at ABA, and a few moved to Siloam Springs permanently. The picture above is an architect's rendering of the 1,100-seat Worship Center built in 1990. In September 2011, ABA became Camp Siloam, open to all churches.

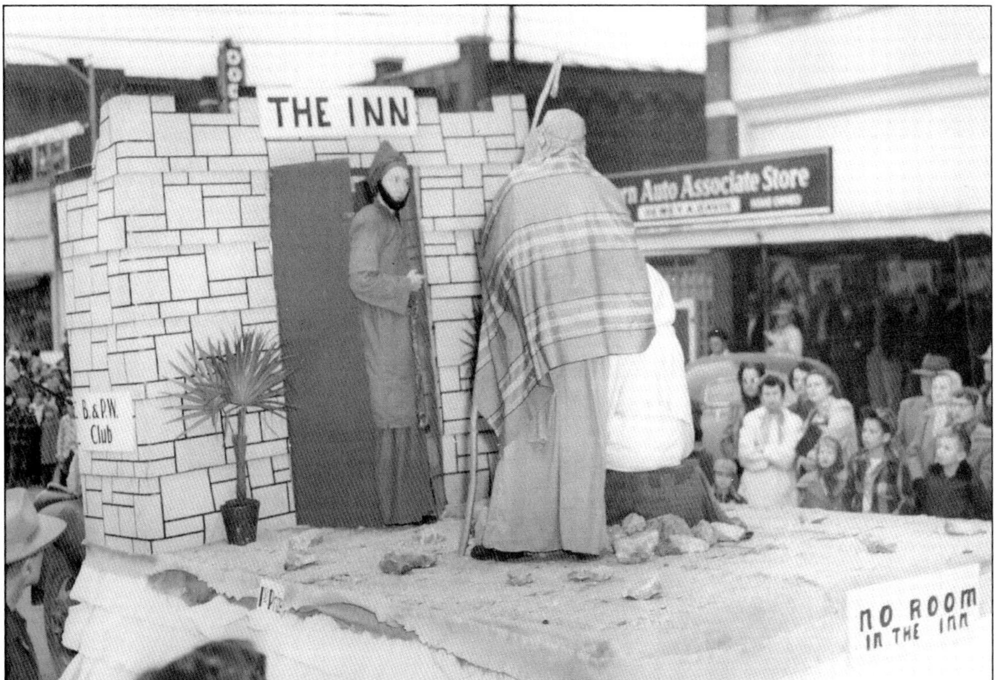

First place in the 1951 Christmas parade went to this float, which was titled "No Room in the Inn" and was built for the local club of the Arkansas Federation of Business and Professional Women. In December 1951, the membership of this club was at 46 and growing. Materials for this float cost $9.09.

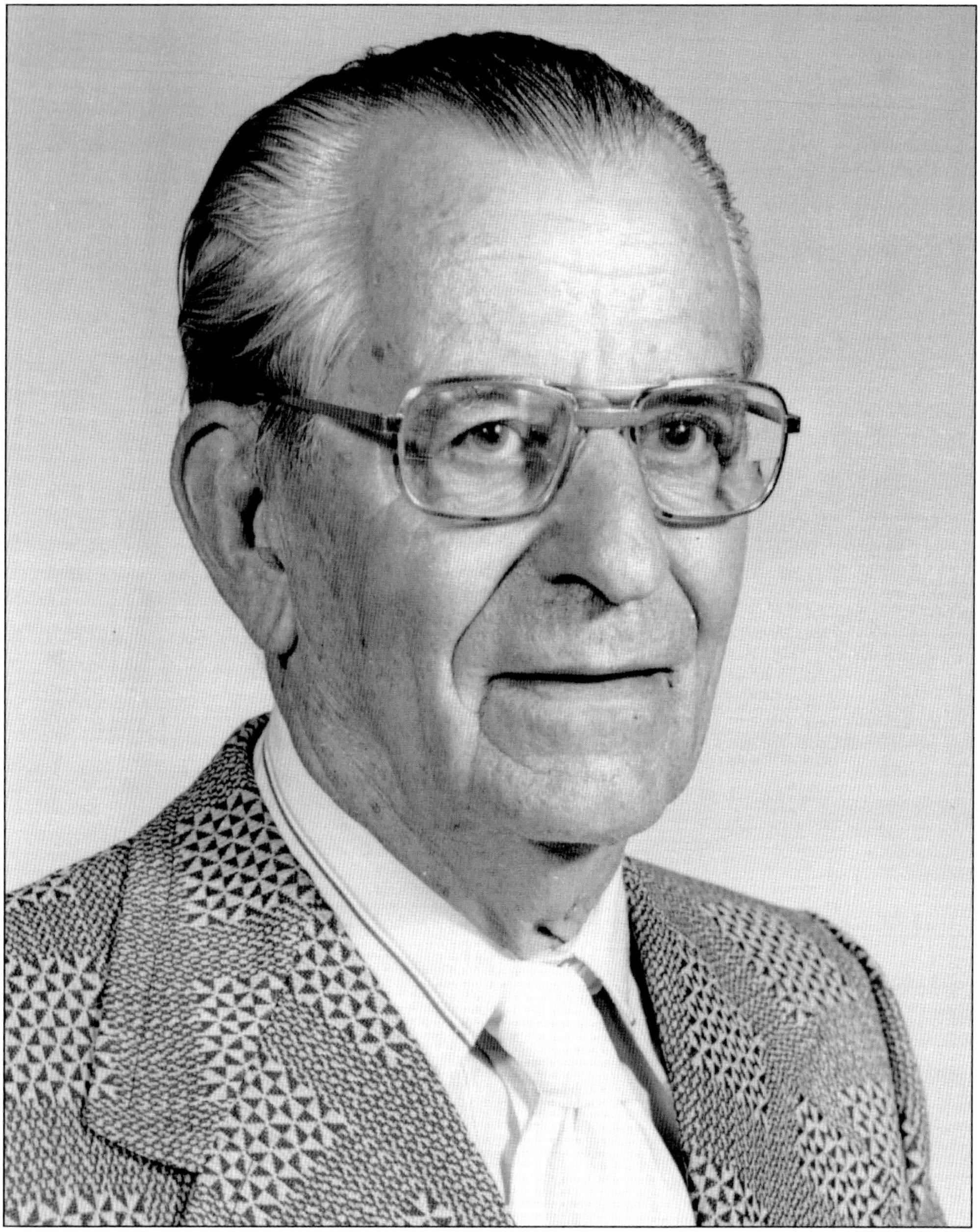

For 50 years, Robert Henry was either on the city council or serving as mayor. He has an unmatched record of service to the city. He was instrumental in the city's purchase of Lake Frances as a reliable water source, which it still is. He was also instrumental is getting many industries to come to town. He supervised the town's recovery from the 1974 flood. He had many other accomplishments for the city, but this is just part of his story. He lived all but the last few of his 101 years on the same block in Siloam Springs—with the exception of the short time in the early 1920s that he spent traveling with a circus. He owned the local semiprofessional baseball team for several years during the Great Depression. They were part of the Ark-Mo League of Arkansas and Missouri baseball teams. He was the recipient of the chamber of commerce 1987 Pioneer Citizen Award. The entire city helped him celebrate his 90th and 100th birthdays.

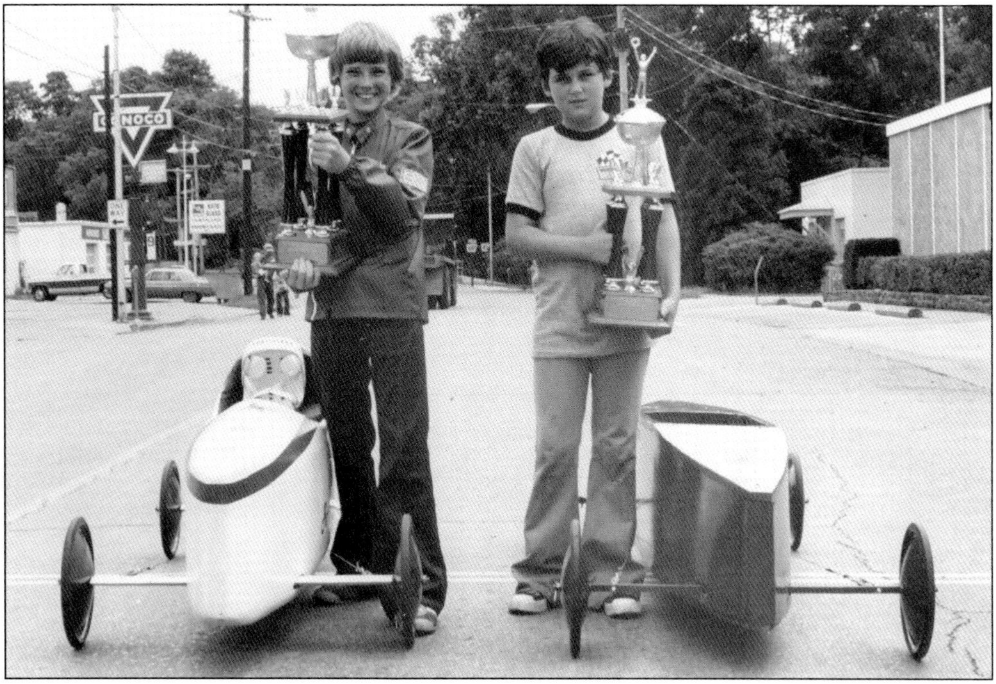

The Siloam Springs Soapbox Derby ran from 1976 through 1978. These photographs are from the 1976 derby. Above are the winners with their first place trophies. Mike Rood, senior division winner, is on the left, with Johnny Mitchell, the junior division winner, on the right. The photograph below shows Johnny Mitchell about to cross the finish line ahead of Ryan Dixon in the junior division competition. The local derby was run on Mount Olive Street, starting at what is now the police station with the finish line near the downtown fire station. Each racer received a trophy and T-shirt. The winner in each division received a champion's trophy, jacket, and all-expense-paid trip to Akron, Ohio, for the All-American Soapbox Derby. Division runners-up also received special trophies.

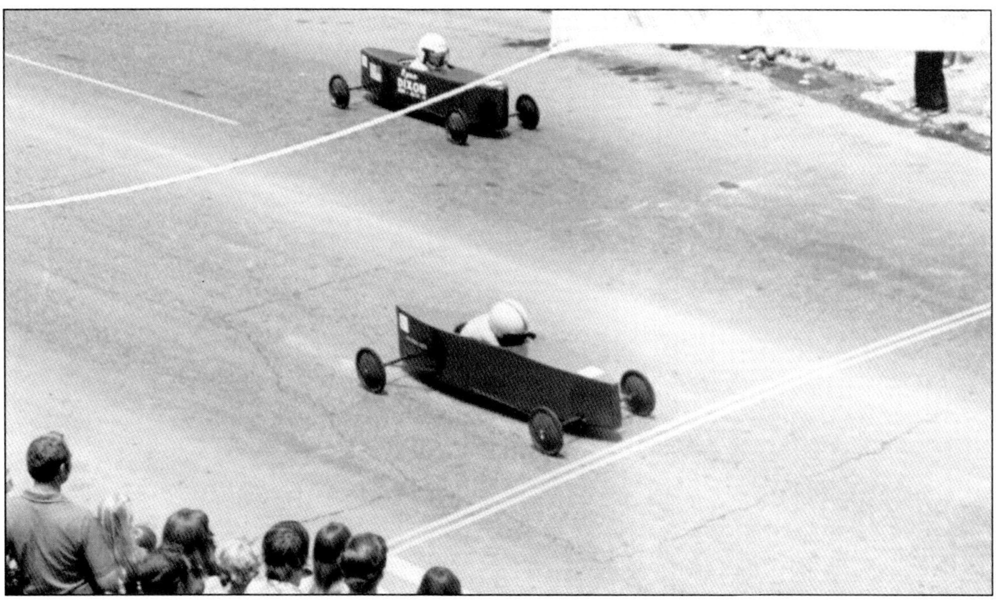

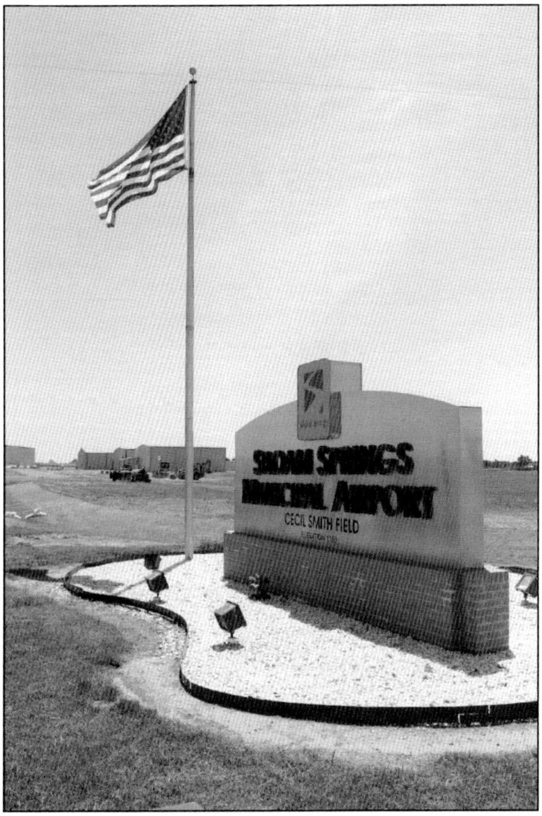

Cecil Smith Field, the Siloam Springs Municipal Airport, is on the east side of town, along Highway 59. It has a 5,000-foot, paved runway that can accommodate most jets and propeller airplanes. It has a beacon and runway edge lights, and the wind cones are lighted. It is the home of Skydive Sky Ranch.

The parks and recreation office was built as the ladies' lounge in City Park, south of the downtown fire station. Parks and recreation is the city department that schedules public use of the parks, sports fields, pavilions, gazebos, aquatic center, and Community Building. The department offers a children's summer camp and promotes use of the Dogwood Springs walking trail.

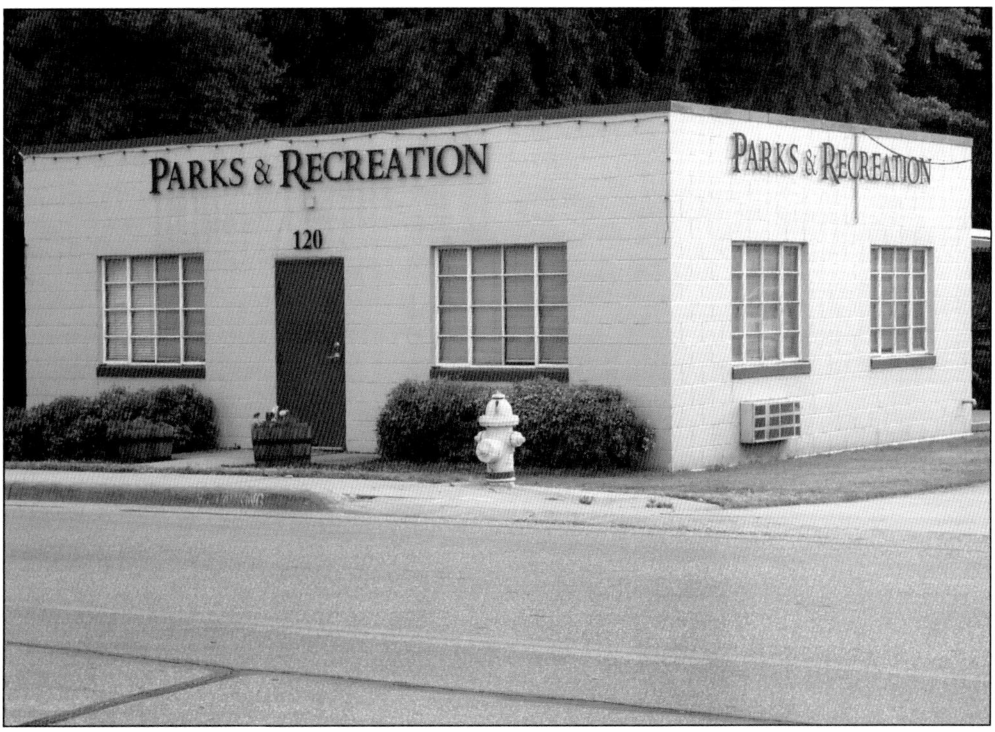

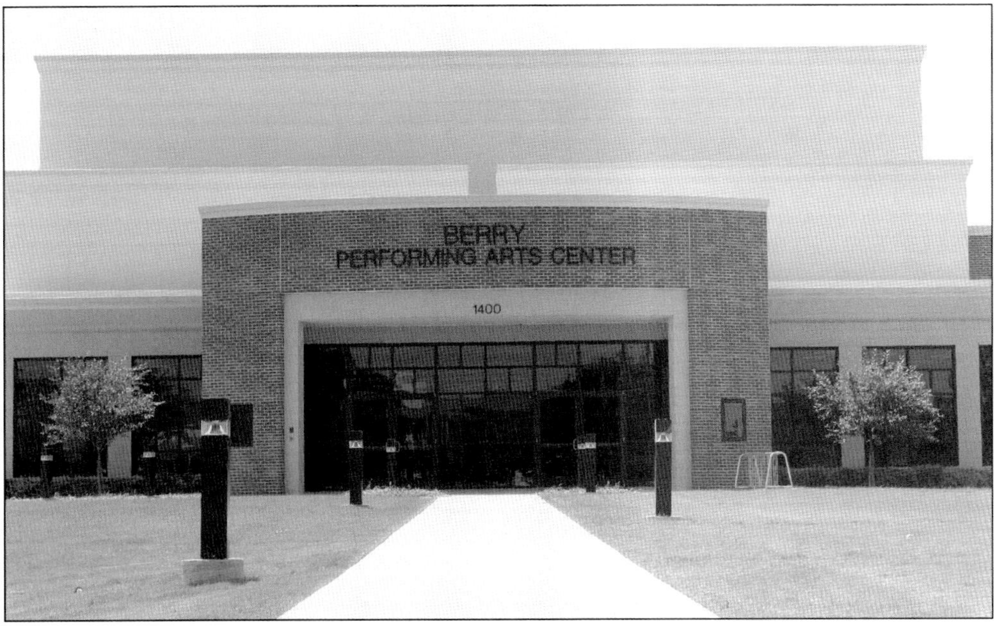

One of the newest buildings on the John Brown University campus is the Berry Performing Arts Center, which opened in 2010. This 28,500-square-foot building seats 492 in the main auditorium. The building is used for theater productions, music performances, recitals, lyceum concert series, lecture series, and choir practice. It even has a recording room. The building cost $8.5 million, all donated funds.

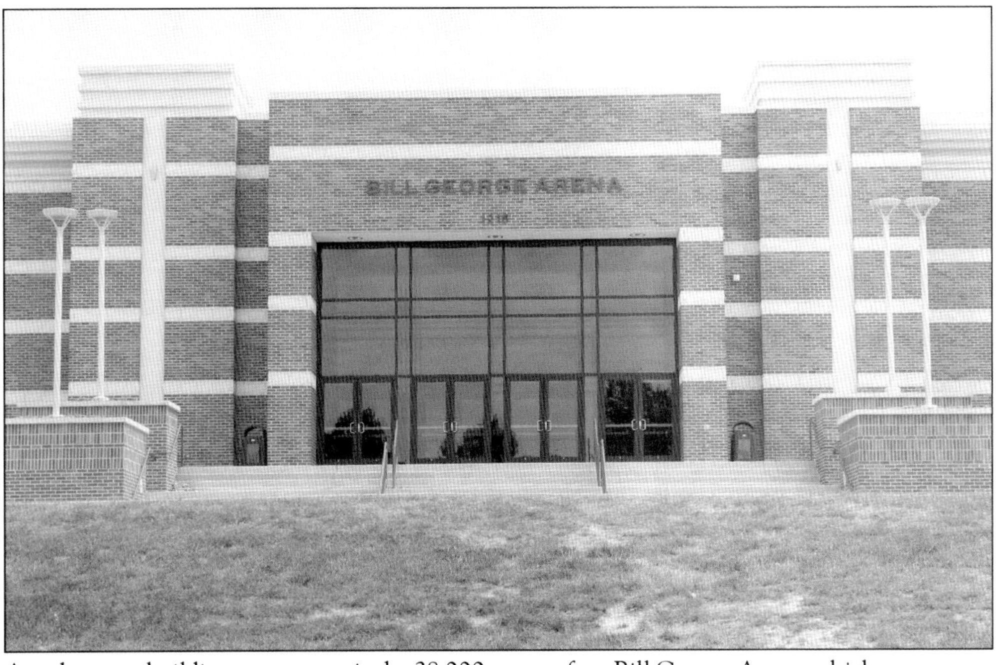

Another new building on campus is the 38,000-square-foot Bill George Arena, which can seat up to 1,750 for basketball games and concerts and up to 2,750 for graduations. This building cost $9.5 million, also all donated funds. Remarkably, the Berry Center and George Arena were both under construction at the same time, and the arena was dedicated one day after the Berry Center.

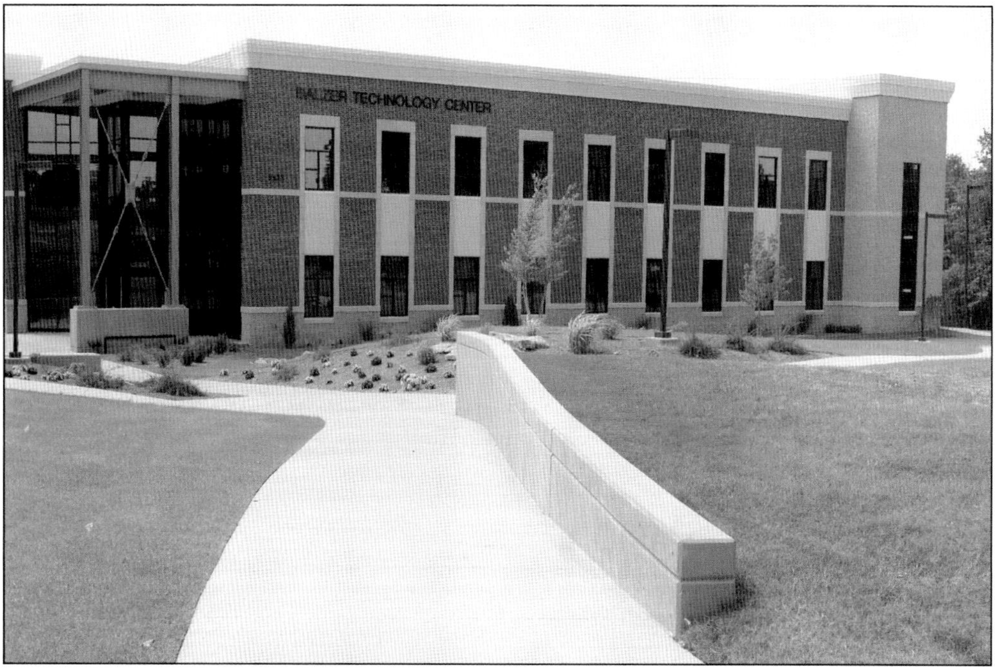

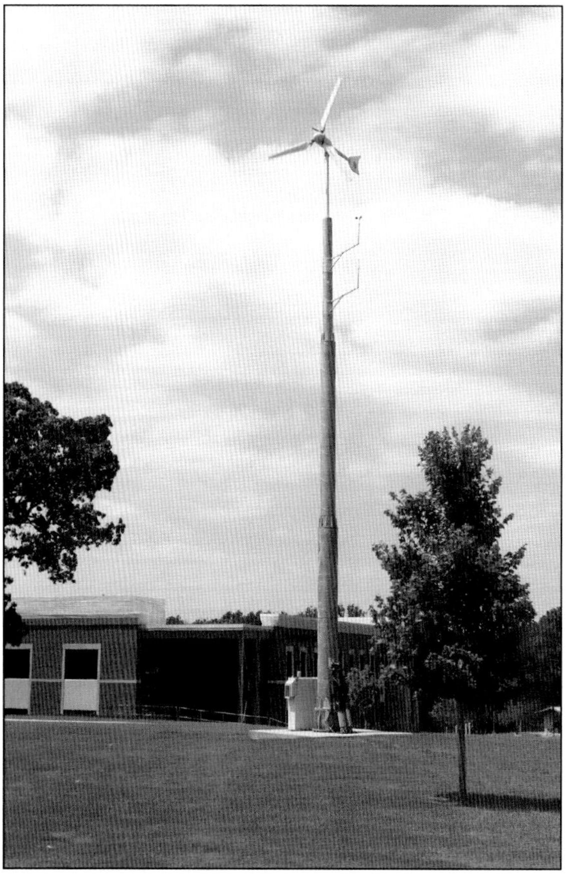

The Balzer Technology Center has an interesting companion structure: a windmill. This 40,000-square-foot building houses engineering and construction management and contains just three traditional classrooms. Most of the building is specialty laboratories. Part of the total $11 million donated to this project is an endowment to fund operations and equipment purchases. This building was completed in 2011 with six faculty and 90 majors in the engineering program and three faculty and 55 students in the construction management program. One engineering laboratory contains a wind tunnel and a jet engine turbine. Construction management areas include indoor spaces for safety training, building projects, and experiments.

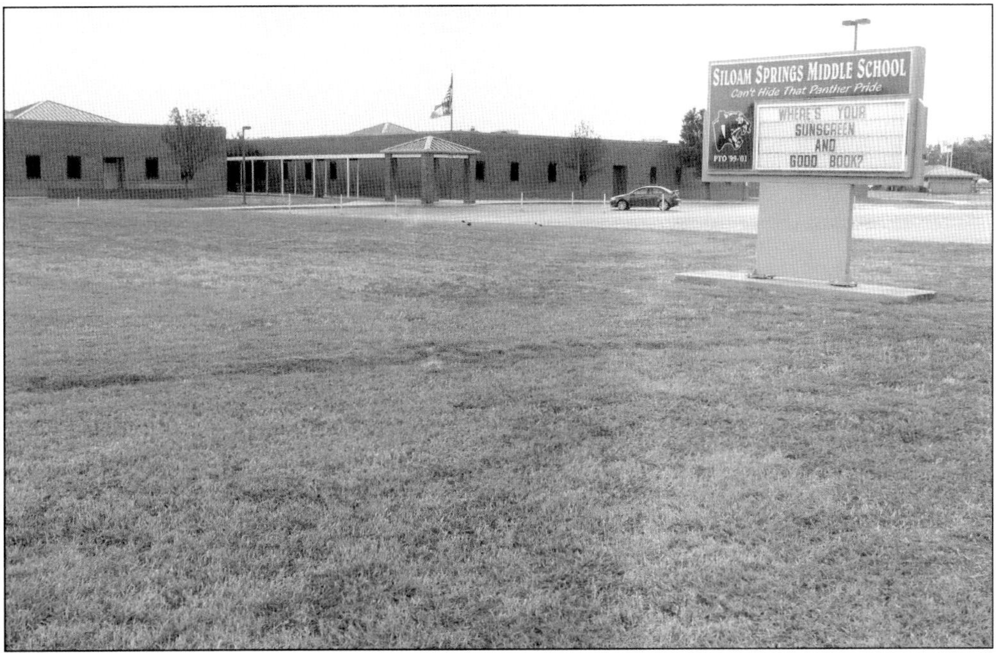

The Siloam Springs Middle School opened in 1995 and was built to house grades six, seven, and eight. Work is now underway to remodel the 1963 high school for grades seven and eight, with the middle school becoming an intermediate school housing grades five and six and Southside housing grades three and four.

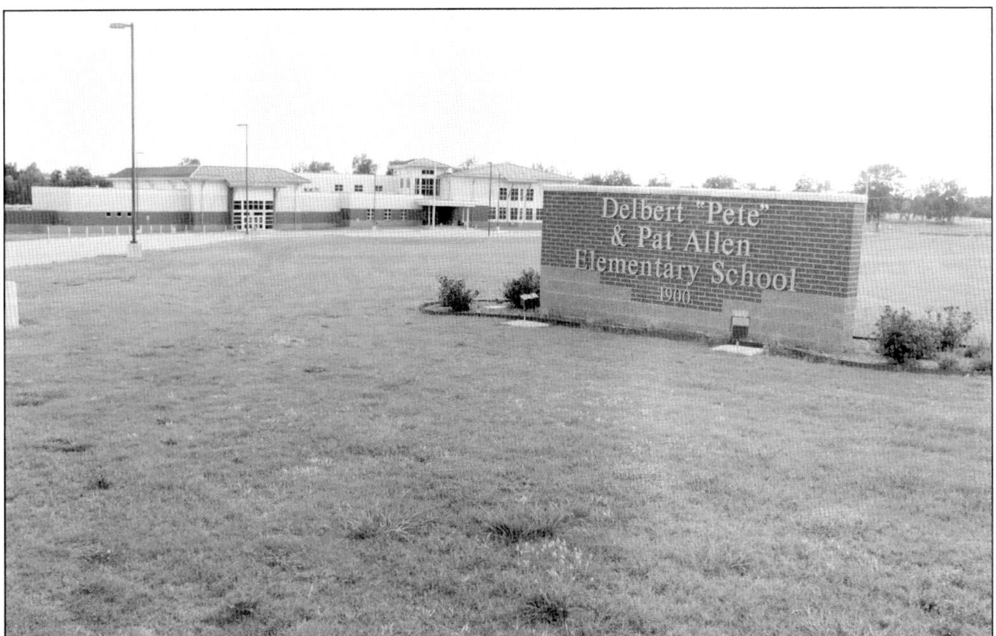

Delbert "Pete" and Pat Allen Elementary opened in August 2006 and adjoins the middle school and Family Aquatic Center property on Mount Olive Street. The school's 92,146 square feet are designed to accommodate up to 750 first- and second-grade students. Ground breaking for this building was in May 2005.

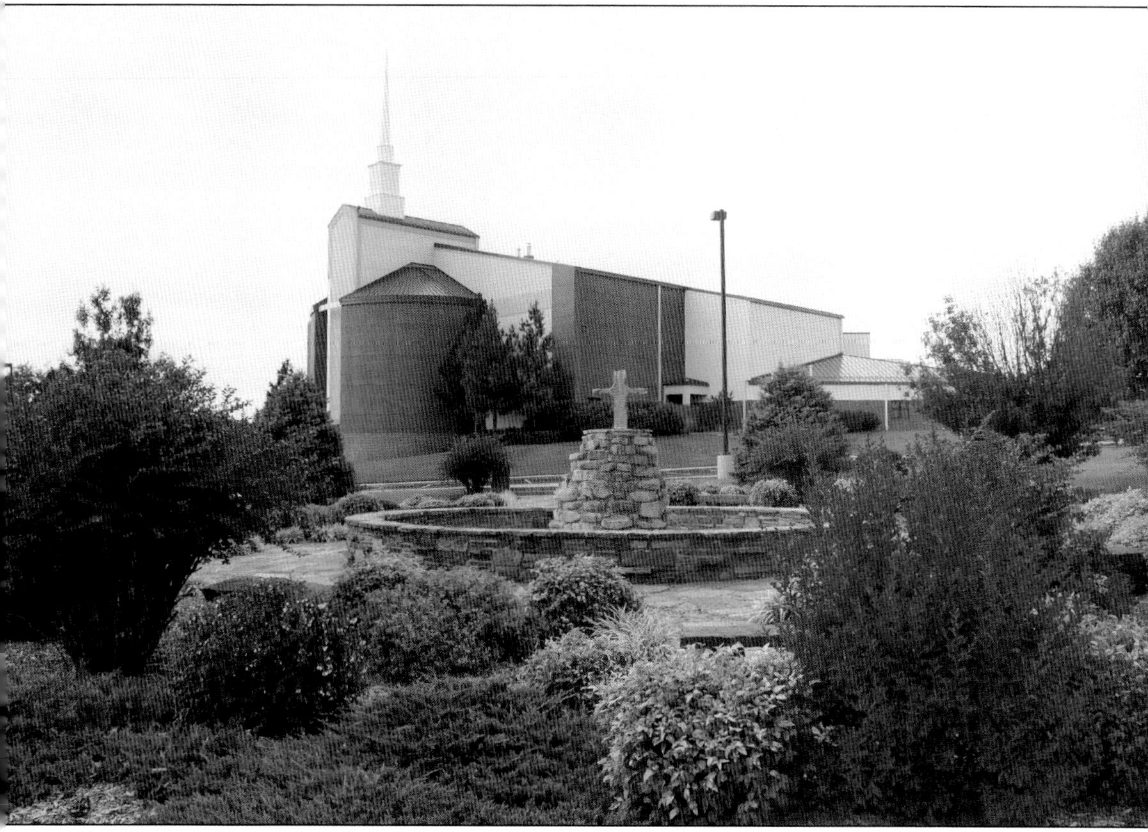

First Baptist Church was founded at Hico in 1868 with 10 charter members. Key Lodge No. 7, Ancient Free and Accepted Masons, was chartered on Lindsey's Prairie in 1854, then moved to Hico, and constructed a building in 1872. This building soon housed the Masons, the Baptists, and Hico School. The church's first building in Siloam Springs was on Tahlequah Street, erected in 1883, with a cemetery east of it. In 1903, the congregation moved into its new building on what is now Broadway. In 1948, members built a new building on this lot and later removed the older building. They purchased 20 acres at the corner of Dawn Hill Road and Highway 43 in 1994, and construction of the new building, pictured here, was completed by the end of 1996. In the foreground is the garden south of the building. The worship center is 25,000 square feet in size, and the youth center is 6,000 square feet. There is also a full-service kitchen. These renovations were completed in 2003.

Fire station No. 1 on Cheri Whitlock Drive opened in 2001. This station houses the department's ladder truck along with other equipment and is where firefighters on duty can sleep, eat, and exercise. This station allows for faster response times to the schools, industries, and houses on the north side of town.

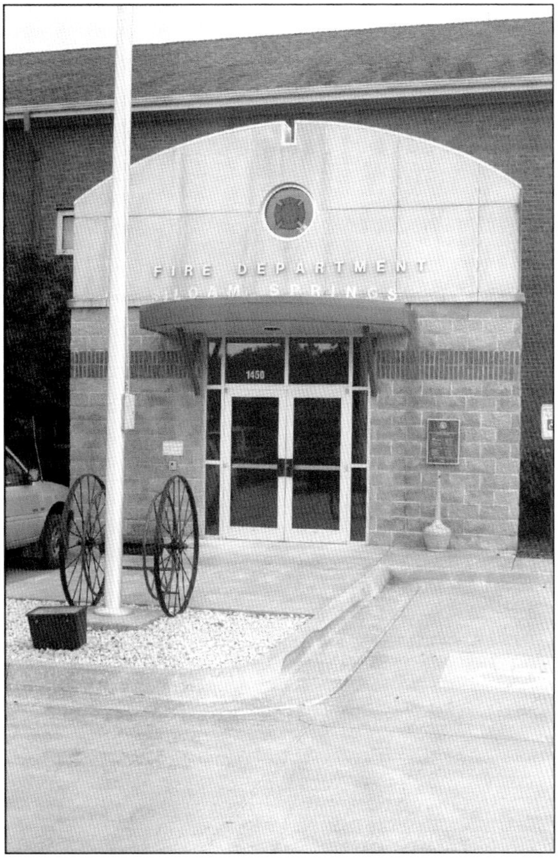

Fire station No. 2 is on Mount Olive Street at Central Street. It was originally designated fire station No. 1 and opened in 1967. This was the location of the 1915 city hall, and the downtown fire station has been at this location since before 1897. In recognition of this history, around the building, there is an old hose cart, a fire bell, and a section of railing from the 1915 city hall.

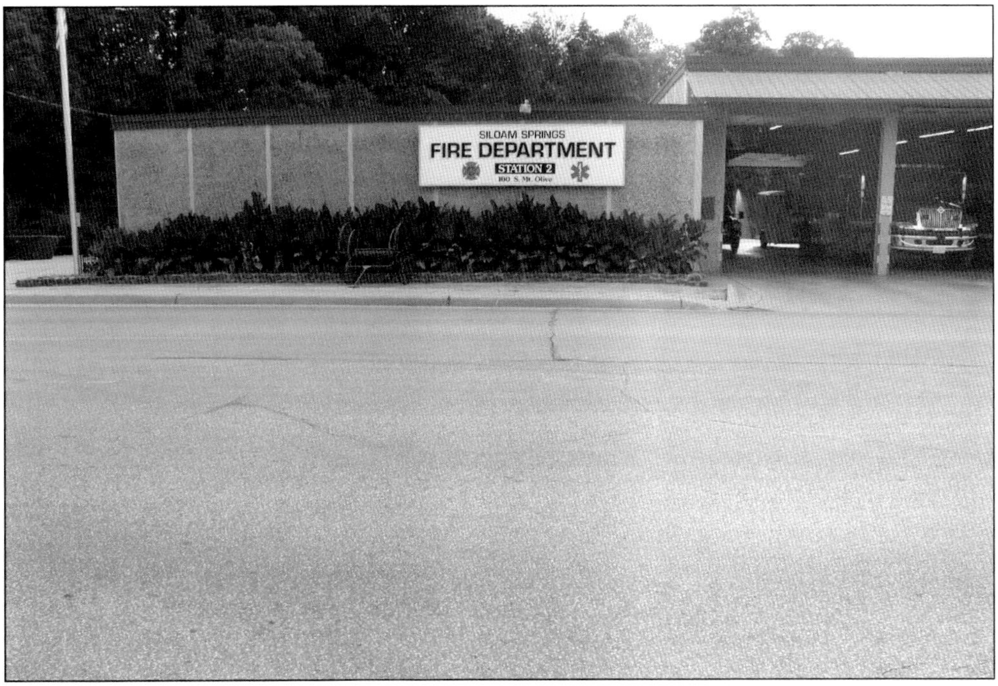

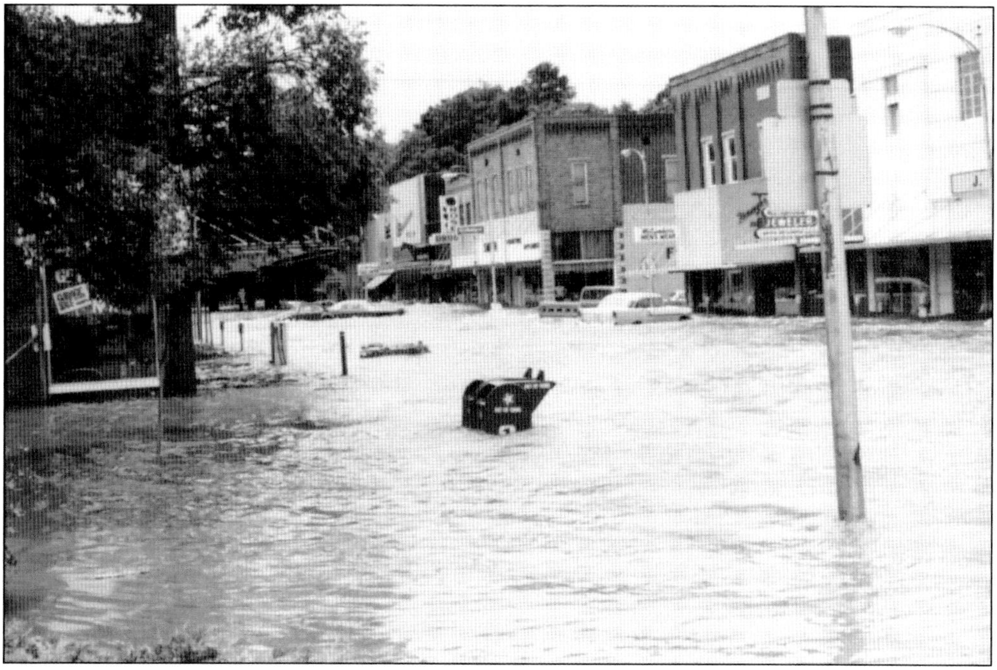

On this page are two views of the June 8, 1974, flood. The photograph above is looking south along Broadway from Central Street. The postal boxes are in front of what was then still the post office downtown. The photograph below was taken looking west along Alpine Street from just east of Broadway. The building at far right is the former State Bank Building seen elsewhere in this book. Note also the "slipcovers" added to the fronts of some buildings downtown at this time. These were generally sheet metal facades added to the front of an older building to "modernize" its appearance. This was popular in the 1960s and 1970s, but most have now been removed.

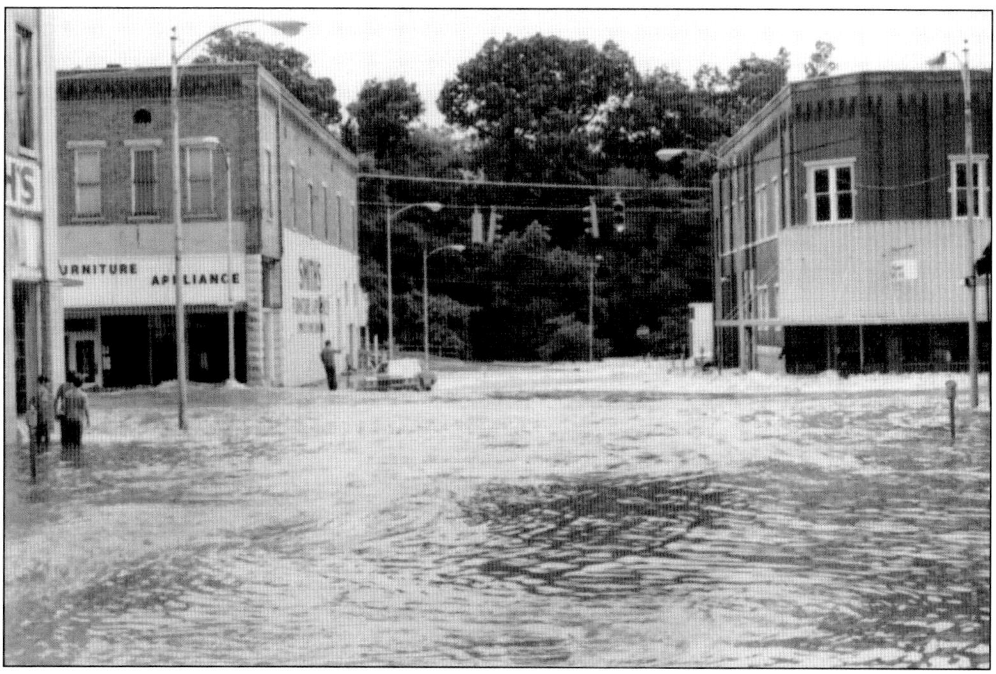

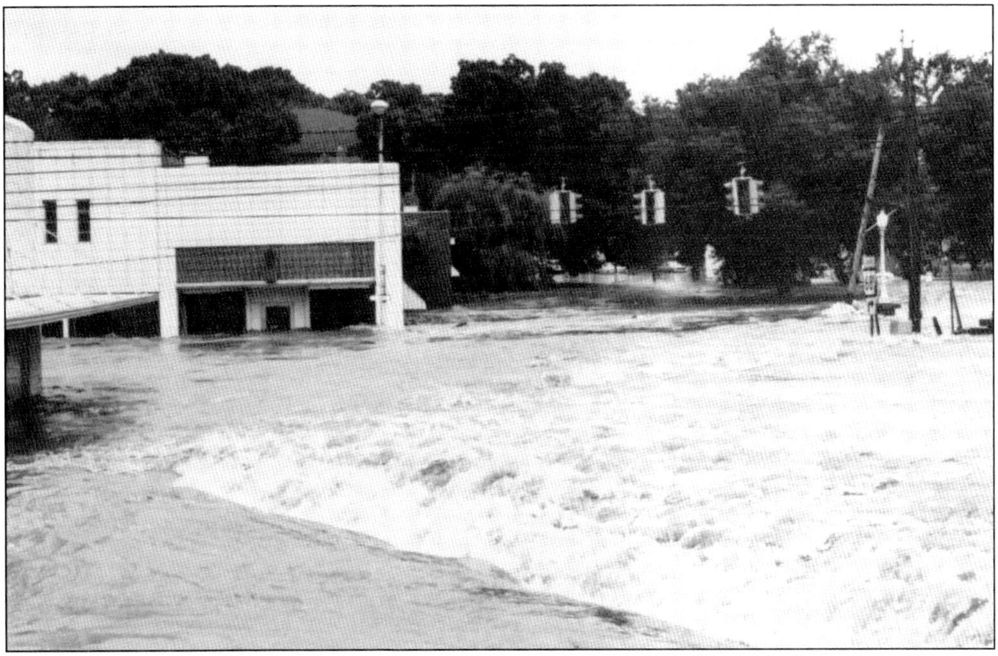

On this page are two more views of the June 8, 1974, flood. The photograph above shows the west end of what was then the Allen Canning Company office, where several office workers retreated to the roof. The view is looking across East Main Street and south on South Maxwell Street and into the Twin Springs Park. The photograph below looks across Broadway and west on Central Street. This flood and the 1892 flood are the two largest recorded flash floods of Sager Creek. In 1974, over nine inches of rain fell on that Saturday morning, leading to a flash flood that caused an estimated $15 to $20 million in damages in Siloam Springs alone. Some parts of the downtown were under seven feet of water.

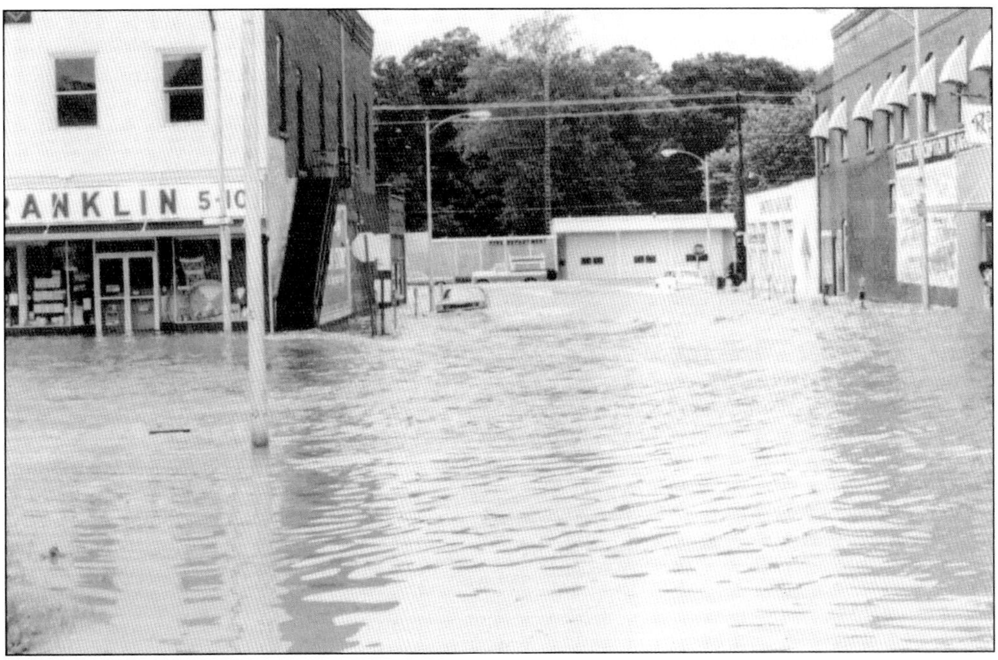

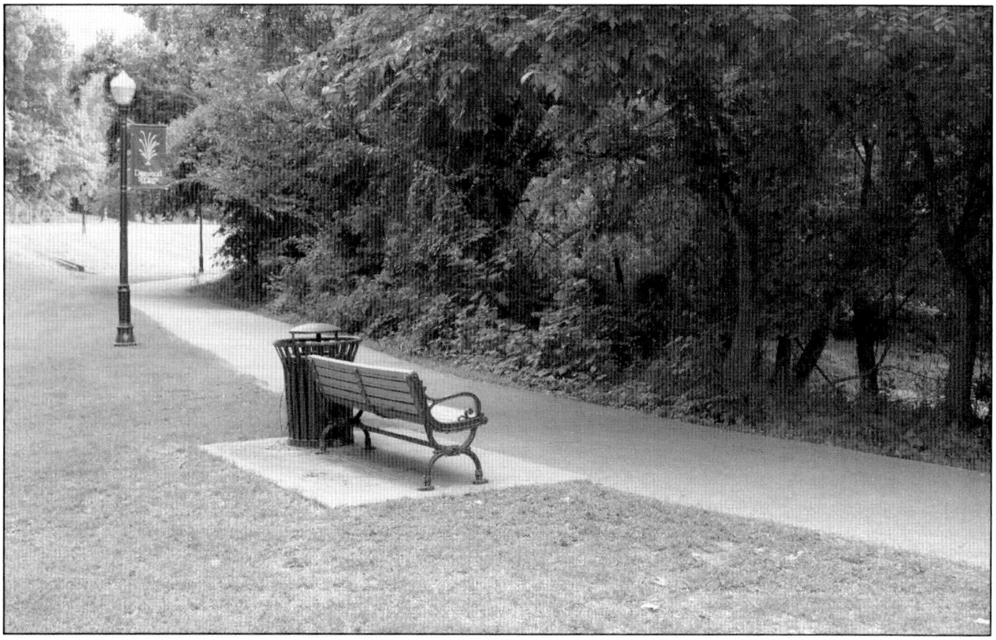

Well-lit walking trails cross Siloam Springs, mostly following the edge of Sager Creek. Benches and trashcans, as seen in the photograph above, are placed in several places along the trail. There are also a few bridges along the trail, like the one seen below. Dogwood Springs Walking Trail was built over a period of several years, starting in 2001, using state matching grants, gifts from the Walton Family Foundation, and city funds and labor. The newest trail was completed in 2010. It follows the edge of John Brown University and connects with the trail from the 1963 high school and the trail running through the parks to the downtown and continuing along Sager Creek to the La-Z-Boy Baseball/Softball Complex.

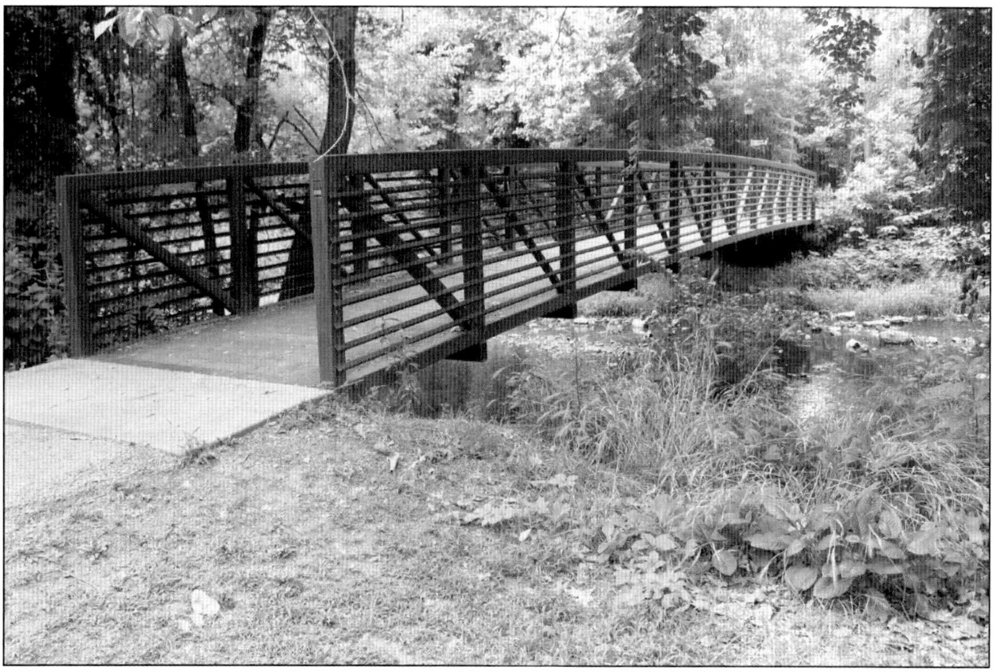

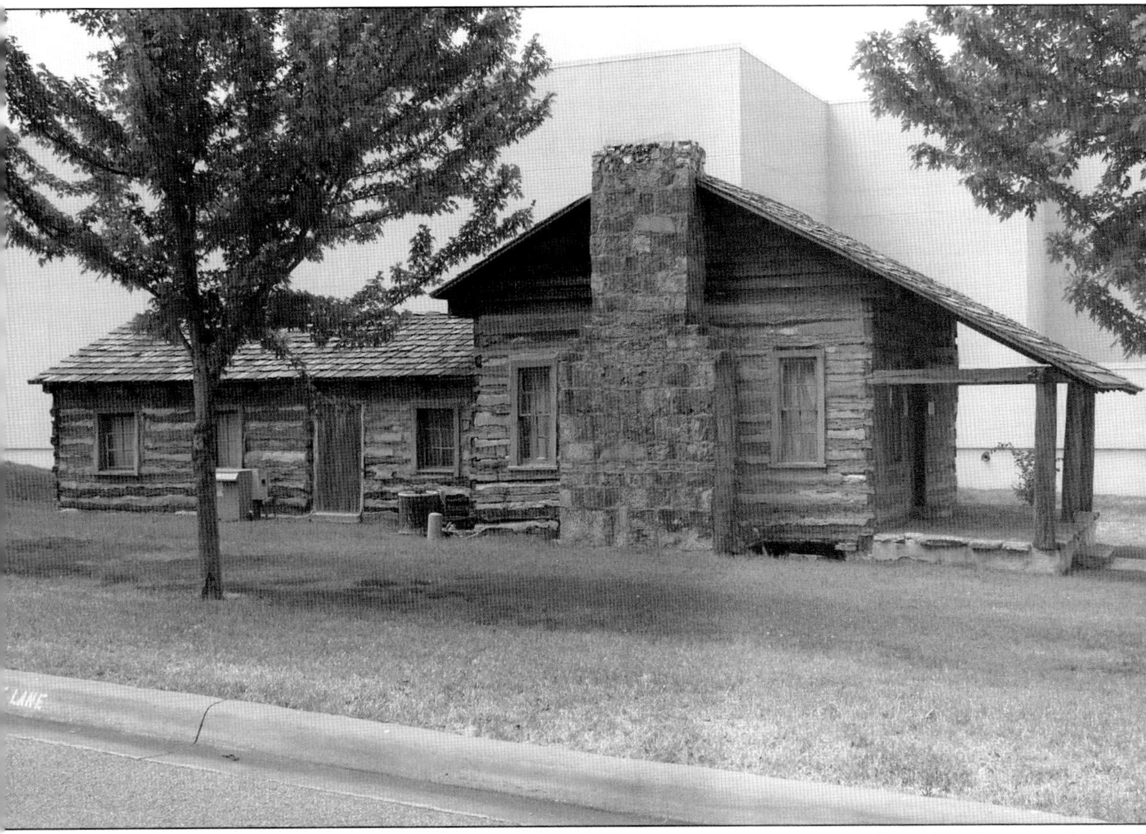

Sager Cabin is seen in this 2012 photograph at the same location it was in when the photograph on page 10 was shot, but the setting could not be more different. New buildings and parking lots now surround the cabin, but as the young trees seen here mature, they should soften the setting. Still, there surely are very few log cabins in the world that have an air-conditioner compressor sitting outside and fiber-optic lines running to them. These features were added when a group of construction management students used the cabin as a workspace and needed to bring in computers. When John Brown University had a herd of Jersey cows, the fence holding them ran up to the cabin. The milk was processed in the cabin. It has also housed classes and, at various times, has housed a faculty member and his family.

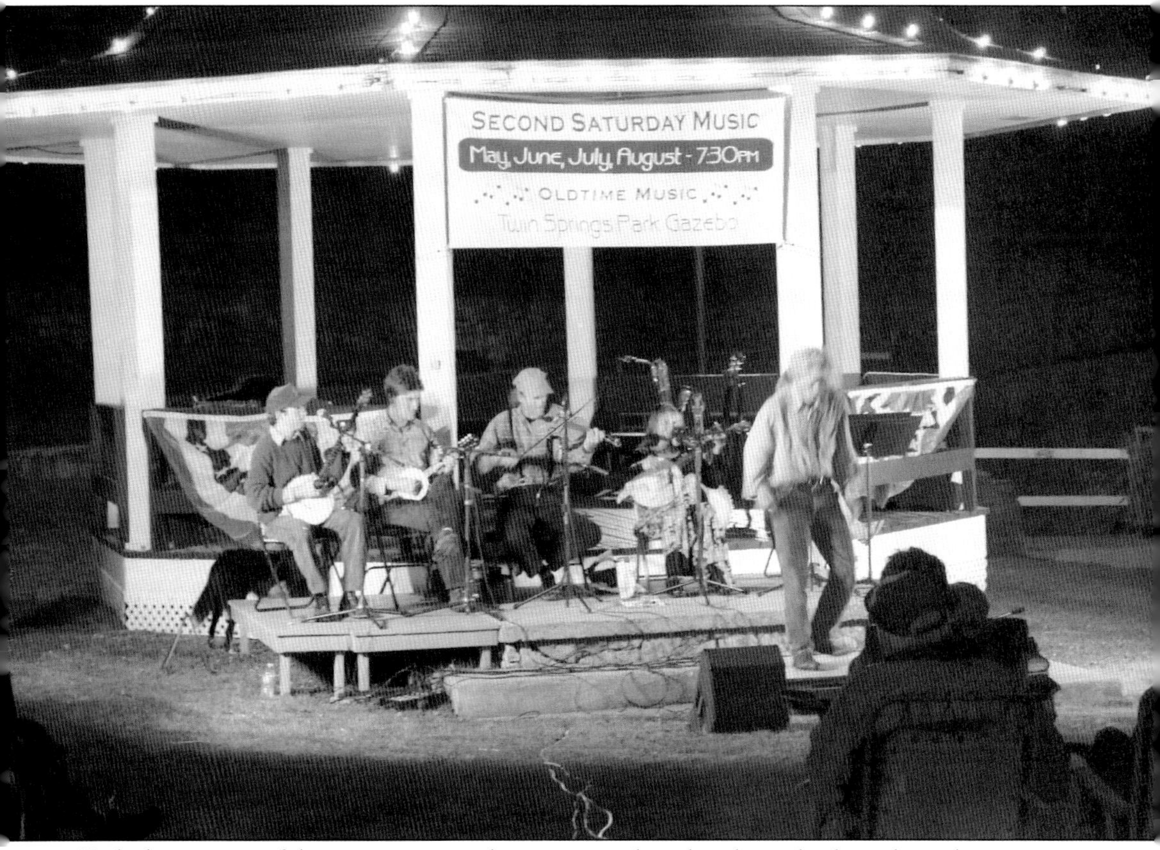

Early descriptions of this town mention that music was heard in the parks throughout the summer. Music is still heard on summer nights, such as second Saturdays in May, June, July, and August during the popular Second Saturday Music series in the Twin Springs Park gazebo. This series brings in folk musicians from across the Ozarks. Bill and Deanna Lisk started this series in 2002 and are still organizing it, with the cooperation of the city parks and recreation department, in 2012. The Lisks and their band Two Cents Worth perform the warm up. These concerts are free, but donations are welcome. This photograph was taken on May 12, 2012, as the Old 78s performed and Kent Beyette joined them to do a little jig dancing. The downtown parks and gazebos also become the backdrop for many weddings and wedding photographs, prom photographs, family photographs, and so on.

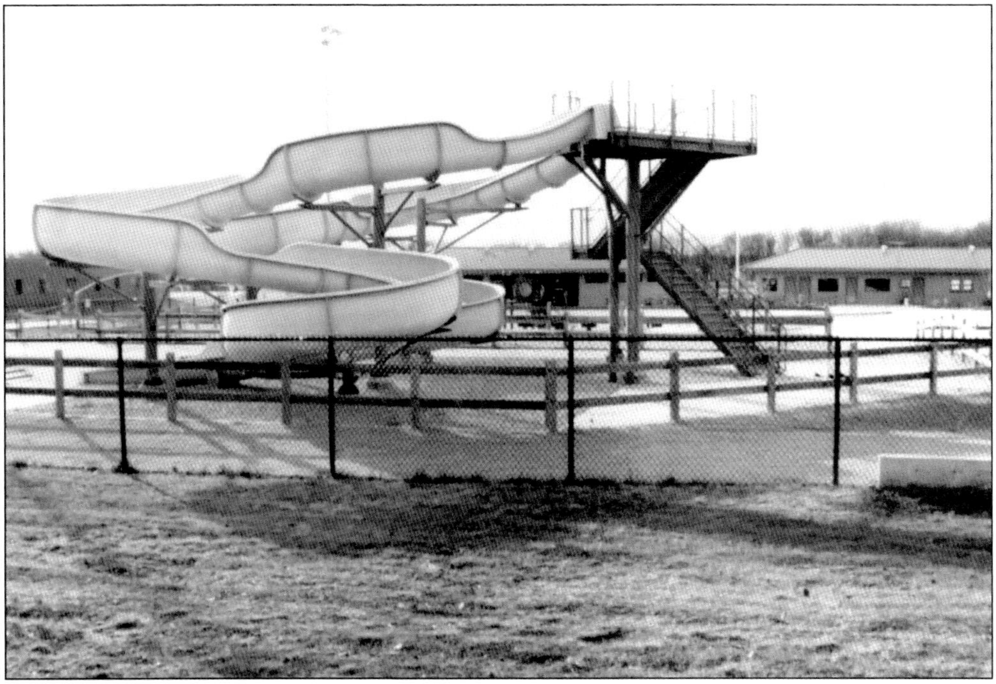

The Siloam Springs Family Aquatic Center opened in 1996 near the middle school and Allen Elementary. It features a slide, wading pool, and a zero-entry pool. Programs include lifeguard lessons, swimming lessons, dive-in movie nights, teen nights, and other special events. The aquatic center draws families from a large surrounding area.

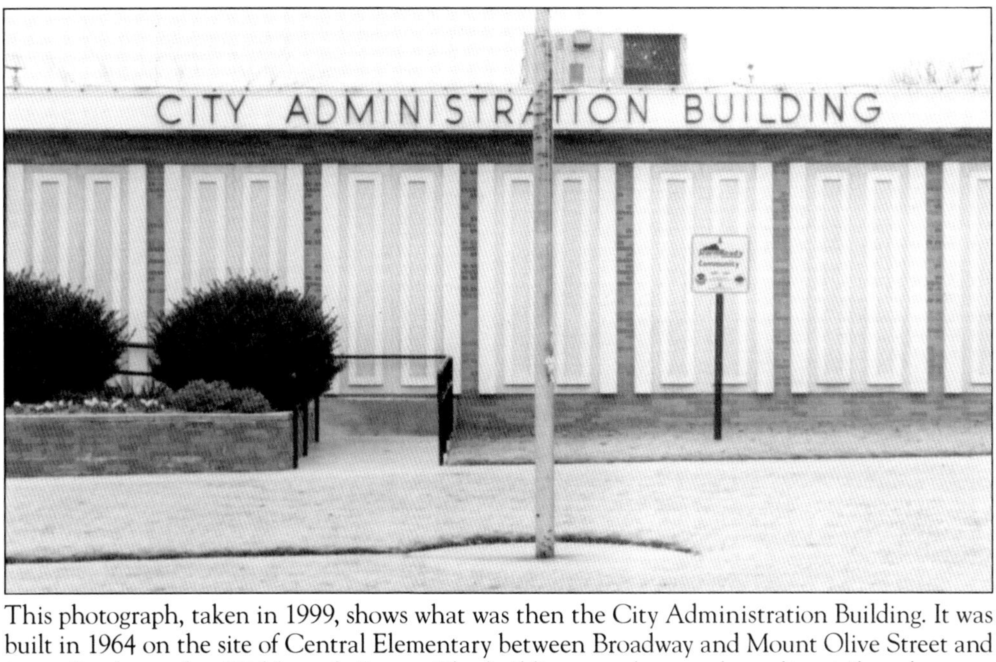

This photograph, taken in 1999, shows what was then the City Administration Building. It was built in 1964 on the site of Central Elementary between Broadway and Mount Olive Street and immediately south of Tahlequah Street. The building now houses the police, jail, and courts. City hall is a short distance south of this building.

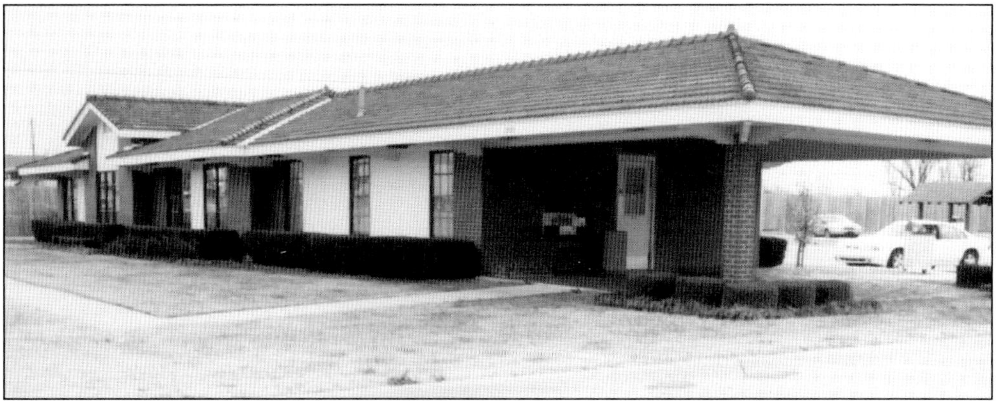

The Arkansas State Welcome Center on Highway 412, located a short distance from the state line, was modeled on the Kansas City Southern passenger depot that once stood in town, and some materials in this building came from the old depot, like the paving bricks used under the portico and beside the sidewalks and the roofing tile. Several items from inside the old depot are preserved as an exhibit inside this building.

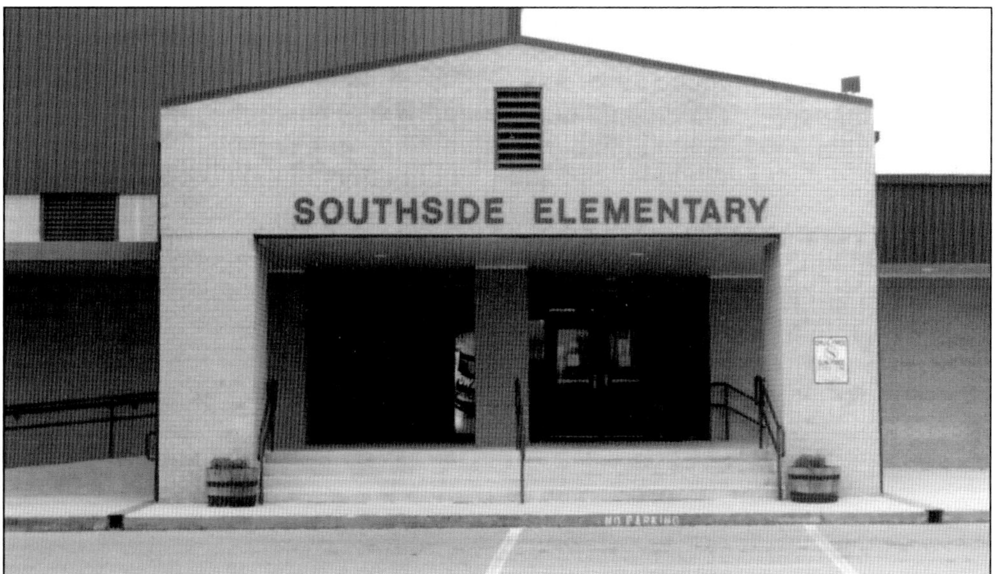

Southside Elementary underwent a major expansion in 1994 and now faces Tulsa Street. The expansion links the original Southside Building on South Wright with the Maple Elementary building on South Maple Street. The 1940 high school was torn down in this expansion, but a monument to this high school was built nearby. The monument includes the Works Project Administration emblem from the building and the names of the school's graduates.

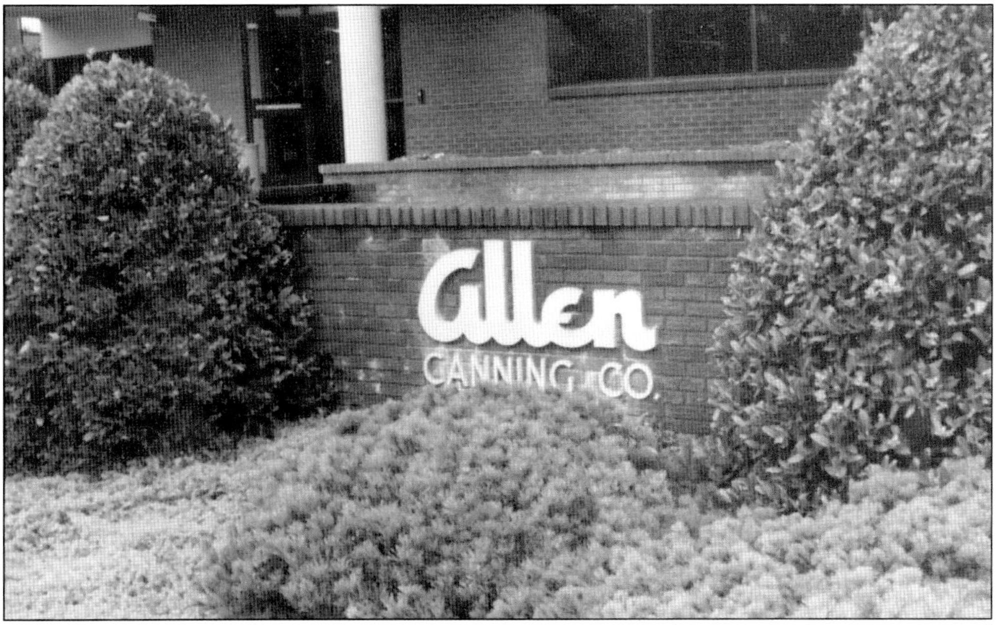

The general office of Allens, Inc., is at 305 East Main Street in downtown Siloam Springs. Earl Allen started Allen Canning Company near Siloam Springs in 1926. The company headquarters was in the middle of the 1974 flood, and employees took refuge on the roof. The company is still family-owned and operates a vegetable processor that cans vegetables under 11 brands. This photograph was taken in 1999.

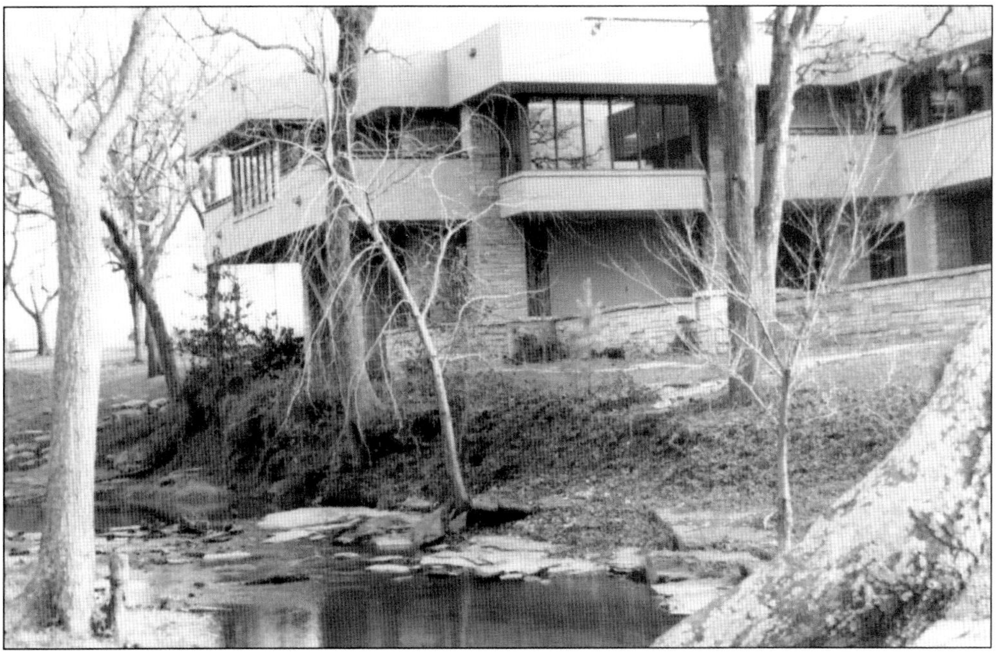

The Simmons Foods corporate headquarters overlooks Sager Creek and part of the walking trail. Plant No. 1, which opened in 1952 as part of the Silver Strike Jubilee, is now part of Simmons Pet Foods, Inc. Simmons Foods provides poultry products for retail, food service, and export. It is a privately held company with facilities primarily in Arkansas, Missouri, and Oklahoma.

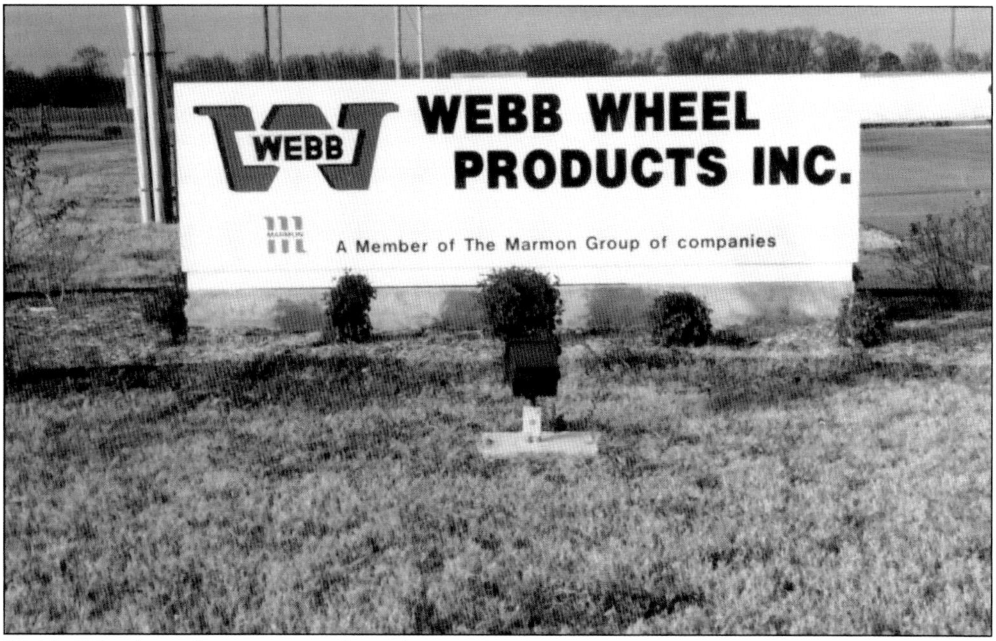

Webb Wheel Products casts and machines wheels, hubs, brake drums, and rotors for trucks, tractors, trailers, and buses. The company began in 1946 and has had a plant in Siloam Springs since 1958. This plant has moved or expanded several times over the years. The plant is now on Country Club Road and makes aftermarket equipment.

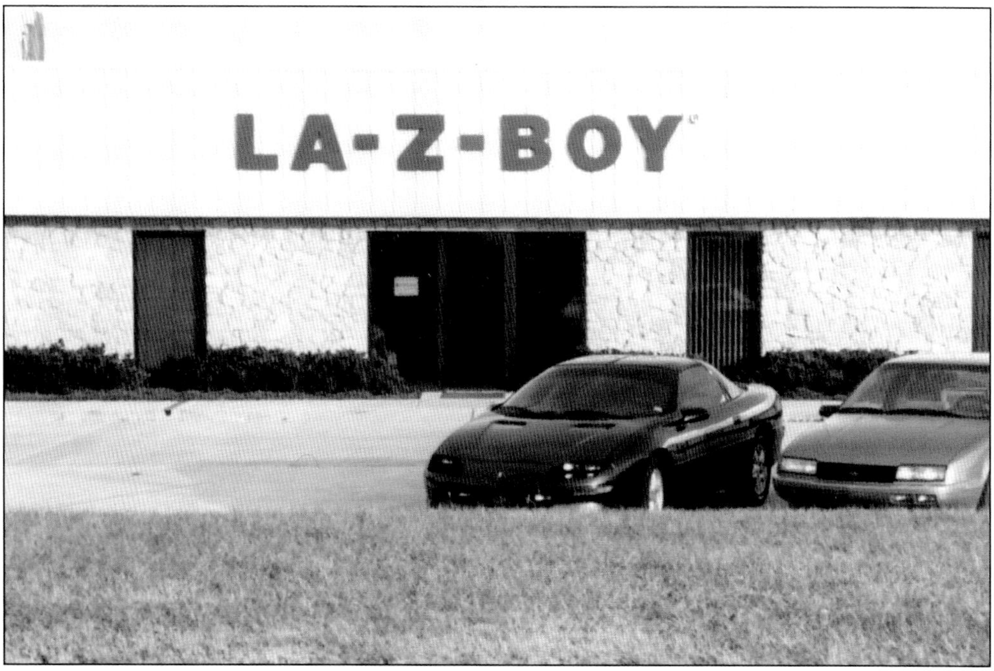

La-Z-Boy established its first plant in Siloam Springs in the former Pet Milk Building at 501 North Lincoln in 1973 and opened its current building at 2601 North Country Club Road in 1995. This 400,000-square-foot facility produces sectionals, sleep sofas, reclining sofas, home theater seating, occasional chairs, lift chairs, and classic La-Z-Boy chairs.

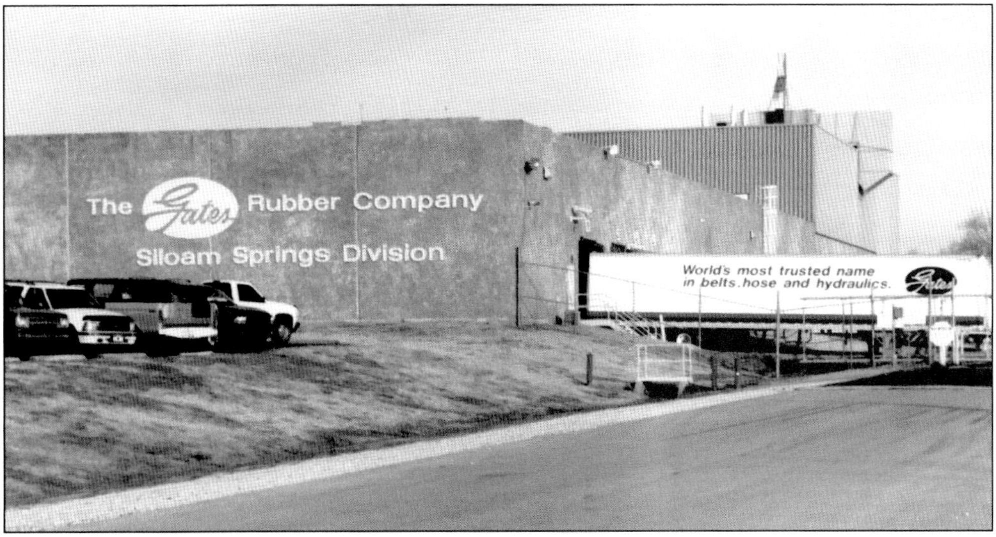

The Gates Corporation makes automotive and industrial belts, hoses, and related products. The Siloam Springs plant was built at 1801 North Lincoln Street in 1974 and began production in 1978. This plant will soon receive a $4 million investment that will increase automotive timing belt production from two million per year to 13 million per year. This photograph was taken in 1999.

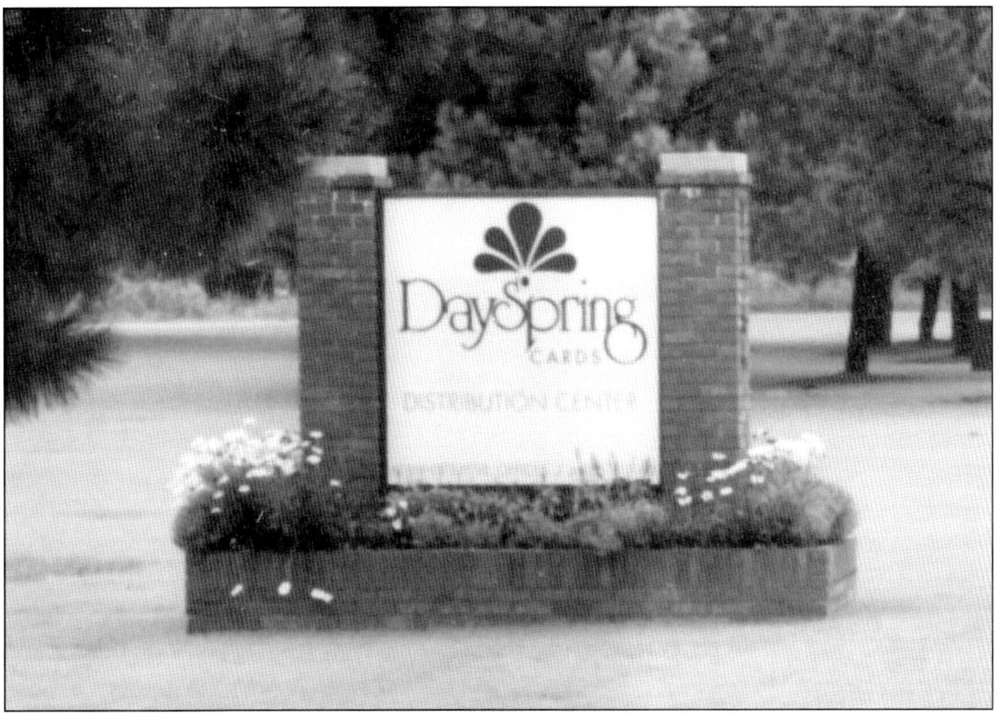

DaySpring Cards makes Christian greeting cards, calendars, and related products, and is now a division of Hallmark Cards. The company started in a California print shop in 1971 and moved to Siloam Springs in 1979. DaySpring expanded its product offerings and gained more market share until it became, according to its website, "the largest publisher and distributor of Christian greeting cards in the world."

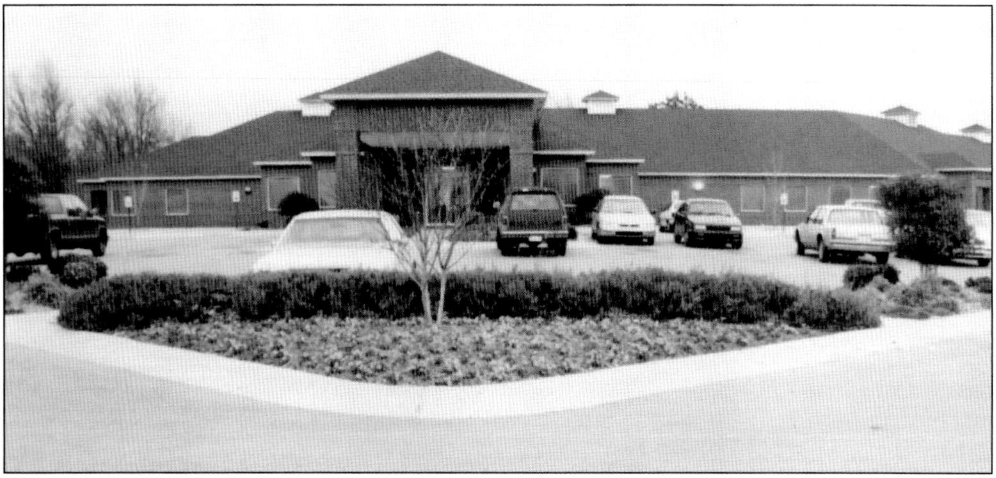

Siloam Springs Medical Center is a 15,000-square-foot building at Holly and Jefferson Streets, completed in 1996. It replaced the first medical center, which was a 6,600-square-foot building at 304 South Maxwell Street. By the end of 1995, there were eight doctors on staff.

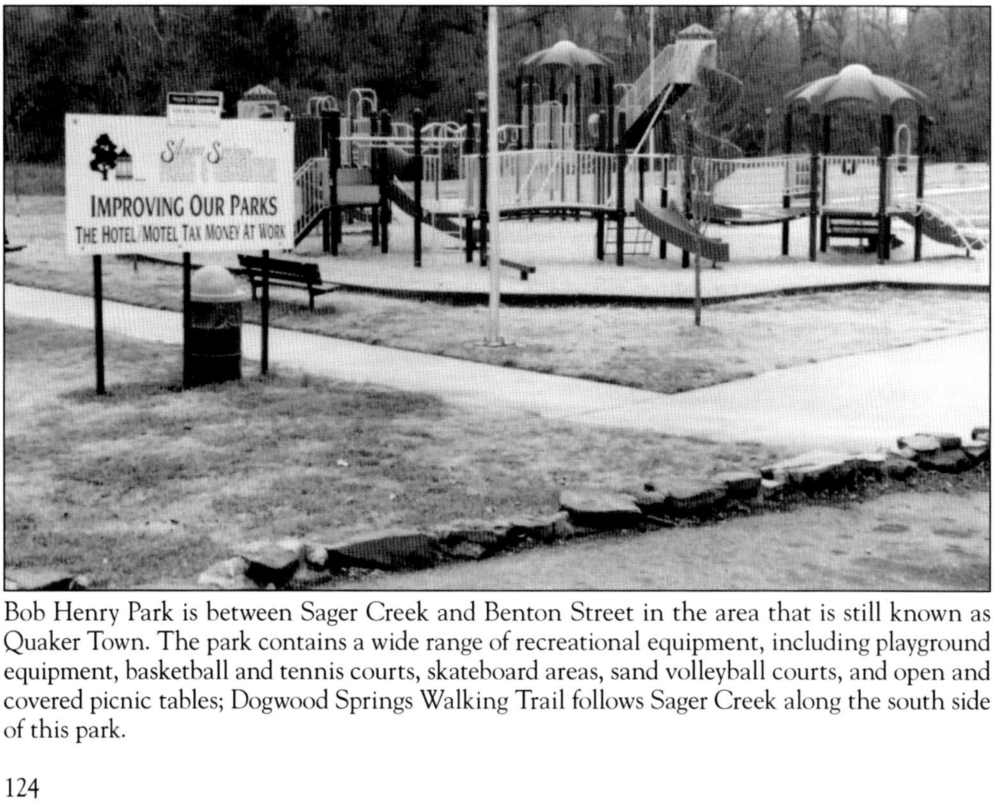

Bob Henry Park is between Sager Creek and Benton Street in the area that is still known as Quaker Town. The park contains a wide range of recreational equipment, including playground equipment, basketball and tennis courts, skateboard areas, sand volleyball courts, and open and covered picnic tables; Dogwood Springs Walking Trail follows Sager Creek along the south side of this park.

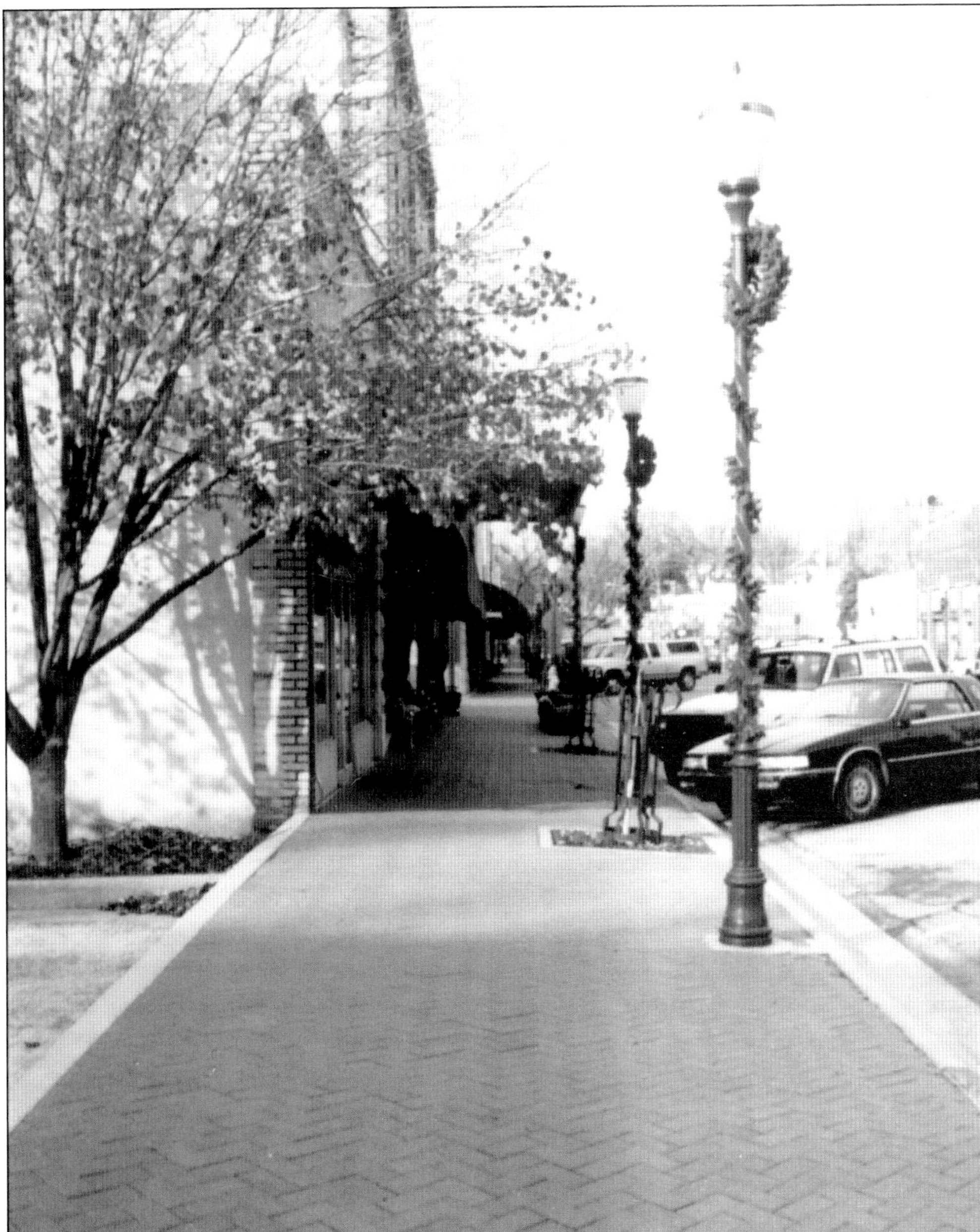

Siloam Springs is now an Arkansas Main Street Community, which represents a major commitment by this town and the state toward the economic health of downtown while maintaining its status as a National Register Historic District. Brick sidewalks and period lighting, installed in 1995, have added to the look and feel of the downtown. Engraved paving bricks are an on-going fundraiser for the local Main Street program. The Arkansas Main Street program is a preservation-based economic development program that has developed a four-point approach to downtown revitalization. These four areas of focus are promotions, outreach, economic restructuring, and design, with committees of local citizens working in each of these areas. A variety of state and local grants are distributed each year to qualifying property owners, and federal and state tax incentives encourage proper restoration projects.

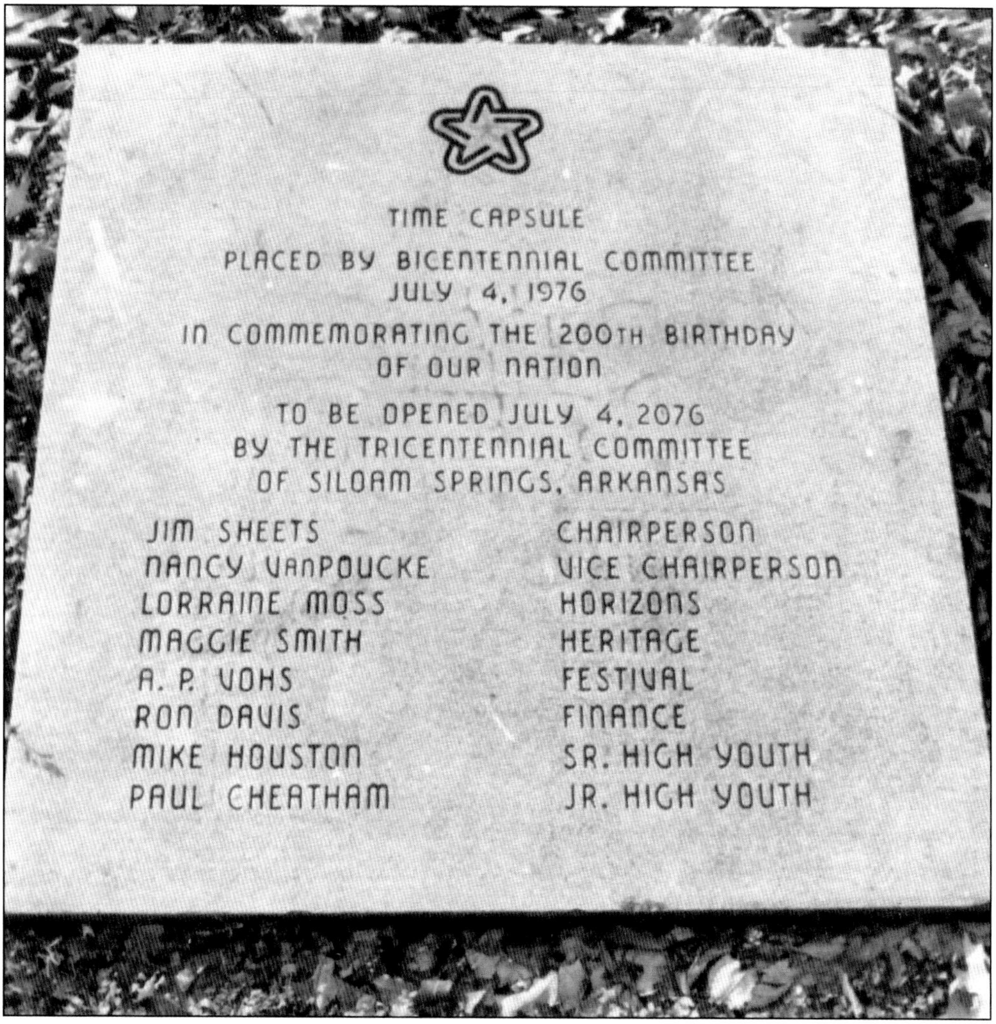

The bicentennial committee dedicated this time capsule in Twin Springs Park at 2:00 p.m. on July 4, 1976. It is to be opened by the tercentennial committee on July 4, 2076. In 1976, Siloam Springs celebrated its 96th birthday. The June 24 picnics were rained out that year, so they were rescheduled for July 4. Later that day were a bicentennial cantata, a doubles horseshoe tournament, and a fireworks display. One major project of this time was the research and writing of a 447-page history of Siloam Springs, titled "Hico, A Heritage—Siloam Springs History," by Maggie Aldridge Smith. She had a table in the Siloam Springs Museum where she received information and photographs from area citizens and did research in the museum collection. This was also the year of the first soapbox derby race in Siloam Springs and the year the monument at the Hico Cemetery was dedicated.

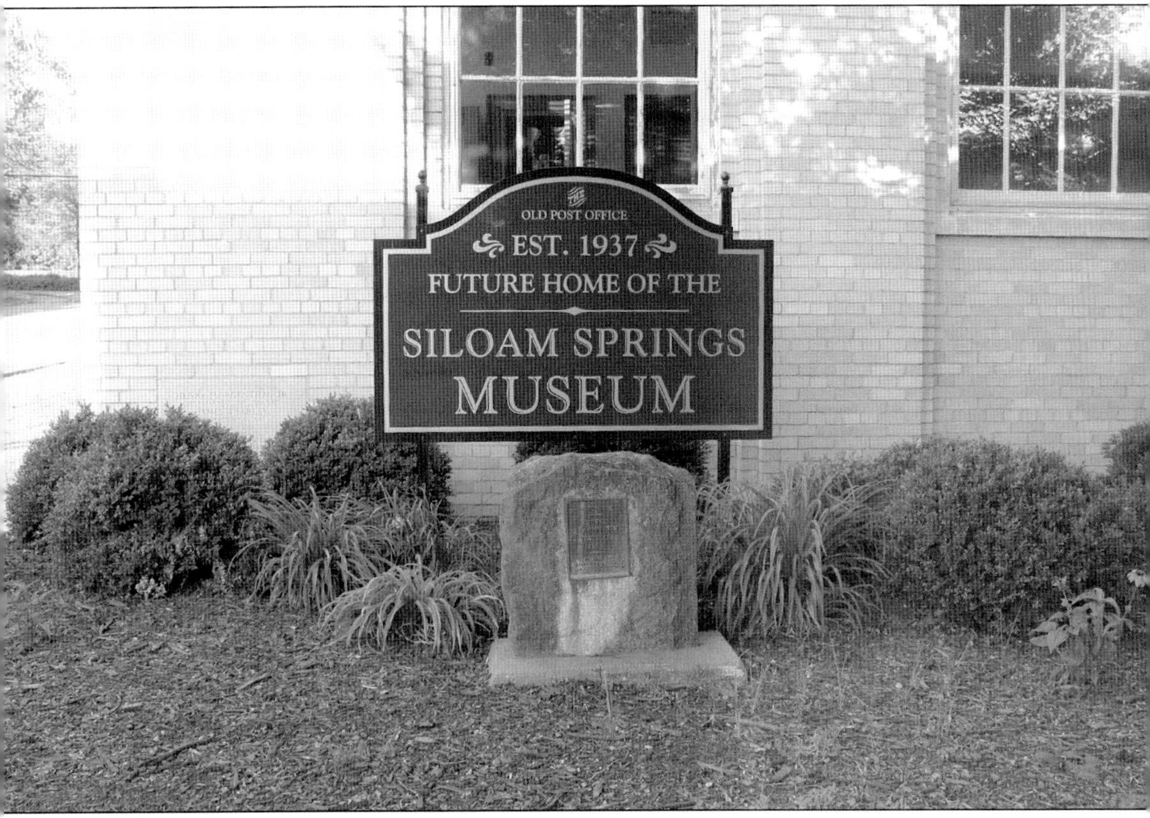

The old post office building downtown is slated to become the new home of the Siloam Springs Museum, providing a much more visible location and more room for exhibits and programs than the building on Maxwell Street. The museum was incorporated in 1969, and its first home was a room in the old Kansas City Southern Depot. The collection soon outgrew that space, and in 1972, the museum moved to 112 North Maxwell Street, which had been completed as the Church of Christ in 1951. Also visible in this photograph is the monument to Spanish War veterans, which was dedicated at noon on June 7, 1937, during the state convention attended by over 200 veterans and auxiliary members. This monument originally stood at the east end of the University Street Bridge over Sager Creek. Since that bridge will soon be replaced, the monument and surrounding plantings were moved to the front of the old post office in spring 2012.